Doreen Lawrence was born in Jamaica in 1952. She came to England aged nine and went to school in south-east London. In 1972, while working in a bank, she married Neville Lawrence.

Since the murder of her son Stephen in 1993, she has campaigned for justice for Stephen and for other victims of racially motivated crime, as well as for police reform. In 2003 she was awarded an OBE for services to community relations. In addition to her work at the Stephen Lawrence Charitable Trust, she sits on panels within the Home Office and the Police Service, and she is a member of both the board and the council of Liberty, the human-rights organization.

Praise for *And Still I Rise*

'You feel pain twice over when Stephen Lawrence's mother writes about the murder of her son. One pain is expected, aching with loss and hurt and emptiness; but the other, less familiar, is also the more affecting. Doreen Lawrence, glimpsed on platforms or television through thirteen years of campaigning, has always seemed so steely, so self-contained. But, in private, she weeps unconsolably ... riage, like her life, frac... ain.' *Observer*

'Public recognition is something Doreen Lawrence never wished for . . . though she has been obliged to become an activist, a fighter, she is naturally a woman of quiet disposition . . . Doreen Lawrence's encounters with officers of the Metropolitan Police and with officials from the Crown Prosecution Service, over a period of many years, transformed her from a quiet mother into a steely, determined campaigner against a system that she had grown to mistrust deeply.' *Independent*

'The social situation this book reveals is disturbing, but most moving is the way Lawrence's life was changed. Her voice is angry, yet throughout she tries to be fair and to understand what happened.' *Sunday Times*

'Her autobiography . . . is a warning, not just a reminder.' *Sunday Express*

And Still I Rise

DOREEN LAWRENCE

with Margaret Busby

ff

faber and faber

First publi~~shed in~~
by Faber a~~nd Faber Limited~~
3 Queen S~~quare~~
This paper~~back edition first published in 2007~~

Typeset by ~~Faber and Faber~~
Printed in ~~England by Mackays of Chatham plc, Chatham, Kent~~

Verse extracts from the following works
are reproduced by kind permission of the publishers:
Benjamin Zephaniah, *Too Black, Too Strong* (Bloodaxe Books, 2001);
Maya Angelou, *And Still I Rise* and *The Complete Collected Poems*
(Virago/Little, Brown Book Group)

ISBN 978-0-571-23459-2

10 9 8 7 6 5 4 3 2 1

To the memory of my son Stephen,
to my two surviving children Stuart and Georgina,
and to my granddaughter Mia.

To my sisters Cheryl and Lorna,
my brothers Charlie, Martin, Mark, Robert and Tony,
to my stepfather Gersham Lindo,
and to the rest of my family who have been there
when I needed them most.

To my aunt Lillian, who has been my reality check
at times when I needed guidance.

To Imran Khan, who has been my shadow since April 1993,
and to Michael Mansfield, QC, Margo Boye-Anawoma,
Martin Soorjoo and Stephen Kamlish, our legal team.

To campaign supporters, to friends old and new,
and to all who have been a tower of strength and more
since the death of Stephen.

And thanks to Dr Maya Angelou for allowing me to use
the title of her poem for my book.

This book owes a great deal to the editorial and literary skills of Neil Belton. His contribution to the text was fundamental, and I am thankful to him. – D.L.

Contents

Preface

Two lives ended one chilly April night thirteen years ago. One was the life of my eldest son. You don't have to be a mother to understand what that means, but perhaps only the parents of children can truly imagine what the loss is like. My son did not die in a car accident or a plane crash. He was murdered by a gang of violent, racist boys, and they got away with it. They remain unpunished to this day.

The second life that ended was the life I thought was mine. Since my son Stephen was killed with such arrogance and contempt I've had a different life, one that I can hardly recognise as my own.

You think that you know your place in the world and that you're safe there, in your part of it, that nothing can harm you except illness or old age. We all have this sense of security, this belief that the world will let us be as long as we do nothing to provoke it. I know I did until late at night that day in the spring of 1993. I wish I could not say so precisely when my life changed, but there it is. There was a knock on the door and voices in the hallway, and I heard my then husband speaking. I wish I had never heard what the voices were saying. After that night I was a different person.

For a long time, it was as if I had to put on armour every day just in order to survive. There were times when I did not want to continue, when I wanted to stop and to return to the security of being the private person I thought I was and maybe still am. There were times when I did not feel like speaking to anyone except my closest friends, and maybe never again to have to speak to more than a few people around a table while we shared food and spoke about ordinary things. Some days I still don't know how I manage to open the front door and go out into the world, and I can confess now that there were days, especially in the days and years immediately after my son's death, when I could not leave my bedroom. Then I'd learn something new – always that slow drip of information on the raw wound – and I would have to decide, again and again, against my own instincts, that I must say something. It would have been easy, sometimes, to roll over and turn my face to the wall, but the voices that so angered me would not have stopped – reassuring, patronising, and lying. And my son Stephen no longer had a voice of his own.

E. L. Doctorow's novel *Ragtime* revolves around a black man in New York, Coalhouse Walker, who is attacked and humiliated by a group of racist white firemen. They cannot bear the fact that he is dignified and articulate. They ruin his car, which he has saved to buy, and cause the death of the woman he loves. He becomes obsessed with obtaining justice against them, and his campaign escalates. He turns to violence, so that in the end he causes a major crisis in the city and among its policemen and politicians. I never dreamed of using violence – our campaign was completely peaceful – but I have sometimes felt like that fictional character, ignored and derided for protesting too much, and going on until I brought the state to admit that terrible wrongs had been done to my son and to my family.

The campaign for justice for Stephen Lawrence changed the way the police in this country view racist crimes. In the course of it I had to get used to people always telling me how dignified I was, as though that were something unusual. There was an implication to my ears that other black people don't behave like this, but I know that they do. There have been hundreds of thousands of people like me, women who have lost what was most precious to them in the world and who have had to go on with their lives. Some are still waiting for justice.

I hope my book will show people that it is possible to come through even the darkest times. I often draw strength from one of my favourite poems, Maya Angelou's 'Still I Rise', which begins:

> You may write me down in history
> With your bitter, twisted lies,
> You may trod me in the very dirt
> But still, like dust, I'll rise . . .

Before now, I had difficulty with the idea of writing about what happened to me and my family, because part of me saw it as selling my soul. Not enough time has passed to lessen the feelings that I first experienced when I walked downstairs to hear what was being said at my own front door thirteen years ago, there isn't enough time in any human life for that, but at least now I think that it might be useful to share my experience with other people. I want to describe what happened to me as truthfully as possible, mindful that in doing so it touches on the lives of others, especially members of my family. I have tried, nevertheless, to respect their privacy, and have only referred to their lives when it was essential to tell my own story.

When people say things like 'You changed policing in this country' I feel a chill, because it sounds as though we're all right now, and it is so easy to find reasons not to keep a close eye on what those with the power in our society do. It is easy to criminalise whole groups of people and not to take seriously what is done to them by others. This book for me is a warning as well as a reminder. May you never experience what I have experienced.

1 Jamaica

When I was a child, I was frightened of lizards, fireflies, the toilet at the end of the yard, the dark. Those were the worst things I could imagine in the rural parish of Clarendon, Jamaica, where I was born on 24 October 1952.

But there was also a loss that I couldn't name at the time. I was two when my mother left the island, and I have no recollection of her at all from that age, only of being told that she had gone away to England. And after that, my grandmother was the closest thing I had to a mother. I remember when I was very young staying with my mother's sister Birdie, and it was fine to be with her. Then at about the age of three I went to live with Granny and I felt truly loved by her. After she died, when I was seven or eight, I went to Aunt Ann and I did not have that comfort any more.

My grandmother had nine children – four boys, five girls. My mother, Ruby, was the fourth youngest. I am the eldest of four, two girls and two boys. There are eight years between me and my next sibling. The other three were born in England after my mother remarried. My father had left home when I was very young. I don't know much about his side of the family, and I was not aware of his existence as a young child, though I was told later that he was there in the background making sure that I was all right, buying food for me and being in touch with my grandmother. I never saw him, however, and it's as though the women in my family have had to cope without men for generations. My mother's father died when she was a year old, and though she had a loving mother she had a hard enough child-hood, which did not make her relations with me any easier when I eventually got to know her.

My father's first name was Blandford, but they called him Burie, I was told that much. People were often given pet names in Jamaica that had nothing to do with the one on their birth certificate. Mine was Joy. An uncle of mine, my mother's brother Leslie, a real country man, claimed to have given me the name. 'On the night you were born you brought joy to my heart,' he once told me, and it was a sweet idea.

My earliest clear memory is of being taken by my grand-mother to the market twenty or so miles away in Spanish Town, where she used to sell the oranges and mangoes and other fruit that she grew. I must have been about three years old. She strung the oranges on their stalks on a bamboo pole so that it looked like the branch of a fruit tree propped upright. She had to stay overnight at the market, watching her produce, and meanwhile she left me with my aunt Lil, who lived in an apartment in a gated yard. We must have got to the city quite late, and that night there was a huge celebration in the streets, noisy and crowded. Masquerade groups wearing vividly coloured cos-tumes paraded in the street outside the gate, a massive carnival that seemed to go on all night. I found the music and the lights terrifying. Some of the masqueraders were dressed like the devil with horns and a long tail, or monsters from the sea, and the size of them and the noise really frightened me. I remember crying and wanting to get safely inside the house. It was all very sinis-ter and loud, and the dancing people wearing masks were leer-ing at me, looking right through me. The town was a terrifying place, in my child's eye, and I was glad to get out of it again to the safety of the countryside.

Clarendon is in the south central part of Jamaica, and in the upper part of the area it is hilly and at the time quite remote. The soil is good and very fertile, but the going is hard and the roads were very bad in the 1950s, and you felt cut off from the big world. Spanish Town, which was run down then and very poor, with a handsome old centre built by slave-owners in the eighteenth century, was the nearest big town before Kingston and it seemed very far away. I was born way up in the valley of the Rio Minho at Crooked River, surrounded by the broken green hills of the Mocho Mountains, and that is where I lived with Aunt Birdie. It is still very lush and beautiful up there, but I remember very little about that time with her except her son, Clive, who was older than me and who always had a runny nose, or so it seemed to this small child. I would walk to church with him, near where Aunt Birdie lived. I can't have stayed still during a long prayer service at that age, but I was expected to be there for all that.

Then it was my grandmother's turn. She lived in a district called Pleasant Valley in the south of Clarendon, at the end of a road that was little more than a track, and in between her and Birdie lived Aunt Ann, who owned a shop near a town called Teak Pen. Sometimes I had to stay with my aunt and I would cry all the time; I really didn't want to be left there, where I felt, in the way that children can so easily pick up, that she was uncomfortable with children. When I cried Aunt Ann used to call me Porridge. Another nickname I was given was Icy, because I would sit there looking impassive and unhappy, and I am sure that certain policemen much later would have found the name fitting for me.

Living with my grandmother I lacked for nothing. Food was plentiful, we had clothes, and I had all the affection a child could ever need. My mother also sent me things from England from time to time, school uniforms and other practical gifts. The uniforms were always navy blue, a blouse and tunic and socks. She did not send toys, and toys were not something that were bought for children where I was growing up; they were made out of tins or broken pieces of machinery and wood.

My grandmother was a very attractive tall lady, tall at least for our family; she must have been about five feet nine (my daughter Georgina takes after her in that). I think of her wearing pastel colours, and embroidered dresses that suited her majestic figure. To me being with her was like being wrapped in a great protective blanket. She made me long dresses so that insects could not bite my legs; she prepared delicious food for me. I never had to sweep the yard or do any of the things that had to be done in the Jamaican countryside, such as fetching water: we had no running water, so water had to be collected from the pond. I wanted to help and begged her to let me carry my own water, so to humour me my grandmother would give me a tiny milk churn and I would toddle along splashing water on the dust.

But I was never made to do anything really burdensome. I felt cosseted and loved. She had spent her life caring for others, especially her own nine children, and she did not grudge me anything. I was the only one of her grandchildren who lived with her. My time with her gives me the best memories of my childhood.

I remember sitting at the back door of her house with my legs dangling, looking out at the trees. The door opened inwards and seemed high to me – I must have been three at the time. It was a one-storey wooden house and like most houses in rural Jamaica it was built on stilts, with a space underneath that was called a cellar, a kind of crawlspace. When it was raining the dogs would creep under the house to get out of the rain. The drop seems too high for a very small child in my memory of it, but I'm sure my grandmother was in the room behind me, watching over me.

My cousin Alvin, my uncle Leslie's son, who was older than me, would come to stay with us from time to time. He was a friendly boy, big for his age, always climbing trees and running somewhere, with all the energy a young boy should have – the kind of energy I saw later in my sons. The house had three rooms: the room that my grandmother and grandfather shared, another room that I shared with a boy called Kenute who my grandmother had adopted, and a general living room and dining area. The kitchen was not part of the house; it was a separate wooden hut a little way down the yard. It had an open coal fire for cooking, and a chimney for ventilation.

There were trees all around the edge of the yard – tangerine, mango and ackee trees, heavy with fruit in the summer, all vivid green and yellow and orange – and my grandmother also grew vegetables. But the main thing was the citrus fruit, for which this area has a perfect climate: those big green-tinted Jamaican oranges, tangerines, limes and grapefruit. It was quite a large yard, a plot of a couple of acres; and Granny sold what she grew in the market in Spanish Town or May Pen, which was nearer, where the Sharp's juice company had a factory and which made the lime cordial that was so popular in England in the 1950s. She worked hard, and every inch of her land produced something useful. She kept a few pigs, and smoked her own meat. She did a lot of heavy lifting, and with that and the selling of the fruit and vegetables she was up from morning till night. Other people kept cows; there was a house up the road where we got fresh milk in cork-topped bottles, the same as the ones in which rum was sold. Part of me misses all that colour and heat, which I took so much for granted. We had big mahoe trees with dusty green foliage and dark red blossoms. There were vines and creepers with white trumpet-like flowers. When I go back to Jamaica now the scent of the pink and white frangipani flowers is so strong, very sweet smelling, almost overpowering. There is nothing here in England like that, or the red of the hibiscus that grew around my grandparents' yard.

The man I called Grandfather was not my biological grand-father. Granny's husband, who died early, was called Howe. My step-grandfather's name was Grant. He had no children with Granny, though he had children from his first marriage. He had

5

married Granny some time after my mother's father died. He was a short, gentle, kindly person, who always wore a loose pair of trousers and a shirt with the sleeves rolled up, and always a hat with a wide brim over his grey hair. He had lost an eye once when he was chopping wood, and never wore a patch over the missing eye. Though I was such an easily frightened child I never found this horrible. He had a donkey, which carried whatever was too heavy for him to lift himself, and like his wife would spend the day cutting and digging and making good. He was the only grandfather I ever knew.

Grandfather was a devoted Jehovah's Witness, and would say to me, 'You're really a true child of Jehovah', nodding his head sagely, but he seemed quite tranquil when the rest of us went to a Baptist church every Sunday. The church consisted of one plain room with benches to sit on and a cross beneath which the minister preached. There were no side walls and as a child when the minister was preaching I could look out at the flowers and the birds instead of at blank walls. You could see docta-birds, hummingbirds with long tails and shiny green bodies. They always seemed to hover over the red flowers. Around the church there were fig and cotton trees, and logwood trees that gave deep shade on a hot day. I would be dressed in my Sunday best: a pink dress with a big bow tied at the back and puff sleeves and smocking on the bodice, with a white petticoat sticking out underneath, little white ankle socks, and a hat. It was a celebration and a coming together, and it was an uplifting experience. I loved the hymns, the whole congregation singing with voices that sounded so happy. Because the services were so long – or they seemed so to me – young children would be allowed to run off and play around the church and come back in time for the final blessing.

In the mornings Granny would get up and make us breakfast, as well as a packed lunch to take to school. Kenute, the boy she had adopted – it was typical of her kindness to do this late in her life – was much older than me and used to walk to school with me every day. He was a tall slim boy with a lopsided and not always nice grin, at least not always to me. He had a scar across his forehead which ran down across his nose, which strangely enough did no harm to his looks. It felt as if we walked for miles to get to that school. As we reached a certain point, Kenute would whistle and out of nowhere among the bushes would come scuttling big, vivid green lizards that had a fan around their throats. They seemed to be provoked by us, I thought by me especially, and their bodies would turn a violent shade of orange and brown as they glared at us, then fade back to green. If a stone was thrown at them they would flare up dark again, and I always thought they were just about to attack me. Kenute knew I was petrified of those lizards. I would stand riveted to the spot and I would be braying like a donkey with fright, choking and unable to breathe. I had to force myself to pass these monsters in order to get to school, and it was unbearable.

When we were coming home, Kenute would do the same trick with the lizards again, so I went through this twice a day. He would also search out a thick, short reptile called a galliwasp that I remember as having a mean golden eye and that was supposed to have a vicious bite, though there are no poisonous reptiles in Jamaica at all. Needless to say I did not know that when I was five years old. By the time we reached the school I had calmed down, and by the time I got home after school I was fine again. I never seem to have complained, so my grandmother never knew that I was so violently upset. Perhaps I was intimidated by Kenute.

Years later, talking to a friend who was a nurse, who mentioned a very similar symptom in a young child, it occurred to me that my reaction to the lizards flushing and staring so angrily was like an asthma attack brought on by fear. There was something so malevolent about those creatures, which were much larger in my imagination than they were in reality, staring at me in the hot sun. They have left me with a lifelong phobia of reptiles. Later, when Granny died, Kenute was old enough to go off and make his own way in life. I don't know where he came from, and I have never seen him again, but I can't say that I remember him with any great affection. It was a secret bullying of the kind that older boys often get away with, taking revenge for God knows what. For my grandparents' kindness to him, maybe.

When he was an old man, long after Grandmother died, my grandfather was living alone in a house surrounded by trees, cut off from the nearest road by bushes and undergrowth. One night a group of young men came to the house and robbed him. He recognised the long scar that came down over the nose of one of them, and said, 'Kenute.' They just looked at each other. Then the robbers stole some money and ran off. At least they did not hurt him.

There was no proper road to the school in Pleasant Valley; people had made their own path by walking. It was very broken country, as I've said, hard and rocky, and the walking was hard because the settlements were separated by hills. The ground was red dirt, so red that it stained your clothes.

My first school was very strict. In those days children in Jamaica used to get caned, hit on the hands with a flexible bamboo rod and though no teacher ever hit me, children around me were punished regularly and would cry at their desks holding their hands to their sides. I was always the small quiet one, did nothing to upset anyone, studied and avoided trouble.

It was at that school that I heard my real name for the first time. On my very first day, my birth certificate went with me, and the teachers began by calling me Doreen Graham. I thought, What are they talking about? Who is this strange person? At home that evening I protested to my grandfather: 'What is this name? I don't like it.' Because of course I much preferred the name I was growing up with in my grandparents' house, and which remained with me, and there seemed to be a threat in this other name with two syllables. If you hear anyone call me Joy today, they will be old friends or close family. Doreen was always my public, formal name, and after Stephen's death I had to become more used to it because that was what everyone I met knew me by. And there would be something wrong in strangers calling me Joy, after what happened to my son.

At school in Clarendon – and this shows how poor and under-resourced the education system in Jamaica was – you had one reading book that you kept for the whole year, a basic literacy text. The next year you got another one, and so on. When Granny was alive she bought me my reading book and I was proud of it and confident, and I did really well in school; when I went to live with my aunt it was a different story.

The wonderful thing about my early years in Jamaica is that out of all the nieces and nephews I was the one all my uncles and aunts knew, and I was surrounded by affectionate relatives even though I missed my mother so much. Uncle Eddie, for example, a regular visitor to grandmother, told me later that everywhere he and his wife went I was always in tow. Everybody claimed a part in my growing up. I was usually the youngest wherever I went, and the smallest child is everyone's favourite. I had a good relationship with most my aunts, but Aunt Lil is the one I knew best when I was living with my grandmother; whenever I go to visit her now in Florida she tells me stories from my childhood, about me standing out in the burning sun in her yard and refus-ing to move, no matter what they did. I would not budge even when someone swished me across the legs with a stick. It can reach 40 degrees in the summer in Jamaica, enough to kill a child with heatstroke. Eventually they had to drag me out of the sun, which I like to think of as early evidence of my stubborn streak.

Aunt Lil lived in that gated compound where the prancing

9

devils scared me so much, but it had become another safe place for me. She was quite a tall, pretty woman who always had a lovely smile. I have trusted her all my life, and knew instinctively even then that she loved children. One of my earliest memories is watching her bathe her daughter Grace outside on the veranda in a tin bath on a hot day.

But Grandmother would also leave me at Aunt Ann's, and come back to collect me on the Saturday nights when she had been to the market. Because I was much less comfortable there I would be ready to go as soon as Grandmother arrived. One night my aunt's husband said, 'I'll take you down tomorrow on my mule. If you go now you'll have to walk.' Did I care? I was walking, no matter how long it took over poor country roads.

I did not realise that they had wanted me to stay because my grandmother looked so unwell that night, and we walked home together very slowly. We could hear the bullfrogs croaking in the grass, and big moths, which in Jamaica we called bats, fluttered around us in the dark. She did not talk much that night and went to bed as soon as we got home.

Her illness seemed very sudden, as it usually does to children. She began to vomit yellow and green matter uncontrollably, in the evenings especially, and I could only watch her get worse and worse. She never got better. One day when Kenute and I were at school the turning point came and a message was sent by one of my aunts to tell us that she had been taken to hospital. I think she had passed out in her yard, and she was in and out of hospital after that until the end. When she came out of hospital for the first time, she was too weak to return to her own house, and stayed at Aunt Ann's place, where there were more people to look after her. And of course Kenute and I had to go too.

One day, soon after I moved into Ann's house, my cousin Alvin, who had come to stay, was sent out to move a cow from a field that was a good way from the house and I decided I was going too. No one was watching me, me so I walked off with him and forgot about the cares of adults for an hour or two. When I came back Aunt Birdie, who was visiting and who had never lifted a finger to me before, began switching me across my legs with cane strips – God, it was painful! – because I had been told not to leave the house. I was about seven or eight at the time. I had not been beaten much until then, but life was about to change.

Granny was my world. Everything that my grandparents could do, even though they didn't have much in the way of money, they would do for me. And it was as if my world collapsed when she died. Once again, I was sitting in class when a teacher called me out to say that she had received a message. She had a very serious look on her face, and leaned down to speak to me very gravely. Granny had died. That was my last day at that school, and I never went back to my grandparents' house. My grandfather stayed in Pleasant Valley for a while, and then seems to have packed up everything to move to a smaller plot that demanded less work, and from then on I saw him only for short visits. Of course I wanted to stay with one of my other aunts, above all Lil, not understanding that she had already moved to England like her sister. I was also fond of my mother's older sister Esther, but it was decided that I must go to my aunt Ann, and sensing already that I would have a harder time with her, that prospect filled me with dread. Even then I knew that my grandmother had protected me from many things. I had to grow up quickly.

At her funeral I saw my grandmother lying in her coffin in a pink dress, looking as if she was asleep, with a smile on her face. Even in death she was a pretty, fair-skinned lady. There were only a few strands of grey in her hair, as she died quite young, like many people who have lives as hard as hers. People came from all over to pay their respects, walking, riding on carts and mules. She was a special person, like a mother to everyone in the district – everyone loved her. It's strange, but apart from my grandfather and my aunt Ann I have no idea who was among the crowds at her funeral; even though my uncles talk about having been there, I don't remember seeing them. As a child all you are aware of is the mass of sad and solemn people, exciting and frightening at the same time.

After life with my loving grandparents, I did not find the experience of staying with my aunt a very happy one. Aunt Ann was a completely different person, as I already had reason to know. She was a harder woman than anyone I'd met, focused on surviving and making money, and was not very patient with children. She should never have been left in charge of her sister's child. She was a handsome woman, thin and vigorous, but she was tired out by the long hours she worked and her attitude didn't make her approachable.

She was a shopkeeper, and it is difficult to remember her without the barrier of the counter that separated her from her customers and from the rest of the world. She knew all the people roundabout, and was friendly to them, but she was also stern, and knew how to refuse favours. If she had given much credit she would have been ruined. Life was very tough then, in a country without any welfare system, and poverty stared many people in the face. If they could not sell what they grew or did not have work on one of the sugar or coffee estates they would have been in dire straits and would have had to move into the shanties of Kingston.

My aunt's shop was on a crossroads. The road to the right led to the main road, where you could get a bus east to Kingston, and another road led north towards the hills where my grandmother was buried; and there was another road up to where my grandfather now lived; and Aunt Ann's house was on the southern road, separated from her shop by a few hundred yards. Everything happened where the roads met. The shop was very busy, a meeting place, general store and landmark. Ann sold food and basic household stuff like candles and string and matches, and the shop was open from early in the morning to late at night. The shelves were stacked with sacks of rice and sugar, and boxes of dried fish and beans lay on the floor. People came to buy their flour, rice, saltfish or herring, which was weighed out and folded up in brown paper for each sale. The shop was L-shaped, and it had a window at the bottom of the L through which customers could be served if my aunt did not want to open the whole shop, say on a Sunday morning, when most people were at church. Otherwise she opened every single day.

Across the road was a patch of level ground where boys played cricket. At other times John Crows – vultures with black wings and a bald head – would land there and hold their wings open, standing for hours before flying off and circling round looking for some rubbish to eat. Down the road to May Pen was my new school. The area around the shop was mostly flat and empty, green scrub and reddish earth, like all that part of lower Clarendon. My aunt kept dogs, to warn her of strangers coming to the shop at night when it was closed. She also had a couple of cows, but they were kept away from the house on some pasture she rented, so I rarely saw them. Her husband owned a mule, which was a sign of real prosperity, a step up from my grand-father's donkey; a mule was almost as prestigious as a horse. They were considered quite well off, at a time and in a place when many people scrabbled on tiny plots or lived off casual labour. But it was not an easy life.

Aunt Ann had a stepdaughter called Gloria, but at the time I went to stay with her she had no children of her own. Gloria was old enough to work, and she really was worked hard, getting up before first light to prepare and open the shop, but at first I was allowed most of the time to run around the yard. My aunt watched me like a hawk; when my boy cousins went off with their friends, playing cricket or for some mischief, I was not allowed to tag along.

Aunt Ann's house, like my grandparents', had three rooms: the one she shared with her husband, the one we kids slept in and a dining and living room. She had an outside kitchen as well as a cooking area in the dining room. Like every house I knew up to that time, it had no running water; we had to go down to the local pond to fetch water for washing and drinking and cooking. Soon I was not excused such chores. Alvin and I had to fill big kerosene cans from the pond and stagger back with them to fill the drum that was kept at the side the house. I could hardly lift it, and water would slosh out of the can while it knocked painfully against my legs.

With no flushing toilet, we made do with a closet at the very end of the yard, which I hated using. There were always lizards in there and I screamed if I saw one in the darkness, sitting there very still or scuttling towards me trying to escape. The colour-shifting ones were still the worst, because they showed how furious they were; another was a pale whitish grey colour and I was told it could suck your blood. I wasn't much better with the beetles and ants.

At night the air was full of the sound of cicadas; they sounded like machines, and the whistler frogs made an unbelievable racket in the trees. In the undergrowth you could see blinkies glowing, fireflies, which terrified me because they made such a loud clicking sound. Country life on the whole didn't agree with me. I was afraid of anything that moved. Since there was no electricity, people relied on kerosene lamps when it grew dark. My aunt kept her shop open until about eleven o'clock each night and we were not allowed to go down to the house, which was about ten minutes' walk away, before the shop shut. By then it was pitch dark, and in the surrounding area only one or two houses would show a light, none close enough to shine on us, and there was no lighting at all on the road going down to the house and we were not allowed to take a lamp with us. Anything moving in the dark scared me, like rat-bats, as bats are called in Jamaica, flitting silently towards your face, so I would never go down to the house alone. The mosquitoes, for some reason, let me alone.

I went back to visit Jamaica after I had Stephen and Stuart, who was a small baby still, and we spent the night at my aunt's house, though I was determined not to stay at the shop until eleven o'clock with my kids. I told her I was going to the house to put them to bed. It brought back to me how scary it was to walk towards the house in the black of night, not knowing what you were walking on, with things flying out of the night. Back then my heart would be in my mouth, and when eventually we reached the door I'd think, Thank God! Gloria and I would light a lamp inside the house and instantly I would feel better.

Though mosquitoes never bothered me, wasps did. There is a fruit called jimbalin, a sort of sour green berry that grows on a tree in clusters, smaller than grapes as I remember them, and it made very good jelly. Alvin and I decided once that we wanted to pick the fruit ourselves in the season for it. We got the idea that if you held a certain green leaf in your mouth you would not get stung by the wasps that were always around the fruit. So, though I was not known for climbing trees, with this leaf in my mouth I clambered up the tree to the branch where the berries were, and the wasps came from everywhere and stung me all over. My eyelids were so swollen with stings I couldn't see. I never believed in the green leaf again, or in any other magical protection.

From time to time Grandfather would visit and give us money to buy things, or someone was sent to bring me money from him. He did all he could, and he did not have much. My aunt would say, as she did with anything given to me, that she was putting it aside for me.

Because I thought my aunt was so mean, I took to helping myself to small items from the shop. One day Gloria told her what I was up to and I was given a hiding. She beat me with a cane switch on my legs. But I had to survive somehow. There was all kinds of food in her shop, yet at times I and any other children who were staying with her would not even have enough to eat. It must have been hard for her suddenly to have to look after us, and she did not find it easy to be caring.

And then, though she was one of my oldest aunts, she had her first child, a boy. She was actually pregnant when Granny died, though we did not know it. When the baby came she was devoted to him and even more neglectful of us. By the time I went back after Stephen was born she had three children. I hope that having her own changed her attitude to children.

Whenever we did anything wrong and were going to be chastised for it Alvin and I – he was my partner in mischief – would hide at the bottom of the L-shaped room, though from there there was nowhere for us to run. Aunt Ann would get a long flexible branch, which she had torn off a tree, and give us a few lashes. Our pranks were not that wicked. One day Alvin and I took all the most expensive balloons and blew them up and burst them. When customers came to buy the balloons, which people used as Christmas decorations, there were none left. But that was the worst that we ever did, and we were given a hiding for it.

As you walked past other people's houses, you heard music by singers like Fats Domino – 'Blueberry Hill' and 'I Want to Walk You Home' – and you might hear Elvis Presley singing 'Heartbreak Hotel,' or local ska groups, but there was no music in my aunt's world. Though she had a radio, we never listened to it, since we spent so little time in the house, except on a Sunday afternoon. Then, when the shop was shut, dinner would be cooked and that was the one time in the week that we ate at the house and acted like a proper family.

I used to get up very early, when it was just beginning to get light. As soon as I had washed and dressed in my school uniform

– a blue skirt with a bib, worn with a white blouse, and white socks and black shoes – Alvin and I would go up to the shop, the centre of our lives, where we had tea and crackers before walking to school. We came back at lunchtime and would be given a roll of soft bread – called peg bread, about six pieces joined together which you broke off to eat – and some sugar and water, a kind of lemonade. In the evening my aunt would cook; for dinner we might have green banana and yam and sweet potato and either meat or fish. Only Alvin and I ate together when we came home, since my uncle was always out tending his land and my aunt would be distracted in the shop.

When I started at the new school I had no books – my aunt provided none, and there was no tuition at home. So there was not much more reading for me; by the time I got to England at the age of nine I still could not read properly. We used a slate and chalk for writing at school, but we never had any of our own chalk or other writing materials to practise at home. As a result I did not progress like the other children, so I was not moved up – they moved you up a grade according to your reading ability. My aunt took no notice.

I missed both my grandparents very much, and I wish I had seen more of my grandfather. He was still alive when Stephen had his first birthday out in Jamaica in 1975. I had corresponded with him and I sent him whatever little money I could, and he knew I was coming to visit. I got a lift from May Pen to the farthest point on the road before it became a track that no car could drive on, and then walked up to his house, which was a rough wooden structure. There was no point in trying to use a pushchair since the track surface was so bad, so I carried my eleven-month-old baby on my hip, plus a bag full of enough baby clothes to last several days (a great pile of heavy towelling nappies). Even though he had nothing much materially, I was so happy to be there. It was just such a pleasure to be with him again.

He passed away in 1982. I had continued writing to him, sending money, and I did not hear from him for several months. Then I had a letter from someone telling me he had died and been buried. I was upset that I didn't know sooner – I would have liked to send flowers, at the very least. That was the end of a part of my life, but I still have memories of a yard full of beautiful trees and a poor house where I was never less than loved and appreciated.

My grandmother is buried at a place called Post Road, which is deep in the countryside and surrounded by bush and trees. She bought the plot many years before, and before she died gave it her to daughter Lil. There was space for Grandfather to be buried next to her when his turn came, as he had always wanted, but in the end his children from his first marriage took charge and buried him elsewhere. It has worked out that my grandmother is not, after all, on her own any more. Stephen is now there with her.

The place is very peaceful. Whenever I am there I always feel a cool breeze on my face, despite the heat. The plot is overlooked by coconut and ackee trees, which have grey bark covered in strange yellow prickles, and it is very quiet and green, far away from the noise and chaos of London. As a child I used to go there with her; she picked tangerines there to take to market. It is the best resting place in the world, though I wish the beloved woman who showed me such kindness did not have to lie there with her great-grandson.

One of the things I regret is that my younger sister, who was born in Britain, never knew my grandmother. At least I had that time with her, which I would not change for anything. When I am asked about people in my life who have most influenced me, it is my grandmother that I name. There was not a mean bone in her body. She had a moral stature that made people want to be like her; she won the genuine respect of those who knew her.

She embedded in me the value of honesty; she treated people

straight, and that is a good lesson. It was one of the reasons she was so well respected, and why people looked to her for advice. She influenced the way I treated my own children. I have always tried to show to them the importance of being honest. Once you tell a lie it is hard not to continue lying – you can't remember the first lie, so you have to tell another lie and another, and it complicates and poisons life. I do not want that complication. I believe in what my grandmother always said: what you don't like for yourself, don't do to anyone else.

I spent a year with my aunt. To a child a year is a long time, and that year with my aunt seemed endless. It was when my aunt took me to get my passport photograph that I sensed my life was about to take another turn. The year after Granny died, in 1962, I came over to England. I was nine years old.

The stories I heard about England were about houses with a fire inside them, so I pictured something like I imagined you might see in Africa – a mud hut with a fire in the middle, smoke curling up into the sunlight. If a plane went by, I used to run along with my face to the sky and shout, 'My mother's on that plane!', wondering what it would be like to fly that high.

I don't remember seeing any photographs of my mother as I was growing up. She remained a remote and imaginary figure. When I came to England, I discovered that she had just one picture of me. We had very little idea of each other. In the photograph she had I was standing on a chair with my grandmother on one side and my aunt Esther, her older sister, on the other. I have no memory of having it taken. The only photo I remember being made of me before Granny died was at a place called Hope Garden in Kingston. I recall going there with my aunt Lil and the photographer telling me to smile. I've often been accused of having an impassive expression, but there are reasons for that, reasons that may have their roots in my childhood, and more recently I have found it difficult to smile to order, like some politician. I just stood there in the garden, cautious of this man I had never met before who was expecting me to smile, so he made me walk up and down and swing my arms like a soldier. He hoped I would find that funny and would laugh, but the picture shows me still staring back with a solemn face.

2 England

My mother was twenty-two years old when she left me in Jamaica and came to England. I don't think she was planning on ever going back, despite the theory that people from the Caribbean came with the idea of staying for only five years and then returning home. I know that as long my grandmother was alive she would not have allowed me to leave the island; and if I had a choice I would have stayed with her to the end.

Where we lived in Jamaica I don't recall seeing any white people. The part of Clarendon we lived in was too poor to attract the rich white expatriates, and if they owned land it would have been further south or east, and there were no tourists. Nor do I remember any Indians. Apart from black, African-Caribbean people, I only saw a few Chinese: there was a single Chinese shop not far from my aunt's in Teak Pen. My first sight of any white people was when I arrived in England in June 1962.

The food on the flight from Jamaica was awful: they gave us boiled eggs and the outer part of the yolk was black. I refused to eat anything, and I became sick and miserable. I had left the basic rural world I knew and suddenly I was miles in the air surrounded by complete strangers. I did not know where I was and what it all meant. I travelled with a man and his daughter who weren't relatives, but who had been asked to look after me. I landed at Heathrow airport, and there I was handed over to another set of strange people. My mother was one of them.

I was very shy and anxious and did not have much to say, even though I had looked forward to coming to England. I had great expectations of arriving and being welcomed into a loving family. But it was not quite like that; it was not like that at all.

My mother did not make much of an impression on me at first; in fact I cannot remember the first thing she said to me, and of course I had nothing, no image with which to compare her. She was a larger-than-life idea to me, and I was expecting to be overwhelmed on first seeing her. Without even a photograph to help me I did not recognise her. It was like meeting a stranger, though one who seemed very familiar. I suppose I could see her sisters in this neatly dressed woman, which was something of a relief. Despite their different personalities, all my aunts looked alike. She was slim, like most of her sisters, well turned out and good-looking, I thought, and I wanted to love her. But she seemed a little disappointed in me, and this did not help.

I do vividly remember, from that first encounter at the airport, my little brother Martin. He was two at the time, nearly eight years younger than me. I noticed his unusual eyes; they were narrow and they were not dark brown, like most of the people whose eyes I knew, but a delicate grey, and they reminded me almost of a cat's eyes (all of his children have inherited his lovely eyes). He wanted to cling to me from the start, and I found great comfort in this chubby little baby – but the amount of clothes he had on! Compared to children in Jamaica, he seemed to be buried in layers of clothing, and this was an English summer.

Luckily for me it was, otherwise I would have been freezing in my yellow cotton dress with its white collar, and I still felt chilly that day. I had a little brown cardboard suitcase – I still have it – and in it were just a couple of cotton dresses. It was light enough for me to carry by myself. My mother was annoyed, it soon came out, that none of the things she had sent for me were in my case, and that there was so little to show for the money she had sent. To her I think I looked shabby and neglected. I had no shoes apart from the ones I had on, and I don't think I had any socks other than the ones I was wearing

We got in the car to drive home; my stepfather's only son drove, a young man in his twenties. My mother was now married to Gersham Lindo, known to his family as Pops. There were so many more cars than I had ever seen in Jamaica, where no one I knew owned a motor car, vast amounts of traffic moving and stopping in ways that I found very strange. I could not figure out the reason for all the stops and starts. I kept looking out of the window at the endless houses that all seemed stuck together – no large gaps between them as there are in the Jamaican countryside, not many trees in the gardens, and only the odd flash of red or yellow flowers. Smoke was curling between the houses, or so I thought, but it was probably London fog we were driving through. The houses all seemed to be made of some reddish brick. Everything else was dark grey and gloomy and frightening.

My mother and stepfather owned a large house in Brockley, in south-east London. Part of the house was rented out; we had the ground floor. They had a sitting and dining room, a bedroom, a kitchen and a bathroom, which was shared, as was the toilet. I slept in the same bedroom as Martin. I had a little bed and he had a cot, but now that he had a sister he did not want to sleep in his own cot any more, he wanted to sleep with me.

As time went on less and less of the house was rented out, so by the time my sister Cheryl came along most of the tenants had gone. My stepfather's son moved with his own family into the bottom part while we lived upstairs. That house was eventually sold and we moved to Greenwich, where my sister and I shared a room and the two boys – by then my brother Mark had been born – shared another room.

There were so many of these white English people, and they seemed so strange, but I just accepted what was there, as children do, and didn't think much about the differences between them and me. Later, when I started school in London and was the only black child in my class, I don't recall anyone treating me badly or being racist towards me.

The only time I remember any strange remarks being made to me was when our class visited the Horniman Museum in Forest Hill. We were shown a video clip of some pastoral tribe in Africa – I think perhaps in Kenya – whose custom was to pierce a cow's vein and drink its blood. As we watched this, another child asked me if I did that too. I was astonished, since I probably knew as much about cows as she did. I can't remember what I said to her, but that was the only insensitive comment that I ever heard in primary school.

I had a very good teacher at first and I learned a lot from her. When I was a child people who didn't rush me and were patient got more out of me than those who expected me to be able to pick things up straight away. I was always very quiet; I needed people to notice that, rather than expect me to keep putting my hand up or shouting out. It was much later that I was first called a pushy person, and I wish I had never had the opportunity to become one.

The first school I attended was the John Stainer Primary School in Brockley, where we lived. In the beginning my mother would collect me every day and take me home for lunch and then take me back again, so I felt very protected in those first months. It was quite a large school, and I had no problems there. I blended in and mixed with everyone, despite being so isolated as the only black pupil. There was one boy who was colour blind and he could not recognise colours when we had to do painting in our art class; he would ask everyone which colours to use and they were never very nice to him, whereas I was, because I liked him, so he made sure to ask me what the colours were so he could finish his pictures. We were both colour blind, in a sense, and I was still unaware of how some people might feel about me.

This childish innocence was still intact when, after a couple of years at junior school, I went to the Christopher Marlowe Secondary School in New Cross, an all-girls' school. I started at the age of eleven, going on twelve, and I was one of the oldest in my first year. It was a racially mixed school; black girls must have made up a third of my class. I was bullied there in my first year, by a group of older black girls, but this soon passed. Many of my friends from my first and second year at that school are still my friends today. My best friend back then, Lorraine, is still very close to me. I am godmother to my schoolfriends Verna and Clara's sons, who are both called Mark and were born in the same year. Most of my friends, as it happened, had Jamaican parents and were born in the West Indies; this seemed to give us a strong bond. It was a time when many West Indian parents were bringing their children over from the Caribbean, and we seemed to find common ground in this strange new world, though I couldn't say we consciously selected each other.

I know now how hard it had been for my mother, one of the early arrivals, when she came to England. She was a machinist, and she took in sewing at home on a piece-rate basis. She had to meet a basic quota in order to get paid, and I remember her crouched over her sewing machine from early in the morning working up women's dresses and suits, her feet pressing the pedals of the machine and her hands moving the cloth forward under the needle. At first the machine was in the corner of the dining room and you could hear it whirring and humming all day; when we moved later she had her own small sewing room. She worked all the time, never lifting her eyes from the job in hand.

Because she worked so hard I was expected to be a second mother to her children, and to carry a lot of weight around the house. From an early age, ten or eleven, I was hoovering, washing, brushing and dusting. We had no washing machine then, and I would either wash clothes by hand or carry them in a big bag to the launderette across the road, put the money into the machine and go back home to do my other chores. I was expected to bathe the younger children and get them ready for school in the mornings, and to feed them. My earliest attempts were less than successful: I remember boiling some eggs until they turned so hard and dry no one could eat them. I soon learned to cook rice and peas, roast potatoes and chicken, saltfish and ackee. By the age of seventeen I could cook anything, and often had to dish up for everybody. This took a lot of time on a Sunday.

This was normal, at the time, for older girls in most Caribbean families. Life was more serious and demanding then for children. Yet I could not help feeling that my mother, who had not seen me for seven years, treated me differently from the others. I was a kind of stranger at home. My brothers were indulged and allowed to run free, as was my sister when she grew up a little, while I had to do the housework and all the things that as the eldest I was responsible for doing. I was unhappy because of this difference, which was common in West Indian families, between the way the children who were born here were treated and those who were born in the islands.

I felt I had no freedom. Occasionally I was able to meet my friends and we would go shopping or maybe to the cinema, but not as often as I would have liked. I had no social life, at least not by my children's standards. It was virtually impossible to have boyfriends. The only time I came into contact with boys was with the ones who would hang about outside the school gate, who were not the ones you really wanted to meet, or when we went for ice-skating lessons and met boys from other schools. I did not have a boyfriend until I was eighteen – and that was the man I married.

I felt resentful of the restrictions placed on me as I was growing up, but all my friends had lives that were not that different from mine. Parents were strict and watchful, and fearful of what the world outside the family could do to their children. My mother must have felt wary of the English world. And I would not have dreamed of arguing my point in the way my children used to argue with me, stating their point of view, like equals. Once Stephen and I were disputing and I said something about him being cheeky.

'Well, whose fault is that?' he asked.

I said, 'It's my fault for being so liberal with you, and if it's my fault for giving you freedom of speech, then you being cheeky is my fault . . .' He felt confident standing his ground, knowing there was a limit to what I could do about it. But I don't need two hands to count the number of times as a child that I dared open my mouth and speak out like that, and if I did I would be struck with the flat of a hand.

To some extent I was the Cinderella of the house. It was worst on Saturdays because then my chores seemed to mount up into a day of drudgery. From about the age of twelve or thirteen, I was always on my own on a Saturday, for the whole day. In the morning, everyone went out and left me to clean and do whatever else needed doing. As a consolation I would put on records and turn the volume up high so that the whole house shook with music. We had many of the early Trojan reggae albums and I liked Desmond Dekker and Pat Kelly – 'The Israelites' was my favourite track, which I played over and over again:

> Get up in the morning, slaving for bread, sir,
> So that every mouth can be fed.
> Poor me, the Israelite.

While doing the housework I would be dancing, moving to the music and the rhythm:

> After a storm there must be a calm,
> They catch me in the farm,
> You sound the alarm.
> Poor me, the Israelite.

Music was a great consolation, and I have never minded my own company, but I can't say that I was happy.

The relationship I have with my sister Cheryl now is so much better than when we were growing up. By the time she became a teenager I was married and had left home. Our relationship only developed after she turned eighteen and put some distance between herself and our mother. After she had her first daughter, who is about six months older than my daughter Georgina, we became very close, as sisters are supposed to be and I once thought we would never become. Cheryl has always got on well with all my children; things that Stephen would not talk about to me he could discuss with her. My mother instigated a lot of the problems between me and my sister by treating us so differently. It is not something we ever talked about openly, but I know that for years Cheryl wanted to have a close friendship with me and felt she could not. My mother did not raise us to support one another. That was a period of our lives we both wish had never happened.

My difficult relationship with my mother was painful for me, and remains so in my memory. I was her first child and perhaps her desertion by my father affected her attitude to me, but I can't say I remember a year when I really got on with her. I felt that she was cold and distant, and that I was a tolerated nuisance in her life. A mother's rejection is very difficult to live with, and while there must have been times when she was affectionate and appreciative of me, it is difficult to remember them, and of course the hurt sticks in your mind more than the good. We had disagreements, and I am very stubborn, but I was never openly argumentative with her. Maybe we could not bond because of the years we were apart. I understand better now what she must have gone through, the constraints of living in England as a young black woman in the 1950s and '60s. I know I tried to make it better, and I often ask myself if I tried hard enough. But how much, after all, can a child mend?

My mother's moods were unpredictable. I would sense a cold atmosphere, an unwillingness to talk to me, if she was upset or unhappy with me. I learned to do my chores properly, so she could not find fault with my performance, and although I was struck by her if she was very angry, the worst thing was the emotional exclusion – her failure to listen to me, to be aware that I had anything to say. I reacted by making sure that I was not noticeable: I grew up as a very, very quiet child. A visitor to the house would hardly realise that I was there.

My stepfather, meanwhile, was doing hard shift work, two weeks on nights, two weeks on days, first at British Oxygen and later in the huge car factory at Ford Dagenham. He was affectionate to me, and treated me well, but I would barely see him for weeks on end. He was uneasy about interfering if my mother and I were at odds, so no one could really influence this tense mother-daughter relationship that never seemed to get better.

With my aunt Lil, who had been living in England for some years now, there was a quite different connection: even when I said things that maybe I should not have said, and she scolded me for it, I never felt she was so angry that I could not talk to her. She was a lifeline for me, living within walking distance, and she would often stop off on her way home from work or at weekends. She married a white man, who later became a local councillor in Lewisham.

I heard more about the bleak days of the 1950s from my stepfather than I did from my mother. She was never one to talk openly, at least not to me, about what she had gone through. Like a lot of people of her generation, she got on with things and accepted what was dished out to her, trying not to dwell on anything, seeing all the hurt and struggle as part of life. One of the reasons I knew more about my stepfather's experience was because I interviewed him later as part of a project I did on people who had come to Britain from the Caribbean in the early days. My stepfather was the first of the family to arrive. He was one of the lucky ones: you heard stories about how hard it was to find places to live, with signs that said 'No Irish, No Blacks, No Dogs', and those were not legends, but he managed to get a room in a white person's house, which was quite unusual. He lived there for some time but was not allowed to bring back any women friends. One day he made the mistake of bringing a girl home, and then of course he had to leave. He talked of sharing with all sorts of people, but the things he remembered were nearly all positive, and he seemed to have no horror stories to tell. He said that back then, if you were walking down the street and saw another black person, you would walk over to shake hands and say hello, because it was such a rarity and you felt so isolated. He came over by boat in about 1953; he landed in Southampton, took a train to Paddington station in London and walked around looking for a room. He was one of the lucky ones, in that he found places to live and got himself a job. Then he started saving money to send for my mother. She came to join him when he had already established a home, leaving me behind.

One of my mother's deepest silences concerned my real father. She would never speak about what happened between them, and remained angry with him for the rest of her life. She took her silence and her anger to the grave with her. And it did not help my relationship with her that he made contact with me when I was about thirteen.

It was a Saturday afternoon, and as usual I was in the house on my own, cleaning or washing. The knocker sounded and I went and opened the door. A good-looking, neatly dressed man stood in the doorway, wearing a suit and a hat. He smiled at me – he always had a smile on his face – and said, 'I'm your father.' I must have invited him in – the thought of one of my children of that age asking a complete stranger into the house would have horrified me – though I have no specific memory of doing so. When my mother came home he was still there. The bitterness she still felt was obvious, and there was a very tense scene, but she did not throw him out.

After that he would come regularly. I was allowed to visit his home, though never to stay the night, and met his second wife and my half-sister. My mother never let any of these visits pass without making some barbed remark, though she never tried to stop them, as far as I know.

We stayed in touch for the rest of his life, and he met all my children, but his visits were fleeting and although I was able to tell him how much his desertion had hurt me and damaged my life, we never became truly intimate. He was a debonair man, always impeccably dressed and groomed, and he was very accepting of me and not in the least resentful of my complaints against him for deserting me. He was no more forthcoming than my mother on what had led to the breakdown of their relationship. People of that generation found it hard to talk about themselves, so I will never understand what left the three of us with such a burden for the rest of our lives.

At school one of my best subjects was Maths; I had a practical bent and enjoyed working with figures, until about the third year of secondary school. I had moved up to a higher grade, but the Maths teacher in that class would make no effort, if you asked her to explain things that you didn't understand, to draw all the students along with her. That was my downfall, and I lost interest. It did not help that I was working so hard at home on the housework, every night and at the weekends. My homework suffered badly, and the teachers never rang alarm bells as they should have done. I am also dyslexic, and this was never addressed as it would be today.

Looking back on schools in the 1960s, I think that the system was set up in such a way that it could not support you once you started falling behind. This was as true for working-class white children, but it had a particularly bad impact on black children.

Many black pupils were not entered for any subjects at O-level. Most of us just did CSEs, and once that happened you were written off academically. In school there was an unspoken assumption that black children would never amount to much, so we were not taught as though we might want to go to university. Our lack of ambition was assumed. And many nights, my mother and stepfather were either working or recovering from work. When they did attend parent-teacher meetings, my mother assumed that my teachers were pushing me on as best they could, expecting that the standard in Britain would be higher than it was in the Caribbean. If she was given a negative report, suggesting that I was not willing to learn, or words to that effect, my mother would accept the voice of authority.

I ended up doing CSEs in English, Maths, Geography and Needlework. I hated History. I found it boring because we were taught only British history, which seemed in the way it was taught to have no relevance to my own background. Now I will read any history I can lay hands on, especially books about the Caribbean and Africa; it is as if I am having my own history lessons now to make up for what I never learned at school.

As a young child I had wanted to be a nurse, until I realised exactly what nurses had to do, and I did not think I would have the stomach for the job. I knew I did not want to work in a factory when I left school, which was what the teachers had been preparing us for. They would say, 'You can do something with your hands,' and that did not interest me. So a group of about three of us, including my friend Lorraine, began to scour the papers for jobs that we might want to do. Because I was fairly good at Maths, I decided to go for banking. I had only four CSEs, but I passed the Natwest Bank's entrance exam and became a clerk in their clearing house in Moorgate. They had just begun introducing computers – they were huge room-sized machines in those days – and I was quick at the calculations that we still needed to do by hand, and could clear errors quite fast.

I enjoyed working there. I had a line manager who must have taken a liking to me. We started work at 8.30 in the morning, but in the winter we had a lot more work to do and you could not leave until it was all completed, and it might be eight o'clock in the evening by the time I went home. Even if it was a penny out, you had to go back through all the files to balance your account. It always seemed to be in the winter that we worked late, and then I had the journey from Moorgate to Deptford, my nearest station, and the walk in the cold and fog. The warmth and colour of Jamaica seemed like another world on those winter evenings. But at least if we finished about 6.30 or 7 p.m., my manager used to say to me, 'Put down 7.30 . . .' He was a decent man, and I appreciated those extra few hours of overtime pay.

The only way in which I felt affected by racism was that while many of the other girls in the bank were made section leaders and promoted, I was not, despite achieving as much or more than others in my department. I had got to the top of my grade, but they wouldn't move me up to the next level. I had an argument with one of the managers and I remember him saying, 'The bank can't give you four hundred pounds just like that.' With the implication, I thought, that there was something unheard of in giving such a rise to a black person. Before that I had not been aware of prejudice against me because of the colour of my skin.

But nothing, not childhood or school or my experiences at work, prepared me for what happened when I thought my life had settled into happiness and middle age.

3   Marriage

Neville Lawrence and I got married in late 1972. Our first meeting was in 1970 when he visited our house with a friend of his who knew my mother. I mainly noticed his height – he was 6 feet 2 inches tall, and he reminded me of Levi Stubbs in the great Motown group, The Four Tops. This tall bearded man, so tall that I had to turn my head upwards to look at him, seemed very adult. I was seventeen at the time and Neville was ten years older. I had only just left school and my peers seemed immature by comparison, especially the boys, the school-gate Romeos and all the rest. I have always been a serious person, even though I would have loved to go to clubs and do the other normal things for a girl of my age, which my mother would never let me do. Neville represented freedom.

He came a few more times with his friend. Our first real date – and even that was with a group of people he knew – was when we went to a concert at Wembley Arena to hear several of the best Jamaican reggae groups, who were on a tour of the UK. When he came to the house to collect me he was driving a dark maroon car (later on he bought a blue mini, which you would not associate with a man of that height, but he loved that car). The outfit I wore – it sounds peculiar and unfashionable, to describe it now – was a red suit with a long bodice coming down over my bum, a flap that buttoned across the middle, sleeveless, like a tunic, with a matching skirt. I wore a white blouse with it. Neville was wearing a dark brown suede jacket. He never had an Afro, his hair was cut very low, and he had this funny widow's peak. I thought he was very handsome.

I had never been to a concert before. In the huge arena, I felt how the crowd went wild when the groups came on, the screaming, the shouting – though I was too composed, too reserved to get really carried away by it all. I know Jamaican people are stereotyped as being very emotional and free and easy, but I don't seem to fit the type. It was like a huge church with all the ecstasy and none of the religion. The concert featured a lot of the best singers of the pre-Bob Marley era: Pat Kelly, Max Romeo and Jimmy Cliff. It was a once-in-a-lifetime event, having all these artists together in one place, and I felt I was stepping out into the world and doing what everyone else had been doing for years.

After that we started going to the cinema – films such as *The Graduate*, *Superfly* and *Shaft* with Richard Roundtree. Black cinema, or at least cinema for blacks, was just beginning to enter the mainstream. Sometimes we visited Neville's friends, and because I was so shy I would never speak – I would not eat, drink, or do anything, I just sat there, feeling maybe less foolish than I looked, but very unsure what to do. I was so unused to the world that my children later took for granted, like a girl from another time, which in a sense I was.

When I met Neville he worked in a leather factory, making clothes, near Edgware Road. We used to travel on the train together in the morning; I would get off at Moorgate and he would carry on. I was living with my mother and stepfather on Ashmead Road in Deptford – we had moved by then – and I would walk from there to New Cross station, where Neville would meet me.

I was nineteen when he proposed – though it was not a conventional proposal. Neville put it in such a casual way that I had to do a double-take to realise what he was saying. We were walking down the street, setting out to work one morning and as we got to New Cross station he said something like, 'Oh, when we are married . . .' My response was a bewildered 'What did you say? What did you mean by that?' As proposals go it lacked drama. There was no romantic business of going down on one knee or making a big performance out of it. That would have been nice, but when it cam to emotional expression, I think he was afraid to risk being knocked back. He didn't say 'I love you'; I'm not sure he ever did. But he cared for me, that much was clear, and I loved him, though it was not an overwhelming, exciting feeling, more of a calm assurance that I was doing the right thing. And there was still that wonderful feeling of knowing someone who had lived much more than I had, and who knew more about life than I did. That was a feeling that would stay with me for a long time.

My father, my real father, was not happy when he found out. He thought Neville was too old. He came round, though, after a few visits to our house, when he could see how Neville and I had a comfortable life and how well he treated me. By the time I had Stephen and Stuart, my father had gone off to work in Nigeria, and on one of his return visits he brought Neville a present. It was his way of saying that he finally approved. By then we had been married for about eight years.

When I think about it now, I wonder why on earth I got married so young. But in the 1970s it was what people did: you left school, got a job, then it was expected that you would marry and have your children. The pattern was more or less the same for all my friends with whom I'd gone to school, although I was the only one who did not have children straight away or before getting married. And it took me a while to come to terms with the very idea of getting married. I didn't say yes at once because I was not sure of myself, despite my strong need to get away from home. I had just started my first job, had begun to have some independence, and I was reluctant to lose that freedom. I was certain that I did not want to have children immediately. At least Neville and I had two years living as a couple before

Stephen was born, and those two years were a good time for me.

My mother did not approve at all or ever of my marriage, as she failed to approve of much that I did. I think marrying Neville was partly my way of escaping the life I had then, and of escaping her domination. I dreaded telling her, and she could not even pretend to be glad when I eventually plucked up courage to make the announcement. She had all kinds of reasons against me marrying him, some of them no doubt sensible enough, but she would have been disappointed if I had said I was marrying a brain surgeon. And of course she would be losing my help around the house. Her own life had been so hard that she had lost all sensitivity to mine.

I had to marry out of all that, in order to find my own way. Marriage gave me the beginning of freedom, of the person I am now.

We eventually got married in Lewisham Registry Office, in front of a few dozen guests. It was my Aunt Lil who arranged everything and who made everything special. She was, and is, a warm and extraordinary person. Her sister, my mother, having disagreed with my choice of husband now disagreed with the organisation of the wedding, so she decided not to be part of it. I got dressed from Lil's house. Someone I knew had made my dress for me. It had a high neck, puffed sleeves, it was fitted at the waist and flared out to the hem, and I wore a broad-brimmed hat. I thought it looked wonderful. It was November, and it was freezing. People were shivering in their best skimpy dresses and suits. My aunt and her husband laid on a wedding breakfast for us and our guests.

I went straight from being at home with my family to having a husband looking after me, and from doing housework for my mother to looking after him. I never lived on my own for a day of my life, not until after Stephen's death. We lived in one room in a family house in Brockley, without even the use of a fridge, so I had to shop every day for fresh food, and we shared a bathroom with other families in the house. Within a year we moved into a nice one-bedroom flat with a fitted kitchen, and life was fine. We never had arguments, except about trivial things, and I felt protected.

Before we had children we often went to formal dinner-dances, the kind where you wore long dresses and smart suits; there was one practically every weekend. We would also spend time visiting friends, and people came round to our house and we would sit for hours talking. We had a modest idea of having a good time, I think, and we lived a very sober life. I was still working at the bank and Neville worked in Edgware Road. He would give me £5 a week – and that would cover the shopping and still pay my train fare to work for the following week. It really was another century.

Those were happy times because for the first time in my life since leaving my grandmother's house I felt needed and valued consistently. Neville was always mending and improving things around the house; he participated in everything and I was never left to do household chores alone. At Christmas time, he always did his share and involved himself with all the arrangements, including decisions about what we were going to eat. He liked having roast duck for Christmas dinner, so he would take care of cooking it. That time of year was important for him. He used to reminisce about Christmas with his family in Jamaica, how on Christmas day in Kingston people went to Christmas market and there was a sort of carnival, and he wanted to recreate a little of that in London.

He never forgot to buy me birthday presents. Even though, like many men, he was not too imaginative about the presents he gave me, I appreciated the fact that he made a special effort. For almost every birthday, he bought me earrings – that was all he could think of; I have always liked gold, so before long I had an entire collection of gold earrings. It was the heyday of leather, and he made me leather and suede clothes in every style that was fashionable: skirts, dresses, a jacket with a high collar and a zip – everyone at the time had one of those jackets but the difference was that Neville had made mine. Since I am so small my clothes fit best when they are made to measure, otherwise the sleeves are far too long, so he always made my coats for me. There was never anything that I wanted that I didn't get, whether for the home or later for the children.

It was in that small flat that my elder son was conceived. When I first realised I was pregnant I was excited, but also frightened about having a baby. During my pregnancy, and every later one, my health was not very good. I was one of those sickly women who can hardly keep any food down early in pregnancy. I had to take tablets to stop me vomiting. After the first few months, my body seemed to adjust and I learned to enjoy the expectation of the baby.

I so wanted my first child to be a boy. I had already chosen his name: Stephen, spelled with a 'ph' and not with a 'v'. His middle name, Adrian, was Neville's father's name, but Stephen was a name that I had always liked, and since my late teens I had thought about that name for my first son, if I ever had one, or Stephanie if I was to have a daughter.

The date that they gave me for Stephen's due date of birth was the very day I had him. He was born at 9.30 in the evening of Friday, 13 September 1974, at Greenwich District Hospital. He weighed 7lb 2oz at birth – big, considering my size. I was incredibly happy when he was born, but I was frightened bringing him home. In the hospital someone is always there to help you, to tell you what to do, how to bathe him, how to hold him. I didn't have the benefit of my mother coming to help, since our relationship had not improved after my marriage. Her coldness and resentment seemed to increase with distance, and I felt again that something in her was taking out on me her anger against my father. She was simply not interested in her grandson. My aunt Lil was living in Brockley by then, and Neville's parents were back in Jamaica, so I was alone in a small flat with a new-born baby who seemed to cry all day.

He was dedicated – christened – at a Baptist church in Plumstead. Then and for what seemed a long time afterwards he not only cried all the time but hardly ever slept, so I was distraught and exhausted trying to work out what to do with him. I kept feeding him, thinking he must be hungry and had not eaten enough, and walked around the flat – there was not much room for walking – comforting him while he howled. Movement soothed him, and then I would rest and he would start again, deafening me. There were days when I felt disoriented and out of control. Then he started crawling – I have photos of him sitting up and trying to crawl – and from then on he was always on the move. He had not liked being confined, and now once he could begin to find his own way around the world, he was a very happy baby. He had such a cheeky expression from then on.

We did not try to buy a house when we were first married; Neville was not interested. He had the mentality of a lot of Caribbean people at the time, that he was not here to stay and would eventually be going back home, so what was the point of buying property here? But once I'd had Stephen I was determined that we were going to have a place of our own, so I started looking at flats. We did find one that we both liked and we had arranged a mortgage, but we needed a deposit of £500. Neville wanted to sell his car, but I told him I didn't think he should. He had left the rag trade and become a builder before Stephen was born; wages were low, and we needed more money. Without a car he would find it much harder getting to jobs. So we stayed, three of us in a space that many people would have found cramped for one. I had, of course, been obliged to give up my Natwest job just before Stephen was born, and we were dependent on Neville now.

Then I became pregnant again. The prospect of having another baby in that tiny flat was not good. And then even that roof was almost taken away from us. We rented the flat through a friend of Neville's who had set up a business into which several people put a thousand pounds each and it went towards buying the house we were living in, and also a shop in Peckham, which was to be rented out as an off-licence and earn us all good money. I ended up paying the thousand pounds out of my wages, a little every month. The scheme worried me; there was something not quite right about it or Neville's friend. I kept asking Neville, 'Shouldn't we at least get some interest off our money?' He assured me that it was all being reinvested in the business; he was always more trusting than me.

I was home one day during my second pregnancy and there was a knock on the door. It was a posse of bailiffs, who had come to repossess the house. 'What are you talking about?' I said. 'We pay rent, we live here.' They insisted that the mortgage hadn't been paid. I told them that we paid rent every week, and managed to get rid of them, for the moment, knowing that if I hadn't been in they would have changed the locks. At least we had a rent book, our only proof that we had been paying rent to Neville's clever friend. When I confronted him that evening he denied everything, and was the picture of injured innocence. But I remembered seeing letters that had come for him, and thinking that they looked threatening, all registered mail and marked urgent; I would leave them in the front hall and every so often he came to pick them up or Neville took them to him. He was not a good liar. Our money was gone.

Fortunately, I had put our names down on the council housing list, so when disaster struck I went to see if the council could find us somewhere to live. We were rehoused in a block of flats, on the second floor. I had never in my life lived in a block of flats; my parents had owned their own house or we had lived in a room in a house, but never in an anonymous block with so many different people. It was an awful place – people peeing outside your front door, rubbish on the stairs, lights in the hall-ways not working. I felt ashamed to be there. We stuck it out for about eighteen months. Stuart was born in the flat when Stephen was two and a half. For all that time he had nowhere to play, and he was an active toddler. There was a play area down the bottom where some older kids used to run about, and one day when Stephen was about four he kept nagging me that he wanted to play downstairs and eventually I said, 'OK, as long as you stay there and don't move away.' By the time I got back upstairs and looked out of the window to check on him, I saw him just about to cross the busy main road, lorries and buses charging along and my son heading towards them. I don't know how I got down those stairs so fast. After that I couldn't let him out. He was there locked up in the flat with me until I could take him out for a walk or to a proper playground. We were both climbing the walls. I badgered the council every day, and even-tually they agreed to rehouse us in a town house with a garage and garden.

It was such a relief. Stephen had been given a bicycle for his fourth birthday and since he could not ride it unless someone took him out, sometimes he would just sit with his feet on the pedals in that second-floor flat, looking wistful and frustrated. We moved to a three-storey house in Llanover Road, in Woolwich, just north of the old Military Academy and not far from the Common. We lived there until Stephen died. There was a play area round the back, enclosed by a high wall, which the children could reach from our back gate, a safer place for them to play than anything we'd had before. We bought the house from the council some years later. I loved it there. I liked the lay-out of the house: there was a living room on the first floor, and a room that Neville and I used as a bedroom. Below us at the back was the kitchen and hallway, and above us were the chil-dren's bedrooms, so Neville and I were at the heart of the house, protecting our children from any harm that might come in. When we first moved there the boys shared a bedroom, but at night they had problems sleeping so eventually we separated them and they each had their own room, until we had Georgina. Stephen was always protective of his little sister; they really had a close bond.

We were happy in that house, which was in a new development. The front doors were close to each other and because we all moved in at the same time as our neighbours, we made friends easily. There were not many black families in the area, but one of them lived next door to us. On our side of the road everyone got on, while you might just say hello to the people on the other side.

I had always wanted to have children. I had probably read too many love stories and had a very romantic idea of married life: the loving husband coming home from work to an ideal family. My own childhood had been so unlike the ideal that I wanted my marriage and my children's lives to turn out perfectly. And for a long time the dream seemed to have come true. I loved family life and watching my children crawl and babble and speak, and then turn into little upright people.

Stuart was a much bigger baby than Stephen: how I managed to carry him I will never know, and he weighed 9lb at birth. He was one of those proper contented babies that you fed every four hours, and then you could leave him – feed him, change him, and he would sleep soundly until his next feed. That was a delightful surprise. Stephen was two and a half when Stuart was born in April 1977, and it looked at first as if he might be jealous of his new baby brother. Then, not long after I brought Stuart home, I was changing his nappy as Stephen was looking on. After studying Stuart for a while, he said, 'Oh, he's got one like me!' And then everything was fine. It helped that Stuart slept so much, allowing me still to spend time with Stephen, so he did not feel left out or that we had no more time for him.

Stephen never liked sleeping. As he was growing up, you would hear him moving around upstairs at night. Stephen was nearly eight and Stuart five when I had Georgina, so they were together for a long time. While they shared a room they would be up there messing about long after we put them to bed. When we gave them separate rooms Stuart would go out like a light while Stephen stayed awake for hours. His curiosity and energy were always amazing to me, and I prayed he would find a creative outlet for it.

Perhaps he was one of those rare people who just did not need much sleep. In the mornings I never had to wake him to get ready for school; he would be up and at it right away. Stephen was full of life, rushing to meet it. I had such great hopes for him.

Stephen always announced exactly what he wanted to do. From about the age of seven he wanted to be an architect. He had a certain artistic gift from an early age and used to make our Christmas cards and birthday cards, and Mother's Day cards for me. His work was always very neat. I bought handwriting books to encourage my children to learn their letters and Stephen quickly picked up reading and writing. By the age of seven he was reading well.

He loved sport. By the time he left primary school he was a good swimmer and could dive and pick up a brick under water. He was a sprinter rather than a long-distance runner; he used to do the 100 metres and 200 metres, and by the time he was nine he had joined an athletics club. Stephen started at Sutcliffe Park and then he changed to Cambridge Harriers. He ran for Greenwich in their junior competition, and when he was fourteen he managed to qualify for the mini-marathon, which is very difficult if you are a sprinter. That was in 1988; he was thrilled to meet Linford Christie and Tessa Sanderson and to help raise money for Great Ormond Street Children's Hospital.

Stephen was good at every sport that he tried. He played football, though he didn't belong to a club; he supported Arsenal, despite being a south London boy. One day he broke his left wrist playing football at school. I had a phone call to go to the hospital. They kept him waiting the whole day, because he wasn't crying even though he was in pain. His best friend Elvin Oduro painted a picture of a girl's face on his plaster cast that was so good it looked like a transfer. Now I wish we had kept it when they cut it off. I hoped and prayed that this was the worst injury that would ever happen to my son.

Stephen enjoyed life. I wanted my kids to be able to look back and remember their childhood with fondness, wanted their childhood to be completely different to mine, so I spent a great deal of time nurturing and helping them. I bought Stephen a Collins pocket dictionary to help him learn to spell – I am terrible at spelling because no one spent time with me, and I did not want him to have the same anxiety about language that I have always felt. We would work at it for half an hour when he came home from school, while I was cooking.

During holiday times, at half-term or at Easter, we would go swimming, to museums, to the cinema. Like all boys his age he loved *Star Wars*, and was very taken with *Edward Scissorhands*, the Johnny Depp film. I took only temporary, part-time employment while Stephen was growing up. I worked at Goldsmith's University Bookshop in Lewisham; I was a care assistant; I did office cleaning. After 1981, I started to work in schools, because that fitted in well with the children's holidays. Whatever job I did, I made sure I could have holidays off at the same time as them, so that they were not left on their own. Georgina was thirteen before I worked three full days a week.

When there was money to spend I would make special trips up-town to the West End shops, and go to the Harrods sale to buy them good-quality things. They were always well dressed – at first I never dreamed of buying clothes from the local market. But once I started studying, it was a different matter; money was scarce and Neville was by that time out of work, so I had to be careful. One day I was out buying Stuart some summer things in the market and I asked Stephen, 'Do you want one of these?' He looked at the clothes and said emphatically, 'No!' It did not matter to Stuart, but it did to Stephen. He had his street cred to keep up, and to be seen wearing market gear was not his style.

When I look back at what life was like then, and how busy I was with three young children, I remember Stephen once asking me, 'Mum, what would you really, really like?' 'Some peace and quiet, please,' I said. My words have come back to me more than once: be careful what you wish for, it may come true.

I think it is essential to have time for your children; we bring them into the world, they did not ask to be here. Even in the kitchen, if I was baking, they were part of it and they helped. At Christmas I made my own mince pies, helped by a conveyor belt of Stephen, Stuart and Georgina. I would roll the pastry and in turn they would cut it out and place it on a tray; put the filling in; put the pie lids on and brush them with milk; then the pies were ready to go in the oven. Those were precious moments.

My children had a carefree life. My marriage was happy. Even though Neville worked long hours when he had building work, he would rush home to be with me and the children. He was not one of those husbands who sit in a pub for hours after work. The only time we had arguments was when I disagreed with him about how he disciplined the children. He was very strict with them, like many West Indian parents, quick to punish them when he thought it necessary by confiscating their toys or stopping them watching television. Occasionally they might get a slap from him, which was a normal way for parents in Jamaica to discipline their children. But looking back, and seeing my surviving children now, I don't think their upbringing did them any harm.

Neville was always harder on Stuart, who would have his toys taken away quite often. It was not a big problem, but I did notice it, and sometimes I felt that I had to stick up for Stuart. Because he was often ill as a child, suffering from both asthma and eczema, I spent a lot of time looking after him, and perhaps Neville was too aware of all the attention that I gave Stuart. He complained that Stuart was always 'under my armpit'; wherever I sat Stuart was in my lap, whereas Stephen was always more assertive and independent.

Only twice did I have to go to the school for anything to do with Stephen's behaviour. The first incident was in his second year at primary school, year 4. Apparently his teacher had torn up one of his books in front of him. I went to the school and listened to what the teacher had to tell me. Stephen had written something and the teacher felt it was not good enough and told him to go away and do it again; but Stephen had decided that what he had done was adequate and stood his ground. Then the teacher tore up his book, which was a ridiculous over-reaction. I told the teacher I did not think that what he had done was such a good idea, that there must be a better way of handling a conflict with a child. I got a lot of respect from the school for not shouting and making accusations in that situation.

The second occasion was in his final year at primary school, when Stephen had a fight with a boy who was calling him racist names. There were not many black children in the school at the time, so the majority of his friends were white and they told Stephen that this boy was calling him names. He had got into a fight and as a result I was called in to see the head teacher. I walked in and listened. Then I said, 'Well, what are you doing about it? It only happened because Stephen had to defend himself. What are you as a school doing?' Eventually the boy did stop insulting him openly; but even after they left school, Stephen told me that this boy persisted in being racist towards him whenever they saw each other.

Those two occasions apart, Stephen had no trouble with his teachers or any of his peers that I know of. At the time of the second incident I was actually working in the school. Stuart went to the same school while Georgina was at nursery. Stephen had no problem with me working there but Stuart did. Stuart as I have said was an asthmatic and he had eczema and he would charge around until his chest got so tight that his whole torso moved painfully when he breathed. I would watch him when I was on playground duty and tell him to stop running around and to calm down – so he made sure to be anywhere but where I was, and would go to another playground to avoid the shame of being reprimanded by his mother at school.

On one family holiday when Stephen and Stuart were small, aged four and two, we went to Cornwall. Neville had made Stephen a tan leather bomber jacket and Stuart had a black one. We were on a hill facing the sea; the wind was blowing in from the sea and I remember watching Stuart screw up his face as the chill went through him, while Stephen was standing with his arms outstretched trying to balance, revelling in it, unfazed by the huge waves and the cold air.

I have always loved taking photos, partly because I had so few images to remind me of my own childhood, and I love looking at a picture and remembering all the circumstances in which it was taken. The image of Stephen that was reproduced so often later, of him smiling and dressed in a black-and-white striped shirt is from a photo I took, never dreaming that it would ever be anything other than a picture for my album or the mantelpiece. He looks so jaunty and confident and just a little cheeky in it, a fit young man ready for life. And once we went on a family outing to Chessington Zoo with a friend who had two girls roughly the same age as my boys. Stephen was about three,

Stuart just over eighteen months – and when I saw the four of them sitting on the pavement, so peacefully, these four kids sitting down, relaxing in the sun, I just had to take a photograph. It will always stay with me as an image of how beautiful children are and how good life can be.

I would not say that Stephen was a perfect child – is there such a thing? He occasionally got up to mischief like any other kid. He didn't have any awareness of danger, and despite my hopes that his football wrist injury would be the last of his hurts, I ended up in hospital with him several more times. Once I went to the hairdresser and I had all three children with me. There was an adventure playground nearby, so Stephen and Stuart went off to play. The next thing I knew they had come back crying and distressed. Stephen had been climbing a tree and he had caught his shin and grazed himself badly. Once again I took him to the hospital, where they cleaned the leg and gave him a tetanus jab.

One Sunday morning he woke us up with his hand covered in blood. There was no bread in the kitchen and since I used to keep a loaf in the freezer, I had called down to him, 'Take the bread out of the freezer and leave it to thaw.' Of course he did not listen to me. He tried to slice the frozen loaf and the knife went into his hand. I remember him coming up the stairs and throwing himself melodramatically on the bed, with one arm stretched out in front of him and blood all over the sheets. I had to get up, dress and drive Stephen to the hospital to have stitches put in his hand.

It was always the Brook Hospital, a Victorian hospital on Shoot-er's Hill that had seen better days. It was a big, redbrick warren of buildings, an old fever hospital that had a casualty department in the centre. From the grounds you could see down the hill to the south, to Eltham and beyond. It had a big water tower near the entrance which could be seen from a long way off. We must have become quite well known there, the number of times I visited with Stephen and Stuart. Once Neville came home and saw things scattered around and no one in the house – I had called an ambulance after one of the boys had burned himself – and immediately came looking for us at Brook Hospital.

Stephen was an extrovert and loved clothes that made him stand out. Once we went shopping and a pair of green leather shoes caught Stephen's eye. Not many people would dream of walking around in green shoes but he tried them on, liked them and I bought them for him. He loved his green shoes. He didn't care if everyone stared. Another time, I remember him wearing a corduroy suit which had a leopard-skin lining with orange in it, and I said, 'Stephen, please – do you really want to wear that? Pimps wear things like that.' But if he saw something that he liked, he would wear it and it didn't matter what anyone else said or thought.

Neville is not particularly fashion-conscious, but I used to be. I was willing to take fashion risks, to say the least. About the time I was leaving school, I bought myself a bright yellow suit with patterned lapels, and some platform shoes; being short, I was looking for height, so I also wore an Afro. When I was working I once bought a two-tone suit which changed colour in the light, green with a shade of brown in it, and I wore that with a crinkly white blouse and pink suede shoes. In those days everyone had a suit like that; incredible as it now seems, they were all the rage. Whatever the latest style, I was willing to try it. Stephen took after me in that.

Once he needed a new tracksuit and being his flash self he wanted one with a yellow trim; there's a photograph of him in it when he was running a mini-marathon in 1988, looking very stylish, with the jacket open, his shoulders thrown back. When he was about to do work experience with the black architect Arthur Timothy in Tower Bridge, I went shopping with him and with money that he had saved we bought various outfits in preparation for his placement. Dressed up to the nines to set out to work, and he looked a picture.

As he got older Stephen would do his homework in the kitchen and be down there for hours; while most children his age went to bed about ten, he was still up at eleven o'clock or later if you let him. While doing his homework, he would be listening to tapes on his Walkman and eating at the same time. He loved soul, R&B, pop singers like Mariah Carey, and he liked LL CoolJ, the early and more melodic kind of rap. He and Stuart had an old record player but nothing to record on, so Stephen would ask Neville to record tapes for him. Neville was very into music – he could spend most of Sunday lying on his back listening to singers such as Luther Vandross, and for his birthdays and Christmas Stephen would buy him LPs.

When my aunt Lil moved to Florida in 1986, I wanted to be able to get on a plane and fly over to see her. She left in August and by Christmas that year I was there. Neville, who never liked flying, made such a fuss about going that I decided just to do it myself. I was already working as a schools care assistant at the time, so I saved all the money I earned, which I could afford to do since Neville's wages paid for everything else. He may have thought that as a woman I would not be able do it or would be too frightened to go. I saved up enough to buy tickets for myself and the boys, and we had a little spending money. Neville took us to the airport and I remember him standing watching us go, looking really lost because we would not be around for Christmas and the New Year. But once we got there we phoned, and we chatted throughout the period I was away. We had a great time and the children loved it, and I felt more independent than I'd been in years.

I began studying again in the late 1980s. I had wanted to go back into education for a long time, partly because I wanted more out of life, and to make up for the lack of encouragement I had experienced as a child. I had begun working as a Special

Needs helper in the local school. A teacher there noticed that I could manage a class if a teacher was out, or if a supply teacher could not handle the students. He gave me a prospectus and said, 'I think you should be a teacher.' That sounded wonderful, but of course I did not have the qualifications. I applied for a teacher training course and was accepted, and did an access course for a year.

After that I could go on to do a BEd degree. I started at the University of Greenwich, where some of the tutors felt that students who came through on the access course route were not as good as those who had taken A-levels. By nature I am quiet and easily intimidated and I found the young students, loud and self-confident, daunting to be around.

I failed one of my second-year exams, partly because I am not good at sitting exams in a room full of people; it makes me very nervous and anxious. I did a part-time year's course in English because I felt I needed to improve my grammar. Then I decided to go back to my degree. Some helpful person suggested that I see a tutor to discuss what I was doing and I decided to take the Humanities degree. At the end of my degree I knew I could do the PGCE, since my intention was to teach in a primary school.

By then Stephen was studying for his A-levels in English Language and Literature at Woolwich College for two days each week, and he was also doing an A-level in Design and Technology and re-sitting his GCE Physics exams. To earn a little money for his sport and his clothes, at weekends he worked at the Fun Junction, a children's play centre, and after that closed down he went to work at a McDonald's in the Old Kent Road. All I was afraid of was that he would not measure up to his own high standards, and I hoped that he would never really fail. He was a popular, active, committed eighteen-year-old. He was good-looking, athletic, 5 feet 10 inches tall. He adored his little sister, he was a Christian, and he hoped to become an architect. He had his whole life ahead of him, and it looked good.

That was my life as it stood in 1993. Nothing much disturbed me, or my confidence in my family's future. Once or twice I discovered that the outside world might see me in a different light. When Stephen and Stuart were still very small, before I had Georgina, I used to go to a young wives' club run by a church. My friend Verna's son had come to stay for a week and I took him with my two boys on a trip organised by the club to Chessington Zoo. I remember other women staring at me with these three young boys and eventually one of them asked Stephen, 'Where's your dad?' She said it with such an edge that I knew she thought that because I was black I would not have a husband. Those were the assumptions that people made, and probably still make. Years later, a white woman was talking about having been married for twenty years and when I said I had been married for twenty-five years I could see how shocked she was. She had assumed that Stephen was born out of wedlock, or that I had lots of kids, or that who I married was not my children's father – those are the stereotypes of black mothers. Even though I was aware of attitudes like that, I would not have said that people were ever really racist towards me.

Nor was I concerned with politics, even though I read the newspapers and was aware of the world I lived in, and its dangers. I would point out to Stephen articles about black youths being attacked on trains or beaten up in police vans. I knew that sort of thing happened, but I was not in the least politicised. When you have children you focus on bringing them up, on giving them love and a stable environment. None of my family that I know of had had any racist experiences, apart from my brother Martin, who when standing at a bus stop once had been accused of looking threatening, as though he was about to rob someone. I was aware, at a distance, of the pressures that bear down on young black men.

Yet stories of killings and assaults worried me, partly because Stephen was such an extrovert. He loved going out with his friends and, since he was a sensible child, we allowed him to. He never thought anything bad could happen to him. When Rolan Adams, another black teenager, was killed for no reason by a white boy with a knife in Thamesmead in 1991, and a march was organised, Stephen wanted to go on it. I told him that I knew the area was racist, and I really didn't want him going down there. I knew enough about Thamesmead to know its bad reputation as an area where the British National Party had a lot of support. But Stephen told me he knew Rolan, and that was why he wanted to be there, and he did go. You can make a fuss and try to protect them but in the end you know you have to let children do what they feel passionate about, because they are growing up and it is their world. Stephen was beginning to assert his independence, like any other teenager.

Little did I know that the kind of people who murdered Rolan Adams would become part of the nightmare that would haunt me for the rest of my life, spreading circles of fear and dishonesty and grief. If I thought about it at the time I saw it as an isolated incident, a warning that there were fanatics in England who hated black people enough to kill them. I could not have imagined how connected all these incidents were. I could not have known then, unless I read and remembered all the horror stories in the local press, about the stabbing of Gurdeep Bhangal, the son of the manager of a Wimpy shop in Eltham High Street, who was knifed because some white boys decided they didn't like the drink they had asked for. He survived, but earlier, in 1992, a young Asian man called Rohit Duggal was killed on Well Hall Road in the same area. I could not have known how his death was linked to other stabbings and to a web of racism and crime in the area. The idea that there was a gang of white boys armed with knives rampaging around Eltham would have sounded like something out of a novel to me. How could I have known any of this? None of this madness, this hatred, seemed to touch me or my family. All I wanted was to improve my own life while I still had time, and make sure my children had a better life than I had been given.

4   Murder

In 1993 I was in my first year of my Humanities degree as a mature student. Though Neville was out of work, we were not experiencing financial hardship, so that my studies were not a great extra strain on the family .

Neville had lost his job in 1990 – there was a downturn in the building trade and the housing market was stagnant – but before that we had always had good earnings. There were times when my part-time wages were all saved because we managed on what Neville brought in. Now he spent a lot of time at home, helping with the children, cooking and being there for them.

My degree involved field trips and the very first time I went on such a trip was in April that year, because before then I had never been able to leave my family alone even for a few days. Now that Neville was at home it was a lot easier, since he could look after the children when they got back from school. I left with the other students on Tuesday, 20 April, and travelled by coach to Birmingham. We visited different places connected with the Black Country and the Industrial Revolution. There were quite a few other mature students on the course and throughout that day when we were not looking at industrial museums and railway stations we would chat about our families and our children. I remember saying how independent Stephen was, and the feeling of pride in talking about my children, and it made the whole day even more enjoyable to think that they were waiting for me at home with all their problems and successes. I felt I'd achieved something worthwhile in bringing them up.

Before I left for that trip Neville was being quite difficult; he was depressed being home and not working and there were times when things were tense between us. But when I got back to London on Thursday evening, 22 April, he came to pick me up at the Woolwich site of Greenwich University, where the coach dropped us off, and we were both making an effort. I remember that it was about nine o'clock.

I asked how the children were. It was the one great thing that we had in common, when all else failed. Despite the strains of unemployment and anxiety, we were holding together well. He said that Stuart and Georgina were at home but that Stephen was still out. This was not something to make me anxious. Stephen was allowed to have his independence; but on school nights I tried to insist that he be home around 10.30 p.m. and at first he submitted to this, but he was eighteen years old, and as time went on he argued more and kicked against the limits we set.

He was, I suppose, going through a typical late adolescent phase: we at home were, generally speaking, always wrong. Some weeks before my field trip he and Stuart had had a petty falling out, as teenagers do, and this quarrel had continued for a long time. He was falling out with everyone in the house, at different times and for different reasons. Some of them were very minor indeed. The dispute with Stuart had begun over a pencil case of Stephen's; somehow Stuart had broken the zip, and Stephen complained, and I was busy in the kitchen at the time and had no time for this fight over a damaged zip. Stephen was not satisfied with that, though I am not sure what he expected me to do. He marched up the stairs again to confront Stuart and I could hear them fighting and arguing. I shouted to Neville, who was in the garage, to come in and sort them out.

Neville became very angry with Stephen when this ridiculous argument escalated, as such things can do between children, and Neville was getting more and more upset with him; whatever

Neville said, Stephen would not have it, and was arguing back and standing up to him until eventually Neville slapped him. Stephen stormed up to his bedroom, swearing wildly. So I followed him upstairs to speak to him, saying, 'Look, go and apologise. You really mustn't use language like that.'

I thought it was all over and done with. That had happened on a Sunday. On the Monday Stephen came down ready to go to school. He said goodbye, went out through the front door, and everything was fine. Then the door opened again and Stephen rushed in and up the stairs. He and his brother could be heard shouting at each other. What Stuart had done was to unscrew every single screw in Stephen's Walkman. Stephen had not realised this until he tried to switch it on, when it fell apart in his hands.

As far as Stephen was concerned, the telling-off I gave Stuart was not enough, so he stopped speaking to his brother. This went on and on. Then he would not speak to Georgina – and in the end refused to speak to any of us. He did Neville and me the courtesy of saying hello but that was about the extent of his communication with the family. Stuart's birthday was on 14 April and we took him to an event run by the Scouts. Stephen refused to join us. Before that, I had talked to him and told him that the way he had been behaving wasn't good enough. 'We're a family,' I remember saying, 'and we need to live together as a family. You can't continue ignoring people like this. If you are not happy at home and you want to leave, that's fine, but while you are here we live as a family.' I thought he might give me a lot of lip but he didn't, but sat and listened quietly. Then he went to his room. I could feel him stretching his wings, more and more, but he was not ready to fly just yet, and I was glad.

After that I noticed a change in him: his step was much lighter, and he would say, 'Mum, I'm going out, do you want anything?' His behaviour was completely different. When we came back on the evening of Stuart's birthday Stephen was home. Our living room was on the first floor and as we walked upstairs he was coming down from the top floor and I heard him mumble something to Stuart.

'What did he say?' I asked.

Stuart said, 'Happy birthday.'

I felt relieved, more than I'd have thought possible. And it had all started over a pencil case. The morning before I left on my trip Georgina came running downstairs, 'Mummy, Mummy, Stephen said good morning!' So there was nothing at home to give me any cause for concern when I went away, and I was feeling good about my children and longing to see them again.

That night of 22 April, Stephen's dinner was in the oven, as it usually was now that he had stopped coming straight home from school for family dinners, another sign of his desire to go his own way. Georgina was sleeping and Stuart was still awake. I went up and chatted to him, and then I took a bath, had something to eat and was getting ready for bed.

We watched the main news on television at ten o'clock, then the local news came on. I remember thinking that it was 10.30 and that it was time for Stephen to be home. But I was not worried; it was just a little prickle of anxiety, the kind of feeling that every mother gets if there is any uncertainty about the whereabouts of her child. I had felt such tremors many times before and knew that I should not give in to them.

Just after the bulletin had finished, about twenty-five or twenty to eleven, I heard a knock on the front door. For a second I wondered who it could be, and then I thought, 'Maybe Stephen has forgotten his key.' There is something about a knock on the door late at night, long after friends or neighbours would call, that makes you feel a little spooked.

Neville went down to answer the door. Our living-room door was open and from where I was sitting I could hear voices and I knew it was not Stephen's voice. Then I heard Stephen's name mentioned. My body came all alive again and I forgot about how tired I was. I rushed downstairs, and the bulk of Neville was blocking my way. I couldn't see who was in the doorway, so I pushed him out of the way and said, 'Well, what about Stephen?' I knew and was already denying to myself that there was something wrong, an injury or accident, hoping and fearing at the same time.

It was a young man called Joey Shepherd who lived with his family in the house behind ours; their front door faced our back garden. He had been to the same primary school as Stephen. He stood there with his father and his younger brother, three white men looking concerned and on edge. They were neighbours that we did not know very well, and we'd never had any real problems with them. Their arrival on our doorstep like this was so unusual that I began to feel something serious had happened, though I was still sure it was nothing that we could not get over. Maybe there had been an accident, maybe he was hurt. Joey said that he happened to be down in Eltham waiting for a bus at the same stop as Stephen. And then he said that Stephen and his friend had been attacked, and he mentioned four or five boys.

The father said, 'Perhaps you should ring the police and find out what has happened.' Without thinking I ran upstairs to the phone, leaving Neville to talk to the Shepherds. I did not know the number of the local police station, had never had to have any dealings with the police in my whole life, so I just rang 999, the one number that might bring help. I told them where I lived and said, 'Somebody has just told me that my son has been attacked.' They put me through to Plumstead police station and I found myself talking to a man who sounded bored with his job.

He said they knew nothing about any incident in Eltham and of course I could not give any details because I knew nearly nothing. I pulled on my coat over my pyjamas. Without speaking about it both Neville and I knew that we had to go down there and see for ourselves. Joey Shepherd had said the bus stop was on Well Hall Road, between an old cinema that had closed down and the Welcome Inn pub, a mile or so south of where we lived, and I had a good idea of where he meant.

By then Stuart had come rushing down the stairs. We told him that Stephen had been attacked and that we were going to find him. He wanted to come out with us but I said we couldn't leave Georgina alone. She was almost eleven, Stuart sixteen, and I was suddenly anxious about them being alone. I was trying to be so calm.

Neville and I got into the car and reached Well Hall Road in about five minutes. At the top of the road there was an old police station, which looked closed that night. The bus stop and the pub, the Welcome Inn, are quite close to each other, so we drove down the road, which seemed grey under the street lights. I was aware of whitewashed houses to our left. There was no one around, as far as I could see. All the life in the street seemed to have packed up and left. The weather was clear and a little cold. We came to the pub, to the bus stop, and we didn't see anything further along the road – no police cars, no flashing lights, we did not see an ambulance or signs of anything having happened, and we should have seen it because it is a straight road. It was almost empty, with only a few cars passing us going north to Woolwich and the city, and this feeling of nothing going on was reassuring: whatever had happened could not have been worth serious attention from the police, and I felt almost relieved. We thought that perhaps he had been taken to hospital, and that we should go and check. I hoped it would be a waste of time and that we would return home to find Stephen waiting for us, cross that we had over-reacted by rushing out to look for him.

Brook Hospital was just a few minutes back up the road, so we turned and drove there. It was just as I remembered it from the last time, red brick and iron stairs outside, lit up from within by bright strip lighting. It had a grim look the way those old hospitals always do and that night it was not somewhere I wanted to be. When it came into sight it depressed me. We drove through the gates into the grounds and around the driveway to the centre of the hospital where the casualty department was located.

Neville dropped me outside the ambulance entrance and went to park the car while I went straight into the casualty department, which I knew well from Stephen's earlier little injuries and I hoped it was something as minor as one of those that had taken him there tonight, if he was there at all. The smell of disinfectant seemed stronger than usual.

When I walked in I could see a police officer and a young black boy standing off to the side furthest from the door. I did not recognise the boy at the time – I was looking for Stephen, and this was not my son, that was all I took in. I walked round the waiting area. There were other people sitting there, the usual drunks with cuts and bruises, but I did not see Stephen.

Just at that moment Neville came in. He recognised Duwayne Brooks straight away, but it was only when he walked over to him and said something that I realised who he was. Duwayne was a friend of Stephen's, though not one that we particularly approved of.

I went up to Duwayne and asked him, 'What happened? Where's Stephen?'

At the same time a nurse came out and walked over to Duwayne and asked, 'What did they hit him with?' Duwayne did not answer. He seemed to be in a state of shock, moving nervously, on the verge of tears. I was trying to talk to him as well, trying to find out exactly what had happened. The tension was terrible.

Other medical people came round, so my attention turned to them: I asked them what was happening, what was wrong with Stephen, where was he, and I said that we wanted to see him.

I must have asked to see him three or four times, and all they kept saying was, 'We're working on him,' repeating this several times.

Each time I said, 'I want to see him,' even more insistently. I was now seriously frightened, but they said no. Then we were shown into a quiet room to the side. Neville and I sat there for a while, not speaking much. After what seemed ages, I thought, 'I can't just sit here.'

I stood up and I went to phone my sister Cheryl. I told her that Stephen was in hospital and that we didn't know what had happened to him. She said she would come down. Then Neville rang his cousin, to whom he was close, and I think we felt that by gathering family around us we were at least doing something and staving off the worst. It was not long after we had made those calls that two women came into the family waiting room. I noticed it was called that, just before they walked in. One was a ginger-haired woman in a dark blue staff nurse's uniform and the other was a doctor in a white coat. They told us, quietly but emphatically, that Stephen had died.

'I'm sorry to inform you that your son has died.' That is what I remember the doctor saying, but she could have said it in some other way. The words were meaningless to me. They may have said he was stabbed; I can't honestly remember. I could not take it in. How can you take in something like that? I think I said something like: 'Died? What do you mean he's died? He can't have died. Stephen isn't dead. No, he's not . . . How do you mean he's died?'

Duwayne, who had come into the room with us, began crying and shouting and hitting the wall.

All I could say was, 'You see . . . the reason why I don't want Stephen to be out?' There was nothing else to be said after that, there was nothing else I could say.

Ever since Stephen had started going out on his own I worried about him. The dangers that I kept seeing for him, he never saw.

He was minding his own business, causing no trouble, and trouble shouldn't trouble him. 'It's not as simple as that,' I would argue. 'If you are in a train make sure you sit in a part where there are lots of people around. When you are walking down a road, walk on the opposite side to where the vehicles are coming, so you can see who's going to stop in front of you.' I warned him against all the dangers I could think of. All except the worst danger, which I never thought about.

He used to get so irritated with me: 'Mum, will you stop telling me these things, stop worrying.' But I couldn't help it. I worried more for Stephen than I ever did for Stuart, since I knew where Stuart was most of the time.

At the hospital that night, I don't remember Duwayne saying anything coherent. He was in a dreadful state, and I didn't press him to speak. Once we knew about Stephen, it was as if no one else existed. Duwayne was alive; my son was gone.

I was numb. Nothing was real any more. I remember that we asked to see Stephen. The doctor told us we had to wait as they were preparing him, some words like that; they meant nothing to me. By then my sister had arrived with her husband. We told them that Stephen had died. We all sat there in silence. My sister was crying; I was not. One or two other family members had come to the hospital; my sister had phoned my brother Martin, and word was spreading.

Eventually the nurse took us into the examination room to see Stephen. His face looked as if he was asleep, not frowning or angry. It was just as if he was sleeping. The only thing that looked out of place was that he had a deep cut on his chin. I remember wanting to say to him, Stephen, now do you understand what I was telling you? I just stood there gazing at him, touching his face; and he was cold, he was already cold.

It must have been after midnight by the time we left the hospital. And then afterwards, what are you meant to do?

Only one police officer was there, who never spoke to us. I'm not sure whether he took Duwayne away before we left the hospital or after. But I know that when we went home, nobody came back with us and we still had no idea what had happened to our son, no explanation from any officer of the law as to how our son had died. My sister could not follow us because her children were home alone, and so Neville drove us back, just the two of us in the car.

It was well into the night when we got home; I don't remember checking the time. We didn't ring anyone when we got home. We did not know what to do, or what to say, even to each other.

Stuart was still awake and he came downstairs. We had to tell him. It was the hardest thing I have ever had to tell him, and I hope I will never have to tell him anything as hard again. I told him Stephen had died – what else could I say, or how could I have said it differently? Stuart cried and cried.

I found out later that while we were out he got on his bike and rode down to Well Hall Road to see for himself. But there was nothing to see, so he came straight home again.

Georgina was asleep and I decided not to wake her.

I don't know how Duwayne's mother found out about Stephen's death, but she came to our house, accompanied by a friend. It must have been the small hours of the morning by then, but normal life had stopped hours before and I did not care. She did not make a good impression on me. How long she stayed I don't know; all I remember about her being there is that she said something about having told Duwayne that whenever there was any trouble he must run. She also said that she was glad it wasn't her son who'd been killed. I cannot forget how she said that – not how sorry she was that my son had died but that she was glad it wasn't her son. I could understand her feeling that, but it was not what I wanted to hear a few hours after my son had been killed.

Eventually I went to our bedroom. I could not sleep. I was still in shock. I just lay there, staring at the darkness in the room.

It is hard to describe what you feel when somebody tells you that your son is *dead*. The word doesn't really sink in; as I said, it doesn't have any meaning. What do you mean, dead? *He's* not dead. And that is how I felt, and how I feel in unguarded moments even now. I still didn't believe he was dead, though I'd been told, I'd seen him, I'd seen his face not moving. I was still hoping that he would wake up, that the phone was about to ring and someone would say it had all been a mistake, and then the front door would open.

In the morning I rang a couple of my oldest friends, Clara and Lorraine, whom I had known since the age of eleven, and before long they were at the house. It was still very early when they came round, before school time.

When Georgina woke up, I was sitting in the living room and Neville was on the telephone downstairs. It was about seven o'clock when she came out of her room. The normal routine would have been that Stephen used the bathroom first, followed by Stuart and then Georgina, because she was the youngest and her school was closest. She sensed at once that there was something wrong. I must have looked terrible. She said, 'Mum, what's up?'

And I could not answer, I really could not answer her.

She went downstairs and she must have overheard her father talking on the phone. Neville was calling relatives and friends, including Stephen's best friend Elvin Oduro, to break the news. From what he was saying, Georgina must have realised that her brother was dead. I can remember her running up the stairs screaming. I went to her and tried to hold her, but her arms and legs were writhing and I could not contain her. She kept repeating, 'It's not true! It's not true! Where is Stephen?'

Eventually I managed to calm her down. It was very difficult to explain to her when I knew so little myself. At the time I did not even know how Stephen had been killed, so all I could say was that Stephen had died and that someone had done this to him.

As more people started coming to the house we had to tell the story over and over again. By this time I was getting more and more agitated. I wanted to know what the police were doing, wanted some exact information.

Stuart cried and cried, though he did not break down like Georgina. Stuart is very like me: we show emotion but don't scream out. In the morning he didn't even come downstairs. I went up and I told both of them that I didn't want them to go to school, I wanted them where I could keep an eye on them and protect them. But they both got dressed and said that they wanted to go.

My friend Rita went with Georgina and Clara went with Stuart, because I could not bear the thought of them going on their own and my friends could explain to the teachers what had happened. Rita stayed for the whole day with Georgina, who was still at primary school, came home with her at lunchtime, and then took her back to the school after lunch. Clara stayed with Stuart for a while, before coming back to me. He came home for lunch too. It must have been a very odd day: how do you sit down in class with your friends around you when your brother has been murdered? But that was the way they chose to cope, perhaps because it was better for them being with their friends than being surrounded by grieving adults.

Georgina was due to go on a school trip for a week on the Monday, 26 April, and again I begged her to stay home, but she was determined to go. As hard as it was to do, I packed clothes for her and spoke to her teacher and was reassured that they would look after her. She would be eleven the following Friday. On her birthday I managed to get a phone call through to her. She said she was all right, but I knew she was still in shock. The children were trying to carry on as though life was still normal.

From about 9 a.m. that Friday the house started to fill up with people – many of them I knew, a lot of them I did not know at all, and how they found their way to us I had no idea. Family and friends gathered around, and they invited people who offered help, and soon the house was full of sympathisers and well-wishers and their friends. It is normal in the African-Caribbean community that death becomes a communal event, a coming together to mourn, and this was a shocking death, so if I had been thinking about it, if I'd been able to think beyond my grief and shock, I would not have been surprised to see so many people. Well-wishers and political groups who had worked with other families of black murder victims came to offer support. The Anti-Racist Alliance was there, I remember, in the person of Marc Wadsworth and Palma Black. I had never heard of them or their group. Ros Howells, who worked with the Greenwich Council for Racial Equality, also turned up at the house, a tall, distinguished-looking woman; I had seen her around in Woolwich, where she worked, though I did not know her to speak to.

Everyone was talking, but by then I had fallen silent. I could not talk to anyone, and I just sat there weeping.

5 In the Dark

At about ten o'clock on the Friday morning two police officers came to the house to inform us that a press conference had been arranged at Woolwich Town Hall to appeal for witnesses to to the killing. Neville went but I did not, because I was not coherent. Instead I watched it on television. Neville was calm but angry, and said that our son's killers should be caught and hanged. By then my sister Cheryl was at the house with us, and my brothers came later in the evening. Aunt Lil in Florida had been told, and I spoke to her on the phone. She broke down, and it made me feel worse that this gentle woman should have to hear that the grand-nephew she had seen so recently had been violently taken away.

My mother – with whom my relationship was as difficult as ever – was also informed, and when I heard that she intended to come down the next day from Northampton, I was not sure that I wanted her there. She had never taken the time to get to know Stephen, or any of my children. What could she do now? Then somebody, I think it was Neville's cousin, took me aside and told me that now was not the time for old quarrels.

She came on the Saturday, and she must have been nervous, wondering how I would react. I can't say that she was affectionate, even then, but she was very upset, as though the loss of her first grandchild had shocked and moved her out of her rigid indifference. I did tell her that I thought she had never taken enough interest in my children. I felt she needed to know that, now that it was too late. I think I was also saying that she had

69

never treated me as though I was important to her. Now I had nothing to lose.

On the Sunday morning before we set off for church she went down to the kitchen on the ground floor (I had not been in the kitchen at all since the Thursday night, I had stayed either in the living room or the bedrooms on the upper floors) and then she wandered back upstairs again, as though she was nervous of being seen in the kitchen by me. So I said to her, 'Look, while you're here in my home there isn't a room that you can't go into, there's nothing that you can't have or help yourself to; everything is there, just help yourself to what you want.' I was concerned partly because she was a diabetic and I did not want her to get ill, and partly because I did not want her to think I was being vindictive about what had happened in the past. I think that broke the ice between us a little, and then we went to church.

During that first weekend people would start coming to the house between seven and eight o'clock in the morning and they would not leave until about two or three o'clock the next morning. They were long, long days. There was no time for reflection or for ourselves. People brought food and cooked for us and themselves and answered the phone. Clara kept a message book beside the telephone and she would write down the name of anyone who called, the substance of the message and the time; I never answered my own phone. Everything that was happening in the house was organised by other people – my life was being taken away from me.

From the day after the murder on, every day from April to June, we had strangers in our home. There was not an empty room in the house. The only time that there was no one else with us was in the early hours of the morning. Because everyone was stressed, those who were smokers were chain smoking cigarettes and it irritated my throat to the point where I practically lost my voice. I remember Cheryl in the end telling people that their smoke was affecting her sister and to go outside, if they had to do it. Despite all the cooking going on I don't recollect eating anything. I remember people saying to me, 'Come on, you have to drink something at least.' About all I could bear to take was some hot water. I lost a couple of stones in weight within a few weeks. None of my clothes fitted. When my sister took me to the shops later to buy something, I had shrunk from a 10 to a size 8 and even that was a little big for me.

On Saturday morning we had been given permission to view Stephen's body at noon, at the mortuary in Greenwich. Two police liaison officers came to escort us there; one was a woman in plain clothes, DC Linda Holden. She was a tall, slim woman with light brown hair. The other was a big-bellied man named John Bevan. The car we travelled in could not carry more than five people; besides Neville and myself there were my sister Cheryl, my brother Mark's girlfriend and a young woman who claimed to be Stephen's girlfriend. This girl had come to the house with my niece and my brother's girl – I think they were sisters – and for reasons that were not clear even at the time joined us for that visit to the mortuary. When she came back to the house afterwards, she was almost showing off to my niece, asserting her intimacy with us in our grief. I had never met her before and I have not seen her since. Stephen may have met her at my brother's house, but his closest friend Elvin Oduro didn't know of her at all. Some strange things happened around Stephen's death; people's behaviour was extraordinary.

We did not take the children with us, which upset Georgina, as she wanted to go. But we did not know what to expect; and nobody had warned us.

At first we were only allowed to view Stephen's body through a glass panel that separated us from him, and I said that I wanted to touch him. The police were there with us, including Linda Holden and PC James Geddis, the officer who had been off-duty on the night Stephen was killed and was passing along Well Hall Road and had stopped to help. It was he who made the call to the emergency services when Duwayne could not get through from the public telephone. These details were starting to emerge from the fog surrounding that night, and I was taking them in slowly and confusedly. The police at the mortuary became agitated when I said that I wanted to touch my son and said no, they did not want me to do that. It felt strange that they did not give us space to mourn our child but were standing over us, as if watching to see what we were going to do – though what they thought we might do I will never know. Neville got quite irate and asked them, ' Would you mind stepping back and giving us some privacy?' We asked to see Stephen on our own, with no one else present, and eventually we were allowed to enter the room where the body was laid out.

I remember they had Stephen's body covered up with a sheet. I remember lifting off the sheet and then I saw his wounds. I noticed some marks that looked like pin-pricks all over his arm, though I did not know what they were and they were not explained to us. (Later, much later, I learned that they were the normal marks left by the post-mortem examination.) I saw that they had already done a post-mortem on him and that looked really horrible, the huge incision down the centre of his body. Then I saw the stab wounds. It was almost as if he had been stabbed right through his arm and into his body, and there was another cut high on his chest near the neck. Both wounds looked like large, wide cuts. It was awful to see this mutilation of my lovely son's body – and there was that cut on his chin. He also had a bruise on his face to one side of his cheek, probably made when he fell. I remember seeing all of that, but I did not know the depth of those wounds or precisely how they had caused his death. I did not hear the exact details until more than two years later, in August 1995, when I heard the pathologist's report at the committal hearings against the young men who were accused of murdering him. But that Saturday, less than two days after he died, all I could think about was the amount of pain he must have been in.

I will describe here what I didn't know then. He was stabbed twice by a large knife on both sides of his body. The knife had penetrated his chest and arm, and both cuts had severed major arteries. It must have felt like being struck by a small sword, a shocking blow.

We were told that he and Duwayne were waiting at the bus stop in Well Hall Road near Dickson Road, and that a group of five or six white boys had crossed the road and caught Stephen as he stood in the mouth of Dickson Road looking to see if a bus was coming. As they crossed the road Duwayne heard one of them shout 'What, what nigger?' and then they were mobbed around Stephen. Duwayne could see that Stephen was being hit with something and turned and ran, and Stephen, despite the fact that, as we learned later, his right lung would already have collapsed, managed to run some way before falling to the ground on the other side of the road. The distances meant nothing to me yet. He lay on his front, his head turned to the left, towards the roadway; his left arm was raised alongside his head. And there he lay dying, while police officers questioned his friend, who had managed to call an ambulance from the nearest phone box.

Already, despite the shock and grief I was feeling, it seemed strange to me that when we had turned up at the hospital on Thursday night the police must have seen us coming in – especially when Neville recognised Duwayne and went up to him – and yet no police officer there said anything to us. No one offered to take us home after we were told Stephen was dead. No one took our address or any other details. I was too upset to think much about it at the time, but it felt as though we were completely isolated and that our wonderful young man's death was of little concern to anyone in authority.

But at least after we left the morgue on Saturday the police took us down to the spot where the attack had taken place.

When they hear that my son was killed in south-east London, people often think of miles of bleak estates and old 1950s council blocks going to seed, but the place where Stephen died is not as rough as people from elsewhere might think. There's a lovely old eighteenth-century hospital at the top of Well Hall Road, set in its own grounds with grass all around it, which was turned into posh apartments after Stephen's murder. Our house was on a council estate, built in the 1960s, well built but with that feeling of being cut off from middle-class Greenwich village a couple of miles to the west. But Well Hall Road was a different world to the one we lived in. It all looked so Olde English. The houses were built to look like something out of a film set in Elizabethan times, with the high slate roofs, whitewashed walls, leaded glass and little bay windows. The streets all have poets' names: Rochester, Congreve, Lovelace. There is green in front of the houses, and plane trees line the road. Right opposite where Stephen finally fell down dying there is a Catholic church built in warm brown brick. It has the look of the 1920s, the look of an Agatha Christie film on TV rather than the gritty backstreets of Woolwich or Peckham. If my son had not died there I would probably think it was a nice area, almost leafy and like a village. I stood there looking and I couldn't believe that such an area could produce people who would commit such a horrific crime. But the Englishness of it was like a mockery now, and the fake old-world features a way of saying to me, You don't belong here in our little world, come here if you dare.

The police started off from where Stephen was attacked, in the mouth of Dickson Road which leads into the Brook Estate, and then drove up to where he actually fell, so I could see how far along the road he had run. It was hard to believe that he had run all that way before he collapsed. I could not stop imagining his agony as he was running. He went down, having lost too much blood, on the pavement outside number 320, Well Hall Road. It was one of those Elizabethan, garden-suburb-type houses. The house was not in great shape; the tiny front garden was patchy and the grass looked neglected; the house needed a coat of whitewash. It seemed the saddest place I had ever seen, and so desolate on that cold day.

After we came back to the house from the mortuary, I sat in Stephen's room looking through his papers and his books, and I came across something he had written for a school project. I remembered taking pictures for this project. Each student had to write something about how they saw themselves in their family, and Stephen had written in his notebook that when I was expecting him I had wanted a little girl. I thought he knew that was not true. I was sure I had communicated to him that I had always wanted a son for my first child. But it seems that somehow Stephen had either never heard me say that or else had misunderstood it. Seeing that was so heart-wrenching, with him not there so I could reassure him that I got exactly what I wanted when he was born. And it is one of the many little things that I can never put right.

On Sunday, 25 April, Rev. David Cruise came to the house and you could see the pain he was feeling. He was the Minister of Trinity Methodist Church, which Neville and I attended for many years, and he had known Stephen since he was a boy of five or six. Stephen's Scout troop was centred on the church hall, and parade days were held there once a month, and he went to drama classes organised by the Scout group. Until he was fourteen he had been very serious about his religion and had wanted to be baptised, but he drifted away, as teenagers often do. Yet the church was one of the places I felt closest to him, and it would remain so after his death. That Sunday David Cruise brought a letter from the Taaffes, a white Christian couple who had been on the scene when Stephen collapsed and who said they had comforted him as he was dying. He read this letter out;

75

in it Mr and Mrs Taaffe mentioned how at peace Stephen had been before he died, which at the time gave me something to hold on to.

My faith is important to me, and it was tested now. I was brought up a Baptist, but I joined the Methodist Church in the late 1970s. It gives me a structure, a strong sense of truth and justice and of equality in the eyes of God. My grandmother was the biggest influence in the development of my belief: watching how she conducted herself in the community, doing unto others as she would have them do unto her. I try to live by that maxim. In David Cruise's church young people were integrated into the church and had a voice, and I liked this, and the fact that it was genuinely open to other cultures. He had spent many years in Africa, and his services brought in music from many countries. As a preacher he was open and tolerant. He became a friend and was always there for us when we needed him – for the renewal of our wedding vows, for example. But I would never need him as much as I did that week.

The question that nobody can ever answer for me is, did Stephen know he was going to die? Young people often pretend to be tough, but I know my own children and they are certainly not hardened or brutalised. So I am sure that in his last moments Stephen would have been asking for me. If only the police who came to him had been more attentive, they might have heard his last words. There is so much that is missing, and these are among the most important, and no one will ever be able to tell me what he was saying as he died.

Duwayne Brooks was in the best position to know. He came to our house soon after the murder, when my brother brought him. We had heard stories, especially in that first week, that since he lived on his own in a hostel, the police were just turning up whenever they wanted to question him or take him in to make statements, regardless of how he might be feeling, and I was concerned that he was in that situation and seemed to have no contact with his family. I wondered why he hadn't gone home to his mother, and why she hadn't come to look after him. It just was not right that he was on his own, and I kept saying to people around me, 'Who do you know can take care of him? Can't somebody take him in?'

I had heard that the police had questioned him that night about whether this was a gang fight, and whether he was in a gang, and that must have been dreadful for him. But I longed to hear from him what had happened and how Stephen had died. The day my brother brought Duwayne to our house, we were in the garden and Ros Howells was there. I said to him that I wouldn't ask him any questions then about the night; I could see how traumatised he was. I wanted him to feel comfortable that he could come back and tell us exactly what had happened when he felt able to do so. There was no point in frightening him or making demands, it would not have been right to do that; so when Neville came and straight away began to question him, I said, 'No, give him a chance and let him talk in his own time.' That is how it was left. Duwayne sat there in silence, unable to utter a word to us about the night of the murder. There was not very much he could have told us, but there was a little, and it was only later that we heard some of the terrible details.

That was, regrettably, the last time I actually spoke to Duwayne. It is very painful to write about this, since he was also a victim of that attack and will probably never be able to live a normal life as a result of it. But it is best to be honest and to say that we had never really approved of Duwayne Brooks; we didn't like the idea of Stephen being with him.

It so happened that Duwayne's mother knew my brother Martin, and that when I went to the christening of my brother's baby, Duwayne was there. Stephen introduced us and I said, 'Oh, you are the one I've been hearing about,' or words to that effect. I had heard Stephen talk about him as someone who was unhappy in himself and never able to apply himself properly.

They had met at Blackheath Bluecoat School. So I was a little wary of him, but at that first meeting there was nothing that made me think that I did not like him.

A couple of days later Stephen came home and told me that Duwayne had said that I had been rude to him. I said, 'Why would I be rude to him? I've only just met him.' In my innocence, all I could think of to explain this impression was to think that maybe because the music at the party was loud he might have assumed I was speaking vehemently to him, but really why would I?

Stephen later told me that Duwayne said that he had only been joking. So from very early in their relationship I felt that he was not somebody I could trust, and I did not like his dependence on Stephen. Stephen was a good student and he had real prospects, he had a stable home and was popular, and I did not want him to be dragged down, perhaps, by this boy whose mother seemed not to care for him very much, who had dropped out of college and who lived in a hostel. There was a time when Stephen was not giving his all to his school work because he was too busy messing around with Duwayne. I should say that I knew nothing worse about Duwayne: there was never any suggestion that he was involved in any wrongdoing or crime, which made the police treatment of him after the murder all the worse.

Elvin Oduro is the friend who knew Stephen best. I am sure that on the night he was killed, had Elvin been available, Stephen would have been in his company rather than with Duwayne. But Elvin was not at school that day. He usually had to pick up his sister after school every evening and Stephen would go with him and take her home. Theirs was an inseparable friendship that I liked.

I cannot guess Duwayne's motives for all the untrue and upsetting things he has said about me and my family. He wrote in a book (which was withdrawn when the publishers acknowledged that it was defamatory, and apologised to me in court) that I was the one who made the rules in my house and everyone went along with my tyrannical ways, including Neville. But Neville took a stronger dislike to Duwayne than me. I remember Duwayne once phoned the house and Neville told him straight, 'Don't call back here.' Neville would never have anything to do with him. Duwayne was in our house only once before the murder, at a time when Neville had not yet come home from work. When Stephen asked if Duwayne could come in, I said yes. I was just about to go out shopping with Georgina. I said as I left, 'I'm trusting you by leaving you in my house and going out – don't make me regret it, right?' When I came back I think he was still there, and I don't remember anything bad happening. Had Neville been there, Stephen would not even have asked his permission because he knew it would be refused.

Duwayne is a troubled and angry young man. I can only speculate as to why he is hostile to me. He seems to resent the fact that the focus of attention since the murder has been on Stephen, and that his needs are never taken into account. I can understand that, but I could not supply the support he needed in the absence of his own family, and I was barely able to cope with my own grief. He might be feeling guilty, I suppose, because he understandably ran off when he saw those boys bearing down on them and couldn't drag Stephen with him. Stephen evidently did not realise what was happening; he saw no reason to run. Perhaps Duwayne was simply more alert to danger.

So it might be that he is haunted by his own conscience for leaving Stephen. Survivor guilt is a well-known effect of violent trauma. However, I have never attached any blame to Duwayne, and cannot blame him for anything that happened that night. I wish him well. And all that really matters to me is the truth about the killers, and justice for my son. The rest is nothing.

On the Sunday after Stephen's death I met for the first time a young solicitor called Imran Khan. Marc Wadsworth of the

Anti-Racist Alliance (ARA) knew Martin Sorjoo, a barrister connected with the Society of Black Lawyers, and had asked them to recommend a solicitor for us. We had never been in need of a lawyer before. Imran Khan was a young Asian man who had qualified as a solicitor eighteen months earlier. He was slightly built, wore glasses and a neat dark beard and was very serious and polite. Before he qualified as a solicitor he had experience of dealing with racial violence and I liked him instinctively. Because every other room in the house was occupied he sat in our bedroom to talk with us, and despite the feeling I had of being crowded out of my own house Imran seemed be able to create a sense of calm around him and to concentrate on what was important. I don't remember much about that first meeting – in the early days Neville did most of the talking – but Imran was very professional in his approach, and from that day to this he has put every effort into seeking justice for Stephen.

That first week is now a blur in my mind. I could not sleep; I dragged myself through the days, taking in what people said to me but feeling helpless and sorrowful. I didn't do anything much; I don't remember leaving the house once all week, apart from going to the mortuary and to church.

At the end of that week I went with my sisters Cheryl and Lorna and one of my cousins, Vivien, to stock up on food at Sainsbury's in Woolwich. I was driving and as we came into the car park two white women were pushing a shopping trolley along one of the aisles. I stopped to let them pass, but for some reason they also stopped, and I tried to manoeuvre past them. The next thing I remember is a shout of 'Fucking nigger.' I was too upset to do anything about it, but my sisters and cousin walked over and confronted the woman who had shouted, and were called 'Black cunts' in return. Cheryl said, 'It was one you bastards that killed my nephew.' The woman then said, 'If he hadn't been in this country he'd still be alive.' She then grabbed a brick out of the boot of her car and threatened Cheryl with it. It was a horrible introduction to the outside world.

The police visited the house more or less every day – always the two liaison officers, John Bevan and Linda Holden. They were both pleasant and sympathetic on the surface, at least at first, though Bevan also had a cheery complacency about him that was a little irritating. Very quickly, however, there was an edge of hard curiosity to their questions. They would come up to the living room and ask us, 'Who are those people downstairs? What are their names?' I thought that this was quite uncalled for – obviously anyone in our house would be either friends or family, or vouched for by them. But Bevan and Holden seemed suspicious and unnerved by them, and acted as though some of these people might just be involved in the murder, as though some family member might be the key to solving the case. It was ludicrous. The way in which black friends and family come together to mourn seemed alien to them.

And the people in our house were all black. The people who killed my son were white. Why should the police be so interested in who was in the house? The officers kept coming regularly, but they were never happy with the people around us who were supporting us, and they were not telling us what was happening with the investigation, or even what was being investigated. They did enquire about Stephen's friends, wanting to know what the people in the house had to do with him. It was as if they had watched too much television, where the murderer is often someone close to the victim, whereas this had been an obvious racist killing by complete strangers. And the bizarre thing was that they constantly wanted information from us, but we were never given any by them.

They asked for the names of Stephen's best friends, and wanted to know about Duwayne Brooks. Once, while we were still prostrate with shock and sorrow, DC Holden held up a pair of thick gloves in a plastic bag and asked us if they belonged to

Stephen. There was something about the way she showed them to us – a blank innocent look, as though to say here is something meaningful and I'm going to catch you out. The gloves did not belong to Stephen, but Neville immediately saw where this was leading. He said that they had nothing to do with Stephen and that his son was not a burglar, that he was not out that night looking to break into houses. Neville is very polite and easy-going, but he was stirred to slow anger by this and he let it show.

We were told that DS Bevan and DC Holden were supposed to liaise between us and the incident room; they were meant to let us know how things were progressing. So I wanted to know from them what they had done with the information they had received from us: had it led anywhere? Did they have any clues as to who the suspects were? But whatever we asked, they said they could not tell us; they could reassure us only that they were working very hard, which meant nothing to me. Concrete progress, the one thing we were interested in seeing, was not something they seemed to know about or were willing to discuss.

There was an air, too, of mysterious, sophisticated operations being carried out that would be too difficult for us to understand. I remember one policeman telling me that they had a 'strategy' and that acting too early would ruin the chances of a prosecution. So we sat in our living room being reassured, while a couple of miles away, it later came out, the suspects cleaned their clothes and disposed of anything that would incriminate them.

Among the names given to us by anonymous callers were those of Gary Dobson and the Acourts, or 'Arecourts' as some of the callers pronounced the name.

It is impossible to tell this story without the benefit of hindsight, because it was only years later that we discovered much of the truth. That first week, while we were being told that the Metropolitan Police had the best detectives in the world, the men in charge of investigating my son's death sent a civilian photographer to sit for a few hours with one policeman outside the family home of Neil and Jamie Acourt, who even the dogs in the Eltham streets seemed to think were involved in my son's death – but not until almost four days after the murder. This man was able to photograph one of the suspects, Neil Acourt, the older brother, leaving the house with a black bin bag full of clothes and God knows what else. The police officer who was with him could not follow Acourt because he had no car of his own; and he had not been given a mobile phone, so he could not call on anyone else to follow Acourt to see what he did with the contents of the bag. The following morning the photographer was there for another few hours, entirely on his own. This time Jamie Acourt left the house, also carrying a black bin liner, and drove off to no one knows where. All that the world's finest detective force had to show for their 'surveillance' was a collection of snatched photographs of the Acourts and their friends, David Norris, Gary Dobson and others.

My understanding is that the police had no idea where these bags were taken. When they did a search of dry-cleaners in the area, they did so weeks after the event, when such an exercise was useless.

One of the reasons that the surveillance took so long to organise, we learned much later – as we learned so much only when it was too late – was that the proper surveillance team was booked on the Monday after Stephen's death to observe another criminal. This was a young black man suspected of 'theft from the person'. The black thief took priority over the white murderers. Even in my darkest moments I would not have believed this possible, and in some ways it is merciful that I did not know it at the time. I still wonder what happened to that young man, and whether the police were able to get a conviction in his case.

Back at our house, meanwhile, I felt that we were under siege, even though I was surrounded by friends and family, and I did not know whether it was day or night. I had lost a lot of weight; afterwards my friends said that I was frighteningly thin. And some of the people around us had their own agendas, and seemed to think that we would go along with them. Various organisations were using our name on leaflets and in statements. One big bald man seemed to have elected himself our security chief and was demanding that we accept twenty-four-hour security from the ARA. Stephen's name was appearing on countless yellow placards of the Anti-Nazi League.

Any time that anyone came with information or a rumour or phoned through with a name – most of it came in the evenings – we would tell Imran Khan, as our lawyer, and he in turn would let the police know. I remember him saying that he had phoned DC Holden to pass on important information and she was annoyed that he had called after midnight and told him to ring again in the morning. Stephen's death was not something that mattered very urgently to them, it seemed to me, and they were not interested in any information that we had. We wanted to help as much as we could so that they could catch Stephen's killers. During that first week, I began to feel that the police had other priorities.

This was very frustrating, because everyone except the police seemed to have a very good idea about who might have stabbed our son to death. From the Monday of that first week we began to hear names of possible suspects. How people knew where we lived I don't know, but pieces of paper would be posted through our letterbox at all hours of the day and night. The phone never stopped ringing, even though we were not listed in the telephone book. Everything was logged in the message book: the time anyone called or knocked at the door with information, along with all the names that were given. Nobody gave me personally any names but then I was hardly ever downstairs; I was in the living room upstairs and I was barely in my own kitchen for the first two weeks. But I was aware that information was flooding in, and this made the police inaction all the more maddening.

I found out five years later that, apart from a number of anonymous phone calls made directly to the police naming the suspects, within the very first twenty-four hours someone actually went to the police station and gave those names and addresses, and the police did nothing with the information. There was also a very explicit note handed in, and a letter was left in a phone box in Eltham. When that letter was not picked up the sender called out the police to a pub car park and while their attention was diverted placed a note under the windscreen wipers of their car. When I heard about this it seemed to sum up the police attitude to the case: you had to shove the information in front of them and even then they did nothing with it. In fact they had dozens of tip-offs in the first couple of days, many including the same names. Even without knowing all this in April 1993, it was hard for me to believe, by the end of that first week, that we live in a society where someone can be senselessly murdered and that the police are so uninterested.

Here is the letter that was addressed to the police and left in a phone box the day after the murder:

The people involved in last night's stabbing are
1. Neil Acourt, 2. David Norris, 3. Jamie Acourt, 4. Gary Dobson.
Names 1 and 2 are also rumoured with Wimpy bar stabbing (Eltham).
Name 1 was definitely seen in the area prior to stabbing.
Names 2 and 1 are ringleaders and are positive knife users.
Names 1, 2, 3 share house in Bourne Brook Rd, Kidbrooke.
Name 4 lives in Phineas Pett Rd.
One of these names stabbed that poor lad.
The names 1 and 2 are very dangerous knife users who always carry knives and quite like using them.

Names 1 and 2 have stabbed before. Stacey Benefield was their victim about 6 weeks ago. He lives in Purneys Road off Rochester Way.
These bastards were definitely involved and must be stopped because they keep getting away with it.
This is not a BNP related incident. (You must stress this.)
Approach these shits with care. Do us all a favour and prove it. Good luck.

It is hard to imagine anything more straightforward or detailed. The young man called Stacey Benefield, I learned later, had almost died when they stabbed him a few weeks before Stephen was killed, but Norris and the Acourts were not charged. Young Benefield was too intimidated to identify them. It was only after Stephen's death that he agreed to come forward, and he picked out Norris and one of the Acourts as the ones who had stabbed him. He felt some safety in knowing that they were also being charged with even more serious crimes, but like all of us he underestimated the incompetence of the police and the hidden influence of the criminal families from which these boys came.

Finally, someone known as 'James Grant', to protect his identity, had walked into the police station less than a day after the murder and told them that the persons responsible for Stephen's killing, according to the message logged by the police, were 'Jamie and Neil Acourt of 102 Bournbrook Road SE3 together with David Norris and 2 other males identity unknown. That the Acourt Brothers call themselves "the Krays". In fact you can only join their gang if you stab someone. They carry knives and weapons most days . . .' Apparently an eager detective had rushed upstairs to tell his boss, DI Benjamin Bullock, that he had a man who claimed to know who the killers were. Bullock seems to have brushed his subordinate off. None of them did anything with this willing informant, and the senior officers running the case later claimed that they were not even told of his existence for over a week.

I found out in 1995, when we were preparing the private prosecution, that the police had lost this James Grant altogether: the police team seem to have forgotten about him for years. Someone in the investigation marginalised him. Grant was very unhappy about the way he'd been treated: the detective who eventually interviewed him, John Davidson, was aggressive and sceptical, and seemed to have alienated him. Davidson's notes of his interview with Grant disappeared, never to be found. Grant had told the police that his source for his knowledge of the killers was a young man who had gone to the Acourts' house on the night of the murder and seen them with wet hair, all five of them, claiming to have had a bath all at the same time. The police did nothing for over a week to track down this other young man. They dragged their feet, mishandled witnesses, slowed things down. Davidson claimed to have registered Grant as an informant, which meant that they would stay in touch with him, but the paper registering this event has never been found. This was, as the barrister Michael Mansfield would say much later at the public inquiry into all these events, 'gross negligence or worse'. The inquiry, chaired by Sir William Macpherson, would later accuse Davidson of lying about this registration. Like everything else in the case during this early and crucial phase, the behaviour of certain policemen was murky, careless and indifferent.

I soon came to realise that the police have an answer – or excuse – for everything. I knew nothing about police work, but it seemed strange to me that they had not searched more thoroughly in the area around the place where the killing happened. The killers had run off into the Brook Estate, but it was obvious to me, looking from the car on the night of the murder, that there was nothing serious being done down there – no roadblocks or barriers or police cars. We found out soon enough that

Duwayne had pointed the police down Dickson Road, at the corner of which Stephen had been stabbed, but they hadn't bothered to search along that road. When I asked the officers why they did not do a house-to-house search and question people on the night when Stephen was murdered, one very senior detective replied, 'You can't expect us to go knocking on doors so late at night.' We were talking about a murder! My belief was that had Stephen been white and the perpetrators black, whatever the time of night, they would have knocked on doors and rounded up every black person they had the slightest reason to suspect.

The white youths being named again and again as suspects, and in great detail in that letter, were known to the police – it was not as if this was a one-off incident. They had been threatening and intimidating people in the area for a long time, white and black; and their violent racist attitudes were notorious. They were an out-of-control gang of youths who had already stabbed several other young men in the area, and though I did not know it at the time, had been named as being at least connected with one of the racist murders in the area, that of Rohit Duggal. The police knew exactly where to find them. Were they so ignorant of what was going on around the estates of southeast London, particularly the area where Stephen was killed, that they could not find a bunch of young white hoodlums? And we were being told, and the police were being told, that these men flaunted their knives and their readiness for violence; two of them, brothers, were apparently known around Eltham as 'the Krays'. What we did not know then was that three of the boys being named to us and the police were members of violent, well-established criminal families, who led charmed lives, like their older relatives, and slipped through the net again and again when it came to police investigation and prosecution.

In this light, and remembering how much we were told about the considered 'strategy' that guided the police who so resented

our questions, it seems strange to me that Detective Superintendent Ian Crampton, who was in charge of investigating my son's
murder that first weekend in April, never recorded in any file his
supposedly 'strategic' decision not to arrest the five boys in
those crucial early days.

I cannot help thinking with some bitterness about one particular incident on the day after the murder, which I learned about
in 1995. An anonymous woman caller rang the police and
talked about the Acourts and Norris behaving like the Krays
and about their stabbing of Stacey Benefield. The incident room
was winding down for the night. There was no night shift, of
course. Someone made a note of her call. I wonder what was on
their minds as they threw that piece of paper into an in-tray and
forgot about my son. A beer at the pub? The meal they would
eat on their way home? How boring it was to have to deal with
the death of some no-account young black boy, who was probably up to no good anyway. And so the killers had another night
of sleep unworried by the police, and another day to get rid of
their knives, their bloody clothes, and to bathe and shower
away the evidence.

6   A Friend from Afar

About two weeks after Stephen's murder, Nelson Mandela came to London, on only his second visit to Britain since his release from twenty-seven years' imprisonment in South Africa. A message was sent to him, through Marc Wadsworth of the ARA, who is a well-connected journalist, and it was arranged for Neville and me to go to meet him at the Athenaeum Hotel in Piccadilly, where he was staying. Stuart came with us, as did my sister Cheryl.

It was 6 May, a Thursday. When we arrived there were crowds of people and cameras outside. It was the first time I had seen so many cameras in one place. I found it nerve-racking, what with the grief I was feeling for Stephen and the feeling that we were getting nowhere with the police, but I was pleased to be meeting Mandela. I had read a lot about him and knew that he stood for resistance to oppression and for black pride, and for a strong moral stand on justice. He said that he wanted the truth of what had been done in the name of apartheid to be known, and I agreed with that. I felt that unless the truth about Stephen's death, which seemed to be blocked, could be told there would never be justice for us. I remember how excited I had been when Mandela came out of prison. I had watched on television when he was released on 11 February 1990, walking so straight and tall and with such dignity out of jail, unbowed by what they had done to him – and that we were actually in the same room as this great man was hard to believe.

The way he spoke was so impressive. He was gentle and courteous, and listened attentively; you didn't feel as if you were meeting a future head of state. He had none of that politician's phoney goodwill. When he smiled you felt he meant it. There was no awkwardness with him of the kind that you often get at a first meeting. We shook hands and sat talking, going through the story of what had happened to Stephen. He was very sympathetic. What horrified him was that he was used to racists killing with impunity in South Africa, but that it was not something he expected to see happening here in the UK. That really shocked him, since he had a high opinion of British justice. We were there talking with him for about twenty minutes. It struck me as incredible that a foreign dignitary as important as Nelson Mandela had made time for us, whereas there had been no statement by any British Conservative government official about the death of our son. Afterwards the press took photographs of us with him and he said a few words for the media. His words were widely reported: 'The Lawrence tragedy is our tragedy. I am deeply touched by the brutality of the murder – brutality that we are all used to in South Africa, where black lives are cheap.'

I also spoke, and spoke plainly. I was very angry by then. I said that I was sure the police knew who the killers were, and still they had not arrested them. 'They are walking, eating and drinking and my son is lying on some slab,' I said. I was well aware by then that if these men were charged they could demand a second post-mortem on Stephen, and the thought of him being cut open again at the behest of his killers horrified me.

Then Mandela had to leave to attend a function, and we had a very different engagement. We were going to meet with the police for the first time later that day.

Another concern was weighing on our minds as we set off for Plumstead police station. Neville's cousin, one of his few relatives in London, had stayed with us the night before with her husband. That morning she was going to come with us in the car, but when she went to wake her husband and give him a cup of tea, she noticed something not right about him; he was not talking, and he is normally a sociable, pleasant man. As we were getting ready to go to our meeting with Mandela, she grew more concerned. He was completely silent, and just sat looking at her with a smile. She realised that she could not leave him and decided to take him to hospital. All day we thought about him, but there was nothing we could do until after we had gone to the police station.

One of my worst experiences in the first week or so had been having Sergeant Bevan and Constable Holden come to my home and tell me again and again, 'You should come down to the incident room to see how hard our officers are working.' All they could offer me was this look at a hive of industry, but no evidence at all of any progress on catching my son's killers. I could only look at them and say, 'Excuse me, but that is your job. Why should I come to see you do your job? That's what you're being paid for.' It was as if they thought they were doing us a favour and they wanted a pat on the back. And their attitude to Imran Khan was extraordinary. When we agreed to come to the station, we said that we would like our lawyer with us, and this seemed to enrage the police. They clearly regarded him as a troublemaker. Their view of us seemed to be that we would be all right if we were not manipulated by this lawyer; that we were simple black folk being led astray.

During the previous ten days, Imran's attempts to get information in writing from the police had run into a stone wall. They resented him even asking, and acted as though we were seeking confidential information that could ruin the case. All we wanted was to know if they were doing something and following up the information we knew they were receiving. And above all we wanted to know why they had not arrested any of the young men as suspects in our son's murder.

What they were doing, as we knew from conversations that we had with Stephen's friends, was questioning *them*, as though these young black men held the key to the mystery of his killing. It was as if they were building up a picture against us, against Stephen. The questions they asked his friends about him were unbelievable – what gang did he belong to, for example, when anyone who had he slightest knowledge of Stephen would know that he had never been near a gang in his life.

So for this first visit to the police station I had decided to write down on some notepaper all the names that people had been giving us daily since the murder – information that we had already passed on to the police. In my innocence I thought that maybe the police needed reminding of them, that if they were only really aware of them they would surely do something.

In the room at the station were Detective Chief Superintendent Bill Ilsley, a tall, skinny, sunken-faced man who did not look too happy to be seeing us, and Chief Superintendent John Philpott, who had grey hair and a pleasant round face. Neville, Ros Howells and my sister Cheryl were with me, and Imran was also there. DCS Ilsley had decided to invite him, since it had become obvious that we would not be content without him. As I walked in the first thing I did was to hand my sheet of paper to Ilsley, saying, 'These are the names of the boys that people have been giving us.' The list included Dobson, the 'Arecourts', and a boy named to us as Catonia (who we later discovered was their friend Danny Caetano, and who was not involved in the attack on Stephen). Then I sat down and I listened. Imran set out what he thought should be done, and everyone was talking.

I said nothing; I just sat quietly listening and observing. I watched this man Ilsley as he folded up the paper I had given him. He kept folding it and folding it into such a small square that it became no bigger than an inch, smaller. I could not believe what I was seeing. Of course he took no notice of me; no one was taking any notice of me, the quiet woman in the corner. As we were leaving – and I had not spoken till then – I said to

Ilsley, 'You're going to put that in the bin now,' and the look of shock on his face was extraordinary. That was obviously what he intended to do with it. If the paper with the names I had given him had been of interest to him he would not have folded it up like that; he would have read it at once, opened a file, put it in the file. Now he was caught out.

'No, no, no,' he said, and he started unfolding it – 'we treat all information that we have coming in very seriously . . .'

And then I left the station.

We went straight from the police station to St Mary's Paddington to see the husband of Neville's cousin, and it turned out that he had had a minor stroke. He had lost all speech and feeling down one side of his body. Looking at him, you could not tell there was anything wrong – his face had not changed but he just could not talk. He could not write or communicate at all. He was in his middle fifties then, and he seemed too young for this to happen to him. We could not help feeling that it showed how the shock of Stephen's murder had a profound effect on everyone in the family. All that happened on the day we met Nelson Mandela.

I was even angrier now. I had felt that the police were doing nothing, not taking Stephen's case as seriously as they should, but the graphic demonstration of Ilsley's contempt for us was so offensive. From then on I was determined not to let up, and knew that I could not rely on them.

The support of Nelson Mandela made an immediate difference, however. Until that meeting in his hotel, the police kept telling us that they did not have enough evidence to make arrests and that they needed more time. If I had known then how badly they used that time I would have been shouting from the rooftops. But the very next day, the police made four arrests, although they had no more evidence on 7 May than they did on 6 May.

It is worth saying again that no one in the Conservative government of this country mentioned Stephen's murder. Michael
Howard was Home Secretary at the time, and was completely
indifferent to Stephen's death. Peter Bottomley was our local
MP, a Conservative but sympathetic to us, and when he came to
the house a couple of days after the murder I asked him, 'Does
John Major [the Prime Minister at the time] know about my
son?'

He replied, 'Well, I don't think so.'

I said, 'Why doesn't the Prime Minister know about my son?
My son was murdered. Why doesn't he know?' Bottomley just
looked at me and could not give me an answer.

Of course he could not answer. No one was interested in a
young black man being murdered; it was not news. As
Bottomley was to say years after the murder, there was 'no
national appeal of any sort' in the media to help catch Stephen's
killers, whereas, he pointed out, there had been an urgent
national appeal that very week for a white woman shot in
Luton. Stephen's murder was briefly reported on the Friday after
it happened. Through having done building work on their
homes, Neville knew a few media people. He contacted someone he knew at the *Independent* in an attempt to get them interested. Then on the Saturday all other news was overshadowed
when an IRA bomb went off in the Bishopsgate area of the City,
causing extensive damage to office buildings and wounding thirty people; the national media covered nothing else that weekend. The local press carried a report, and on the Thursday
following Stephen's death a group of pupils from his school
went to the area to lay flowers and photos were taken. The cap-
tion in the paper mistook Neville's cousin for 'Stephen's mother', myself. We were not besieged by the media. Our meeting
with Mandela, however, was on the nine o'clock television
news.

That Friday, 7 May, Neil and Jamie Acourt and Gary Dobson

were arrested and put on an identity parade, which was aborted. We heard about it on the news, like everyone else. At first we were not told their names, just that three boys had been arrested. When we complained of being the last to know, we were promised that if anything further happened we would be told. Then on Monday we were called by Detective Sergeant Bevan and told that two more boys were to be arrested but that we should keep it quiet. Within half an hour, it was on the news.

Gary Dobson claimed, I was later told, that on the evening of the murder he had gone round to borrow a CD from the Acourts, and that it was Bob Marley's *Legend*. This was how he explained his presence at the Acourt house. The irony of these young racists enjoying the music of this black apostle of peace and understanding was incredible.

David Norris was arrested after coming to Southwark police station with his mother and a high-powered lawyer who had represented many gangsters (including Norris's father: if we had known about him at the time we would have had a clearer idea of what we were up against). Like the others, Norris was released on police bail until required to return to take part in identification parades.

On the 13th, Duwayne picked out Neil Acourt at an identity parade, and Stacey Benefield and his friend Mattie Farman picked out Norris.

Luke Knight was not arrested until 3 June. He claimed to have been playing Nintendo at home on the night of the murder, and was supported by his mother, though she admitted to going to bed early that night. But Knight was picked out by Duwayne Brooks at an identity parade.

We did not know who these people were and we had no idea what they looked like. But they certainly knew what we looked like, and we were sure they had something to do with a couple of frightening incidents around our house. One night a tyre on our car was punctured with a screwdriver; ours was the only car in the road to be vandalised. Neville heard something and went out to look early in the morning, and I was acutely anxious until he came back inside. Another night my brother's girlfriend left our house after midnight, and not long afterwards we got a phone call from her. She said that as she was leaving she saw young white men watching the house and they began walking towards her. She rushed to get into her car, shut the door and drove off. She said she looked in the mirror and saw that the four boys were standing together across the road, just staring at our house. On her way home she stopped at Shooters Hill police station and reported what she had seen. They said that they had never heard of the Stephen Lawrence murder and did not seem very interested in hearing more about it. Neville rang Imran Khan, who informed the police working on the case; though they later said that a police car was sent, I was not aware of it.

That was terrifying, realising that those boys must know where we lived. (It was not until June 1993 that Greenwich council had a special letterbox fitted to our door, which was meant to suffocate any fire bomb dropped through the box and set off an alarm.) When the boys' names were mentioned, there was an obvious reaction of unease in the neighbourhood; whoever was connected to Stephen's killers knew how to spread fear, and was well informed.

I told Detective Chief Superintendent Ilsley about people watching our house but he didn't want to know. You would think, from his reaction, that we were making it up and being melodramatic. He said, 'Watching your house? Don't be silly, no one's watching your house. What boys?' When I explained further, he made a hand gesture as if brushing it aside and said dismissively, 'Oh, they're just thugs.' He couldn't seem to imagine that we had serious concerns about our safety, or what those mere 'thugs' were capable of doing.

On 8 May, the Saturday after we met Nelson Mandela and the day after the first arrests, an anti-racist march took place.

The organisers had originally planned to have it in central London, but after they heard about Stephen's murder they decided to use that as a focus instead and to hold the march in Welling, south of where we lived in Greenwich, round a British National Party building that housed a 'bookshop', but which was in fact an organising centre for racist thuggery. We were not there, and had no connection with the organisers, but we heard the stories about the fighting that broke out among the demonstrators and the police. The following week we did an interview with the *Daily Mail*. The paper had done a report about the march and the violence, the burnt-out cars and broken shop windows, and they put a photograph of Neville and me right in the middle of all those images, as if to imply that we had caused the riot. We wished to make it clear that we did not want Stephen's name associated with that sort of violence and that we had no control over groups who might try to use our private tragedy for their own political purposes. That was when we remembered that Neville had done building work at the house of Paul Dacre, the editor of the *Daily Mail*. Neville was able through other journalists to reach him on the phone, and asked him, 'How could you do that, and you know me?' Since then the paper has been surprisingly supportive to our cause, as I will later describe.

That demonstration was to have very serious consequences for us. One of the people who went on the march was Duwayne Brooks, and like many of the young men on the march he was photographed by the press and police. Hundreds of protestors were throwing things at the building and battering cars, which I did not approve of, but I could understand their anger, since Stephen's death was one of several racist murders in south-east London. As it would later turn out, the police were more concerned with this outburst of anger than they were with what had caused it.

*

Although we had been to see Stephen's body at the morgue, we knew we would not to be allowed to bury him for some time. Once arrests had been made, there was the prospect of further post-mortems, so Stephen's body would not be released to us. And until that happened, we could not even plan a funeral. It was dreadful not being able to do anything. We were living suspended lives. I tried to keep up normal routines, making sure my remaining children were all right, but I also needed to channel my energies into something else. For the time being, there was nothing I could do for Stephen.

I tried to apply myself once more to my studies. I had not finished the first year of my degree course when Stephen died in April. I still had my first-year exams, and it was suggested that I postpone them, but I felt that if I postponed I would never do them. There was some course work still to do and I completed it and handed it in. I asked to sit my exams in a room on my own instead of being surrounded by other people – I knew that would be the only way I could only focus and cope. The only other person in the room was a pregnant woman, and that is how I took my first-year exams; and, in spite of everything, I got through. I was still numb with sorrow, and the pain of knowing that his killers had not been brought to trial could not be eased. But at least I had done what I set out to do, and I could promise Stephen that I would apply myself to his case with equal determination.

7   Burying Stephen

Stephen died in April; his body was not released to us for over six weeks. We were told from the start that his body would not be released until the whole procedure of bringing charges had been completed. Once those lads had been arrested, all five of them in effect had the right to insist on separate post-mortems: Stephen could be opened up five times. They seemed to have more rights as suspect murderers than we did as grieving parents. They could hold Stephen's body for a year if they wanted to, and I could not bear that, and argued that the process should be cut short. So it was agreed with the coroner that there would be one independent post-mortem, and he took responsibility for ensuring that whatever information came out of that would be disseminated to the solicitors of all those charged, so that each did not have to go through the same procedure. Once the order was given, and the examination carried out, they let us have Stephen's body.

The first decision to be made was where to bury Stephen. He often used to walk down Cemetery Lane in Charlton on his way to Elvin's house and I would ask him if he was not frightened, walking past the cemetery late at night, but he seemed to find the road peaceful. We had been thinking that might be a fitting place to bury him; but then I was speaking to my aunt Lil in Florida and remembered the plot of land in Jamaica where my grandmother was buried and I thought, Why not bury him with his great-grandmother? Aunt Lil asked her sister Ann in Jamaica to have the grave dug there. Then we had to go through the bureaucratic procedures over here involved in taking the body back to Jamaica. Exporting the dead is not easy.

At the same time we were organising a service in London for the people who would not be able to go to Jamaica. I wanted it to be held at Trinity Church and Rev. David Cruise to officiate. I chose the order of service, and the songs and who was going to sing them. David came and we sat down and tried to pick things that would have been right for Stephen, young and not too morbid. Elvin Oduro made a tape recording of Stephen's favourite songs, and we had it playing as people entered the church. I remember 'Hello Mama Africa', the song by Garnett Silk which had come out not too long before and which Stephen used to play all the time. I remember that line 'Oh Mama Africa, you make me know what life is worth.' Every time I think about those dark days with Elvin, he was like someone who had had his arm cut off, so lost was he without Stephen. He put all of his energy into everything connected with Stephen. He painted Stephen's face on a banner and I remember looking at it and saying, 'Elvin, that's not really Stephen, you know.' He said, 'But that's how I saw him,' really stern and confident.

The service took place on 18 June. I wanted people to walk behind the hearse. I wanted all traffic in the area to stop. We walked from our house with Stephen's casket. Because I was so angry at the way the police had treated us and at what they were doing, or not doing, I wanted everyone to know that Stephen had died. I wanted the whole area to know about it, I wanted people to remember that day and what had been done to Stephen. So I had arranged that we walk all the way to the church, down major roads; normally it would have taken about twenty minutes to walk that distance, but it took much longer that day. All shops along the way were shut, with their shutters down, and all roads were closed.

Stephen's hearse came first, then Elvin and Leon, another friend of Stephen's from school, carrying the banner that Elvin had painted, wearing dark suits and walking very slowly. From Llanover Road we turned left on to Herbert Road, which is normally a busy road, but that morning there was no traffic, only crowds of mourners, black and white. The funeral procession moved with great dignity and solemnity. The mood was very sombre, as though everyone had a feeling that this was something that needed to be witnessed, and that something shameful had happened that must never happen again. We walked to the very end of Herbert Road, then turned right on to Plumstead Common Road, another busy main road where traffic was again at a standstill. All the shops along Herbert Road had closed, and people came and stood in silence outside them as the hearse was going past.

By the time we got to the church on Burrage Road there were hundreds of people massed around it – there was not a vacant space left near the building. Crowds of people whom I did not even know were there, as well as the MPs Diane Abbott, Paul Boateng and Peter Bottomley. I had not invited anyone. People heard about the funeral and just turned up, and I was glad that they did.

The church was full to overflowing; they opened the doors and the crowds of people spilled into the hallway. Then they were channelled into the church hall, which was packed, and loudspeakers had been set up there as well as outside in the street so the people who could not get into the church or the hall could hear what was being said. For me it was a very hard day. I wished to remain in control, to keep my grief private, but I was shaking inside and at times I could barely stand up.

During the service Stephen's cousin Karina sang 'Tears in Heaven', the song Eric Clapton wrote when his son died. David Carlisle, who knew Stephen when they were at church together, played the piano. My cousin Grace read a eulogy and Rev. David Cruise spoke. He spoke as if he knew that someone had been hurt, and hurt in the heart. One of the things he said was:

'Racial hatred is in our midst and we ignore it at our peril.' Everyone was so angry, in a very quiet way, and it came out in the speeches that people made.

After the service, people filed past Stephen's open coffin. Stuart and I had gone to see him after he was dressed – my brother's girlfriend and my sister dressed him – but we did not take Georgina with us, so she had not seen him at all since he died. As she sat there, watching everyone else walk past, since we would be the last to say goodbye to him, she kept crying, 'I want to go, I want to go,' and I was saying, 'No, we have to wait for a just little while, wait a little while,' and trying to hold her back. At last, she was able to see him and to bid farewell to her brother.

It was strange that Stephen didn't look much different from when he was alive; I knew that usually after people die their colour often changes, but Stephen's didn't – he looked a little darker but not as dark as people often look after death. And he still appeared to be sleeping, at peace, as he had looked when we first saw him in the mortuary.

When I see photos of Georgina from that time, she was just up to about my shoulder, yet within a couple of years she began to tower over me. She had to grow up quickly in many other ways too. We have all lost, but my children lost a lot of their innocence. Stuart lost his teenage years and Georgina lost all of her childhood; she was ten when Stephen died, and the rest of her young years were dominated by Stephen's case, the endless twists and turns of failed investigations and trials and inquiries.

I did not want any police officers in the church. They asked if they could attend and I told them their place was outside, policing the streets. I had become hard towards them, and had no wish to give them any public relations benefits.

Afterwards Neville put out a statement that said: 'We are finally able to put Stephen to rest. We, however, will not rest until all of Stephen's murderers are caught, convicted and punished appropriately.' He ended: 'The racists must be told that the burial of Stephen is not the burial of our campaign for justice. It is only the beginning.'

A week after the service in London, we left for Jamaica. Stephen was to be buried there on 3 July, and we arrived a week and a half beforehand. His casket travelled on the same flight as us. When we landed in Jamaica and had to go through customs, at first the officials were very stern. 'Why are you visiting?' To bury my son. 'Where is your son?' Somewhere in the airport here. Once they realised the situation, it was different. The Jamaican High Commission in London had not warned anyone that we were coming, even though they knew. It was people from the British High Commission who came to meet us; the MP Paul Boateng had contacted them, thinking it might make things easier for us at the airport, though in fact since they had no jurisdiction there we still had to queue for a long time at customs before we got through. But it must be said that we got more support from the British High Commission in Jamaica than from the British government here. The High Commissioner, Derek Milton, attended both the church service and the burial.

As a child in Jamaica I knew nothing about funerals, apart from my grandmother's when I was too young to remember much. It was strange now to see how certain things were done, the customs that were followed. Everything was speeded up and loud. After the service in the church, which was in May Pen, we had to travel down to the burial ground in Clarendon, a drive of a good hour and a half. The roads were poor, but the hearse – an old black American Cadillac converted so that it had a platform and a high roof – took off at speed. We were following in a separate car, and there was no way we could keep up. Loudspeakers strapped on top of the hearse were blaring out gospel music as it raced to the burial ground.

By the time we caught up they were already carrying the casket to the burying place, which is away from the road. They were hurrying, and I was wondering what the rush was. Then I realised that in the country, with no electricity, everything had to be done before it got dark. The service had taken place at mid-day, by the time it ended it was two, and then there was the drive to the burial site, where songs and hymns were sung over the grave – all that took time and the light was going.

The grave was a concrete tomb, and Stephen's coffin slid inside, rather than resting on the earth, and then they cemented up the opening. That was all done while we were there, and I was grateful for that, because we had heard rumours of people being turned out of their coffins and the coffins stolen and I did not want that happening to Stephen.

As the burial ceremony was ending and I was walking away a commotion broke out among the men. My aunt had said, 'It's traditional to bring some rum to give to the men who prepare the grave,' and that had been done. It had not seemed like a good idea to give the men drink before they were finished, how-ever.

I got back to the grave in time to see Stuart taking off his jacket ready to fight – someone must have said something nasty to him – and then I saw a man pull a knife. I was terrified. I just grabbed Stuart, shoved him into the car and shut the door.

I said, 'What the hell is happening? I've just buried one son because someone stabbed him, I'm here at his funeral and some-one else has got a knife out?'

There had been some dispute about payment for the workers. We had already paid most of their money apart from a final instalment, and Neville said to them, 'We're all going back for a drink and some food. Come and have something with us and we'll give you the balance of the money there.' Perhaps they did not believe that would happen and thought he was trying to pull a fast one, so the situation had become heated. To be paying money over Stephen's grave did not seem decent, but after that we just settled up and let them go on their way.

As we drove off I was thinking that I could so easily have lost my other son over some petty misunderstanding with the men who had just buried his brother.

8   The Cost of Murder

My marriage died the same night Stephen died, though I did not know it yet.

The Neville I knew was always doing things around the house. If I was cooking, he would help; he would do his share of cleaning. On Sundays he made breakfast and I would make the dinner. Now all of a sudden he was not doing a thing. Stephen's death brought out a completely different person in him, and made me realise how much damage violence can do to a whole family and the way it lives.

In Jamaica when we went to bury Stephen we stayed with a friend, Karita, whom Neville had known for years, and her husband Hubert. Their children and mine were roughly the same age. Hubert would take his wife to work in the morning so that he could have the car during the day; Neville would go with them in the morning and then he and Hubert would be out for the whole day. The burial coincided with school holidays, so all the children would go off together, while I was left on my own with just the housekeeper. I spent most of my time up in the bedroom.

It was then that I first noticed a difference in Neville's attitude towards me. Now when he came back in the evening, after his days out with his friend, he never asked me how my day had been, or showed any interest in what I'd been doing. In fact I would have spent hours sitting on the bed, or trying and failing to read a book.

We were there for a long time, from the end of June until

August – Stephen was buried on the 3 July – and Neville was like that every day. Occasionally Karita was able to take some time off and would take me to Montego Bay or some other resort place, but otherwise I would be in the house on my own. I became more and more miserable.

The evenings were better, when the children and all the adults gathered together, and there was a semblance of normality. Neville and I could put on a united front then, and enjoy the company of others, if not our own. On the 29 July, while we were sitting around on a hot, peaceful day, the two families talking and laughing, the phone rang. It was my sister Cheryl, who had returned to London a week or so previously. She had just listened to the news and had heard that the Crown Prosecution Service (CPS) had dropped the charges against the accused boys because, in their assessment, there was 'insufficient evidence to provide a realistic prospect of a conviction'. Soon afterwards Imran Khan rang, quiet and calm, but outraged by what he had also heard at the last moment.

I went to my room, devastated and unable to speak. A few days later we returned to London.

Many other people, I learned on my return, were also outraged, and the decision of the CPS was widely denounced. The day after the announcement, Imran and Cheryl had sent out a press release on our behalf. Imran was quoted as saying that he feared the discontinuance could spark racial unrest: 'It is quite unbelievable that the police have been unable to secure the evidence required to commit these youths for trial after three months.' Cheryl said: 'We were constantly told by the police to trust them and that they were doing all they could. It obviously wasn't enough. As Nelson Mandela told us, black lives are cheap.'

Peter Bottomley, MP, appealed to the local community not to take the law into its own hands, and urged the Attorney-General to ask the CPS for a full explanation of their decision. The Anti-

Racist Alliance said the decision was proof that 'there is something rotten at the heart of the Crown Prosecution Service when it deals with racist murders'. I could not have put it better myself.

In our absence, Imran and Cheryl, together with a number of people from the campaign, had met Peter Lloyd, the junior minister at the Home Office. As it was described to me later, it was a big meeting, the minister flanked by officials and advisers. Cheryl and our lawyers demanded an inquiry, an independent examination of what had gone so terribly wrong in this case. Lloyd made soothing comments, giving smooth assurances that the police were giving this the highest priority and that he was entirely confident they would do their best to find hard evidence in the future. But even three thousand miles away I could feel the brush-off.

While we were still away there had also been a big demonstration against the decision not to charge the suspects, with people in the Stephen Lawrence Family Campaign protesting outside the CPS building. This campaign was an informal group that had come together to publicise what had happened to Stephen and the racism and lack of interest that we as a family were suffering at the hands of the police. Among those who were involved were Ros Howells, people from the Anti-Nazi League, and Marc Wadsworth and Palma Black from the Anti-Racist Alliance. My nephew Matthew was involved, as was my sister Cheryl. Certain people in the campaign provided links to the unions, who had a public voice that we lacked. The TUC and its General Secretary John Monks were very supportive, and eventually set up the Stephen Lawrence Task Group to tackle institutional racism at work. We had been forced to take control of the campaign because in the weeks after Stephen's murder various groups were attempting to use us for their own ends.

One of the first events the campaign had organised was a candle-lit vigil two weeks after Stephen was killed, in which children from Stephen's school, Blackheath Bluecoat, took part. Then in mid-May we had organised a 'human chain', when people joined hands to form a link between the place where Stephen was killed and the place where Rohit Duggal was killed, which was across the roundabout, near the cinema on Well Hall Road, a distance of about 250 yards. Because it meant that the traffic was stopped we had to get police permission, and that was difficult because they did not want to be accommodating.

I never dreamed that this campaign would have to be sustained for so long, and that we would have to battle against such grinding official resistance. It had never crossed my mind that the five boys would not even have to face a court. The campaign now seemed like a lifeline, and I thanked God for it.

Through Imran Khan, we asked for an independent outsider to examine the papers in the case to see if there was enough evidence to bring a private case against the suspects. The CPS refused, saying that it would set a bad precedent. We again demanded a public inquiry into the police handling of the case. Peter Lloyd at the Home Office demanded of us in turn evidence for such a step – evidence that could only emerge in the course of an inquiry, and which we were in no position to provide. While this circular argument was going on, we did not know that Deputy Assistant Commissioner David Osland, the boss of Crampton and all the other police officers dealing with the case, wrote to Paul Condon, the Commissioner of the Metropolitan Police, saying that 'our patience is wearing thin . . . not only with the Lawrence family and their representatives but also with self-appointed public and media commentators'. How dare we question them, after all? The police then decided to commission a review, in order to show the world that they took our protests seriously. It would of course be an internal review, carried out by another policeman – the idea of some outsider looking at what they had done or not done was unthinkable. This was due to be completed before the end of the year.

Stephen's murderers had walked free, and I felt that I was the one in prison.

Neville refused to return to our house in Llanover Road, and I was not in any fit state to argue with him. We would, I suppose, have been sitting targets there, since those boys knew where we lived and what we looked like; but it was also my home. We had been to see Greenwich Council about being rehoused but nothing had come of it. We picked up some clothes from our house and went to stay with Neville's cousin in Marylebone. Stuart had just got a temporary job in McDonald's and wanted to go back to work, but from where we were staying it was too far for him to travel. He spent a couple of nights with my sister, and then family friends said he could stay with them. It was the worst time for the family to be separated – Stuart down in the south-east of London, Neville and me up in the north-west; but the school term had not yet begun, so at least Georgina was still with us.

I felt completely isolated. Though Neville and I felt equally angry about the decision to let those boys go, it was as if our emotions could not connect in any way. We seemed to be living parallel lives, no longer touching except in the most ordinary domestic matters, and often not even then. It was such a contrast with what my relationship with Neville had once been, when he would never leave the house without making me a cup of tea in the mornings. Now I seemed not to be there for him.

He would spend the day on his own, outside the house; nothing brought us together. One afternoon I went to church with his cousin and when I came back I thought, I just can't sit here. I went wandering and I noticed a canal that looked very peaceful, it must have been the Regent's Canal, and I sat on a bench looking at the water and the trees. I was there for hours. Eventually I decided to get up and try to find my way back, and as I was walking I saw Neville. He asked me where I had been, and said he had been looking for me. I realised then that him missing me had become a rare event.

I used to disappear quite often like that. I did not feel that there was anyone I could talk to, if I could not talk to Neville. Even when I did say something to him about how I felt about how he was behaving, he looked at me blankly as if I was imagining what I felt or that something was wrong with me. The feelings of separateness grew wider and wider.

Eventually Greenwich Council gave us a house in Charlton. Even then it was difficult to get Stuart to come home; he probably did not want to face the atmosphere of tension and grief. But I insisted. I could not stand the fact of him being away. When he came home, he spent a lot of time in his room, the door shut on the rest of us. He became very uncommunicative, and days would pass without him speaking very much.

Neville was behaving more and more strangely, too. I said to him, 'Look, what's important now is the children – nothing else matters. We took Stephen for granted and now he's gone.' I was concerned that he should build up a relationship with Stuart. 'You have lost one son, don't risk losing another,' I said. I tried to encourage Stuart to see a therapist, or anyone with whom he might be willing to talk. I wanted to hold the family together, and I worried that he was particularly vulnerable. At sixteen, he could go either way; here was a young man who had been doing really well at school but after his brother's death his GCSE results were not as satisfactory as they could have been. Stephen died in April 1993 and Stuart had to start his exams in May, so it was a difficult time for him. He started going to Woolwich College, and he knew I was there for him. But he and Neville had always had a difficult relationship; now it was even worse. Neville would claim, 'Stuart doesn't want to know,' and I said: 'Even if that's what you think, just sit in the room with him. When he's ready, he will talk to you. Just be there – that's all you need to do.' But Neville seemed unable to listen. Rather than the gap narrowing between them it got wider, and it became so wide you could run a ship through it – in fact you could run a whole country through it, as I was soon to discover.

We had both changed. I wanted a much closer relationship with the family now; I wanted us to appreciate one another even more than we had done before. I could not conceive of losing any of my children. Now that I knew how suddenly it can all come to an end, I had to enjoy every moment of my children, to let them know how much I loved them. It was as if a great crack in the earth had opened up under our feet and I had to make sure that my children knew how dangerous the world was and how important they were to me. That was what I tried to say to Neville: to beg him to appreciate all of them. Staying together as a close unit seemed to me the only chance we had of coming through our grief. But he was sunk in depression, and things just seemed to go downhill. While the three of us – Stuart, Georgina and me – were in the living room watching television or talking, Neville would be upstairs alone. I tried to talk with him about what he was going through, but he could not acknowledge that there was anything wrong.

It did not help that he had nothing to occupy him. The children and I had things to do to distract us from brooding on our grief: I had gone back to studying for my university course, Stuart was at college and Georgina had just started secondary school, while Neville was at home alone with time on his hands, just as he had been before Stephen died, only now it was infinitely worse.

Before, when he was not working, he had been such a help and support around the house, but now everything had turned around and I had to take on all the responsibility for the domestic chores. When I came home, I had to cook, dish up and clear up, before I could think of trying to do any of my course work. In that house in Charlton the kitchen was too small for a dishwasher, so we had to wash up by hand, which we had not done for years. Neville would eat, get up from the table, take his one plate, wash it, go upstairs to the bedroom and stay there. It was as if he had just shut down. Yet if anyone called around to visit he would come down and laugh and talk as if nothing was wrong. He was capable of going out and speaking in public about the campaign; but when it came to the family, he had lost heart. The murder seemed to have consumed the person he used to be.

Meanwhile, there was no good news in the world outside. In September the CPS decided that no action would be taken against the two white women who had shouted racist abuse at me and Cheryl in the car park in Woolwich, deciding it would be 'difficult to rebut' the woman's claim that she had taken a brick out of her car for purposes of self-defence. The likelihood of conviction was too small, they said. I could not help feeling that they empathised more with the white women faced with two angry black women than with the bereaved relatives of a murdered young man being racially abused.

Paul Condon refused to meet us in mid-September, and in his letter turning down a meeting he used the language of injured pride and outraged dignity. He spoke of the review he had set up, but made it clear he thought that there was really nothing to be reviewed: 'I would not wish to comment on specific aspects of the investigation in advance of the review being completed . . . In general terms I would like to take this opportunity to refute the allegations that the Metropolitan Police view this case with anything other than the utmost seriousness. Any impartial view of events since 22nd April shows that this is simply not true.' The behaviour of his officers seemed to be prejudged.

After Stephen's funeral, I went back into the second year of my Humanities degree. Doing the course helped me be stronger; I could switch my concentration to my studies, away from my personal grief, so that it did not consume me in such a way that I couldn't function. My personal tutor, Bridget Leach, became a rock of support for me, after Stephen's death, within the university. I was able to sit and talk to her about my work and she was always there to help. Some of the other tutors were not so accommodating, and there were unpleasant and insensitive encounters with tutors who seemed entirely unaware of my circumstances, one of them making a point of refusing me an extension on an essay I had to write. People use power in sad ways.

I must admit that I did not attend university every day. I was so focused on what had happened to Stephen and on developments in the case. I could not understand how anyone could be aware of a killing as brutal and senseless as this and not be angry about it; the police seemed to lack some essential moral fibre that might have made them outraged enough to make sure they caught Stephen's murderers. People in the area couldn't understand why those boys who were so notorious, who were feared and disliked all over Eltham, were not even questioned until after our meeting with Nelson Mandela, when the police suddenly felt the need to make arrests.

We had regular meetings that autumn with Detective Chief Superintendent Bill Ilsley and Chief Superintendent John Philpott. In my talks with Philpott I felt that, given the chance, he would have been more communicative with us. At times it was as if he wanted to tell us something, but could not. It was something about his body language: when certain matters came up you saw him push himself forward as if about to say something, but then he made eye contact with Ilsley, or maybe remembered his position, and that he was not leading the investigation. But his boss, Ilsley, was a different person altogether. I had always found the older officers to be more obstructive, and certainly more resentful of a pushy black family daring to question them. They did not like having to justify themselves to people like me; that attitude was clear from the outset. I could sense racism in everything they said and did – the barely concealed irritation, the stony faces, the assumption that we were being manipulated by Imran Khan. We would ask them questions: has anything new happened? What have you done with the information you were given? Are you able to arrest anybody? Are you able to identify anybody? Each time I asked a question they could not answer it. They always claimed, 'Nobody's talking.' They sheltered behind this myth of the wall of silence, when we knew, and later investigations proved, that information had been pouring over the wall from the moment news of the murder circulated around the area.

If someone has given you information and afterwards asks you about it, you would expect to update the person on where the information had led. We never got anything from them. The police had their own wall of silence.

I once asked if they had considered putting a plant in the cell when the boys were in custody to get information by listening to them. Ilsley was offended, saying, 'No way, we don't do things like that. Where do you get these ideas?'

Detective Superintendent Brian Weeden was supposed to be the senior investigating officer working on the case – DCS Ilsley was his boss – and in that first year his hostility to Imran Khan, and it seemed to the fact that we were using a solicitor at all, was very plain. He invited us to see the incident room – provided we didn't bring Imran. This we could not accept. I first laid eyes on him at the adjourned inquest in December 1993, and first met him the following year.

At the time of these meetings with Ilsley and the others I did not know about the attacks that contributed to the borough of Greenwich being called 'the racist capital of London'. Nor had I learned that the father of one of the boys – David Norris's father Clifford – was associated with corrupt police officers. He was wanted by Customs and Excise for major drug dealing, and at this time, during the autumn of 1993, he was on the run in England somewhere, as he had been for the past four years. He seemed untouchable.

Meanwhile, the various groups that had taken an interest in Stephen's death were tearing each other apart and were in danger of destroying our campaign, which we wanted to keep focused and dignified. Back in the summer, the ARA had suggested that there should be a demonstration in central London in October, a peaceful show of anger and concern at the way Stephen had been treated by our justice system. The Anti-Nazi League (ANL), which we had by then come to realise was a front for the Socialist Workers Party, wanted to hold it in southeast London around the BNP 'bookshop' with its blue steel doors. At a meeting attended by Imran Khan the argument was put to a vote. The central London march was agreed. While we were away in Jamaica burying our son, it emerged that the ANL had organised a demonstration in the south-east regardless of our wishes and of the vote at the meeting. My nephew Matthew, my aunt Lil's son, was chairing a meeting and it was suggested that because he was of mixed race (his father is white) he had no business being there and that his wishes and ours were irrelevant. Matthew was so upset that he walked out. It seemed that the ANL saw themselves as having a 'wider responsibility' to the fight against 'Nazism', as they insisted on describing British racism, than to the campaign to get at the truth about Stephen's death. We were asked to choose between the two marches. Instead we sent a letter to the ANL and the ARA, asking them to stop using Stephen's name. 'His name means a lot to us,' I wrote. 'It is too precious to be used in a cynical way.' We wanted to distance ourselves from all other agendas than the search for justice for our son. In the end both marches went ahead, which was a waste of good people's energy, and the one in south-east London turned into a violent confrontation with the police, with militants on the demonstration shouting for the BNP shop to be burned down.

At home, the effects of this terrible strain, and the constant work, and our frustration by the police and the judicial system, were ever more obvious. Whereas Stephen had stopped confiding in me at about the age of fourteen, Stuart's openness continued until he was sixteen. After his brother's death this intimacy stopped. He went through a deep depression and Stephen was not discussed in the house. As a family we did not talk; and as time went by no one else wanted to talk about Stephen in the way that I wanted to talk about him. And Stuart just drifted. He became very angry, no matter what I said or how I handled it, so I grew cautious of saying anything, trying to avoid a row. I was worried about him, because of the stories I had heard about Rolan Adams's brother Nathan and what happened to him after his brother's death, such as him putting his hand through a glass window and severing an artery in an attempt to harm himself. I dreaded that Stuart might become equally distressed, and that could so easily have happened.

I remember saying to Neville at around this time that material things don't count, that Stuart and Georgina were all we had left. Stephen's death did not happen just to me and Neville, it happened to them too, though they might not be able to articulate their feelings fully. I thought about the fact that when Stephen died they both chose to go to school the next day. It made me determined to try to keep to an everyday routine for them, making dentist's appointments, ensuring Georgina had her packed lunch, encouraging them to take part in sport. My heart was not in it, but I knew I had to go on. Georgina had even gone away on a school trip, though I'd begged her not to go. I had a fear of either of them leaving my sight for more than the daylight hours. But they did not want to accept what was happening and the fact that the house was constantly visited by strange people, whereas before we had led such quiet and private lives. They probably needed space and the only place to find it was at school.

The riot at the British National Party building in Welling came back to haunt us in the autumn of 1993. Of all the young people shouting and throwing things, only six were ever charged with anything criminal. One of them was Duwayne Brooks. In October, an incredible six months after the event, he was charged with violent disorder and criminal damage over the riot. It was astonishing how seriously the police treated this terrible crime by a young man who had seen his friend stabbed to death two weeks before, how they combed through hours of television film and video and images which they seized from newspapers. They found a photo of him with a piece of wood in his hand. It was a model investigation, pursued with energy and determination. I wish the officers who spent so much time on this case had been working on Stephen's. And one of the effects of their work was to further discredit Duwayne and to weaken his reliability as a witness. He was the one close eyewitness to our son's death, and a great deal depended on him.

9   Winter

I am good at appearing composed, at wearing a mask, but I still had moments when I would lock myself in my room and not come out for two whole days. I would not speak to anyone; I wouldn't drink or eat.

The bad news flooding in on us was like a constant insult, disappointment after disappointment.

In August 1993 the internal review, which was meant to examine how the Metropolitan Police Service had conducted their investigation into Stephen's case, had been launched by Detective Chief Superintendent John Barker. At the time we were staying at Ros's house, after coming back from burying Stephen, but in early September we went to meet Superintendent Barker at our house in Llanover Road. We told him of all our anxieties, our concerns and complaints, everything we felt had gone wrong, and how we felt that the investigation team had focused on our family rather than Stephen's murderers in the early days of their work. We spoke about what the officers did and did not do, how I had given names of suspects to the officers and they had done nothing about it, and how we were treated in general by them. Barker was a personable, tanned, well-dressed man in a brown suit with matching shoes, and he seemed to show real concern for us. He was, as usual with senior policemen, accompanied by a couple of junior officers. He said that he would do his best to get to the bottom of the case, and assured us that while he could not give us a copy of the report, as that was for the Commis-sioner to decide, he would give us feedback on whatever he found. We would know exactly what had happened during the early stages of the first investigation.

We never heard from the man again. All we learned about his report in the year of Stephen's killing was the conclusion of the review that the media reported in November:

> The investigation has been progressed satisfactorily and all lines of inquiry correctly pursued.
>
> Liaison between the victim's family and the investigation team deteriorated at an early stage. This affected communication and confidence between the two parties.
>
> Press and media relations were hampered by the involvement of active, politically motivated groups . . .
>
> This has been and remains an investigation undertaken with professionalism and dedication by a team who have experienced pressures and outside influences on an unprecedented scale.

I felt demeaned by the complacency of this conclusion, and by the hostility that reeked from those sentences about our family and our supporters. The only political motivation that I or Neville ever had was the desire to know the truth about our son's death. It was as if all that Barker cared about was protecting the police from 'outside influences', and instead of improving their methods he was concerned with further insulating them from public scrutiny.

Five years later, at the public inquiry, the inquiry chairman declared that there was no point in calling Barker as a witness. In effect, he was dismissed as utterly unreliable. It was a lesson to me not to take people at face value.

Imran Khan approached the barrister Michael Mansfield, QC, and he agreed to act for us. When the first inquest into Stephen's death opened at Southwark Coroner's Court on 21 December 1993, we were advised by Mansfield that it was not a good idea to continue with it then, because all sorts of information could come out that might prejudice any chance of prosecuting the boys later. We first needed to get the evidence against them. The police, however, wanted to go ahead with the inquest. The Crimestoppers organisation had put up a £5,000 reward for anyone coming forward with information and some useful new material had come through, they said.

Days before the hearing Imran Khan received a call from Noel Penstone of Greenwich Council's Race Equality Unit, who had passed on a new line of enquiry to the police. The suggestion was that one of the suspects or someone very close to them had confessed to a teacher. The police had not, apparently, responded to this information, and we wanted to get to the bottom of it before the inquest decided on the cause of death. When the coroner heard all the arguments he decided to adjourn the inquest, and we were grateful for this decision.

About five weeks before Christmas, David Norris was sent for trial at the Central Criminal Court for the attempted murder of Stacey Benefield. We had hopes that at least one of the boys would feel the weight of the law. Someone who was there told me that Norris was very soberly dressed in a suit and tie, and was attended by his well-dressed blonde mother. Stacey and his friend Mattie Farman looked like rough skinheads by comparison, and there was a strange atmosphere in the courtroom. Norris was acquitted, which seemed to shock even the police and the lawyers. This added to our sense of depression and that there was something rotten in the state of justice.

If only we had known how rotten. We later learned that the driver taking Norris to and from the jail was approached by a juror and told that the verdict was going to be not guilty. Even though the police and the CPS suspected that the jury had been nobbled, no application was made for any person on the jury to be discharged. The same juror approached the driver later in the trial to say that he wanted to offer young Norris a job. This juror who was so helpful to Norris was found to be awaiting trial on charges of handling a stolen cheque, and to be involved in a fraud amounting to £100,000. The CPS never charged the man or even reprimanded him, and they did not order a retrial. The charmed life of the Norrises continued; David's father, Clifford, was still on the run and nowhere near being tracked down.

The juror in the Benefield case much later apologised in the *Daily Mail* to our family – 'had I known then what I know now', and other phrases of that kind. All those public apologies washed over us, all too late and none of them any use.

Neville made no plans for our first Christmas without Stephen; his delight in the carnival aspect of the season was gone. Georgina had always loved Christmas, and she wanted this one to be even more special because Stephen wasn't there. We put up a Christmas tree for her, and she went shopping for presents with her pocket money. On Christmas Day I wanted to place some flowers on the pavement where Stephen had died. As I was getting ready to go out Neville decided he would come too. So we all went down to Well Hall Road, but there was still a stiff distance between us while we stood by the empty roadway where our son had died. The lights in the houses set back from the road were not for us. It felt incredibly bleak, and I felt that we were alone in the world at that moment. We came back home in silence.

Usually Neville would have helped me in the kitchen at Christmas, but that year he didn't even keep me company in the kitchen. I cooked, but I was too upset to eat. I knew he was grieving but I also knew that the children needed him to make an effort, to at least try to make things normal even if he would inevitably fail.

Georgina had bought two presents for everyone. She

wrapped them separately: one was from her and one was from Stephen.

That Christmas after Stephen's death was my worst ever, living in a strange house in Charlton and cut off from everything that had become familiar to us. (In fact, I haven't had a good Christmas since, though none have been as bad as that one. Now, I try always to leave the country at that time because it makes me so miserable to be close to places that bring the memories back.) All the way through Christmas Day I cried. That night, my brother came round. Neville was upstairs as usual, though he came down when my brother arrived and talked to him.

After Christmas the situation got even worse. At one function we had attended, Peter Bottomley, trying to be supportive as our local MP, had kindly invited us to his house in Guildford on Boxing Day. I had not even heard the offer being made to Neville. I knew about it only after he had accepted and then I felt obliged to go. Ros Howells had also been invited.

On Boxing Day we got ready to travel to Surrey, though I did not feel in the least sociable. By this time Stuart had gone to stay with his godfather, and we decided to drop Georgina off at Neville's cousin's house, rather than taking her with us. After picking up Ros we drove to Guildford. I was not talking very much, and Ros must have sensed the tension. She tried to make light of it, doing her best to make conversation on the journey until we got there.

In a social environment, Neville was able to laugh and chat, while I withdrew into myself. That day was very painful for me. Peter Bottomley's in-laws, Virginia's parents, were very sympathetic to us, but it was a normal Christmas celebration for them and they had nothing to make them sad; for me it was torture, sitting among all these people who were having a good time.

On the way back Neville announced that he had invited two couples round to dinner with us the next day. I did not know if

I had enough food in the house, and one of the couples was vegetarian. He needed to have other people's company, and they were nice people; but it was the last thing I wanted. I could not help letting him know that I was upset. By then we had picked Stuart up but Georgina was still staying with Neville's cousin.

The following morning, in tears as usual, I got up and went down to the kitchen to start preparing the evening meal. Neville was upstairs in the bedroom. Stuart was in his room. I was alone in the kitchen cooking for people whom I did not want to see. All of a sudden I thought to myself, I can't go through with this. In front of the guests I would have to be smiling, laughing, and I knew I could not do it.

I rang Ros and told her that I needed to get away, and asked her to find me somewhere to go. I remember saying that I needed to be able to come home by myself when I was ready. I told her not to come to the house, and arranged to meet her round the corner.

I finished cooking, then went and told Stuart, 'The food is ready. Just help yourself when you want something.' By this time one family of guests had arrived. The woman came in, asking me, 'How are things?' I cannot describe what it was like to have to try to maintain a polite front at that moment. That was one of my darkest days. I don't think anyone realised how I really felt.

I went upstairs and got a plastic carrier bag, threw in a change of underclothes, my toothbrush and a book to read; I didn't even take a comb. Then I walked out.

It was raining while I stood there waiting for Ros. She drove up, her concern written on her face, and drove me to somewhere in the direction of Brockley, and I cried all the way. I was still crying when we arrived at the house of a friend of hers, Sybil Phoenix, who was active in the black community but whom I had never met before. I found it embarrassing to go to people I did not know, but they took me in and were very kind to me. I was shown to a bedroom and sat there crying. Ros went back home, and that is where I stayed.

I remained there for the rest of that day. It was a Wednesday. The next day Sybil had to go to a speaking engagement but her husband was home. In the morning before she left she made me a cup of tea. I did not leave the room all that day, except to go to the bathroom. I read the whole of the book I had brought – a Terry McMillan novel, I don't remember which one. Hours later I heard a knock on the door and it was one of her sons asking if I was all right. I said I was. The room was dark, apart from when I put the light on to read; I never opened the curtains. At about six o'clock that evening that I went downstairs. Sybil's husband had cooked some food and I sat and ate a little, then I went back upstairs. I stayed there for the whole of the next day, venturing down again late in the evening. It was Friday, coming up to New Year's Eve.

After I had left home that lunchtime, it seems that at first Neville told the guests that I had gone to the shops. They waited for some hours and when I had not come back and people were asking where I was, he began to get worried. He rang my sister, he even rang Imran Khan – though how would he know where I was? My sister came to the house, and everyone was now panicking about me. I understand that my aunt happened to phone from Florida and she overheard Neville telling my sister – who answered the phone – not to say anything. Aunt Lil demanded to know what was going on, saying that she wanted to speak to me. They had to admit they did not know where I was. Ros did not call them until about eight o'clock in the evening to explain my departure. I phoned home two days later, when I was feeling a little stronger, and phoned my aunt in America, who was relieved to hear from me.

On the Saturday afternoon I took a cab home. By then the rest of the family had gone to Neville's cousin's house, and I rang them to say that I was back.

Neville came in that night as if nothing had happened. He could not acknowledge that my distress had anything to do with his behaviour. Nevertheless, I apologised – the night before I left, we had had some heated words about his making arrangements without consulting me, so I apologised in case I had said things I should not have said. Neville took my apology to mean that I apologised for everything else, that he had nothing to be sorry for. The fact that he asked no questions, and that nothing more was said, made things worse. He still sat around the house, just as before. And this went on for further weeks and months.

My family had always been supportive towards Neville. Aunt Lil suggested that he should come to Florida for a while; it might help him to be in a different environment. In the spring, he went over there and stayed for six months. My uncle found him odd jobs so that he could pay his way.

In London, meanwhile, I had to deal with the aftermath of Stephen's death, looking after the children, working part-time to pay the rent and carrying on with my studies.

I was deeply hurt that someone who had always showed me that he cared was no longer interested in anything to do with me. I know that he was shattered by the loss of our son, but we had all lost Stephen; Neville seemed to feel that the loss was his alone.

Nothing in my world was as it used to be.

At around the time Neville left for Jamaica, the CPS were asked to drop the case against Duwayne Brooks for his role in the disorder around the BNP shop. It was suggested that it was not in the public interest to go on with it. At the time, of course, we were not privy to the CPS's correspondence, but we did see it years later. They stonily refused to discontinue the case, and the same lawyers who had decided to drop the case against Norris, Dobson, Knight and the Acourts grew indignant at the idea of letting Duwayne off – 'There can be no question of the prosecution not proceeding on the basis of the evidence available . . .' Their spokesman said that it was 'totally improper' to suggest that it should be dropped on public interest grounds. His diligence in hounding this vulnerable young man was impressive.

We also found out that the Crown Prosecution Service asked the police to note their impressions of the boy on the night of the murder and afterwards – they were seeking to establish that he was disturbed at around that time, and that his presence at Welling was caused by grief and shock. Thirteen policemen, with amazing unanim-ity, said that he was aggressive, uncooperative, 'anti-police', arrogant and excitable – the litany of clichés about young black men. There was no sympathy for him whatsoever, no suggestion that he had been traumatised by what he had gone through. All this would contribute to our difficulties in the years ahead, and contribute to the protection of the killers.

10   Alone

In the early summer of 1994 Neville and I met in Jamaica in order to put a headstone on Stephen's grave. We needed the headstone to be ready for 3 July, the anniversary of Stephen's burial, so before leaving London I had paid for the headstone, and for an inscription on the granite, with the dates of Stephen's birth and death. A photograph of him was to be incorporated in the slab. The High Commission helped by flying the headstone out with some military equipment.

After I had collected the headstone from the Jamaican Army in Kingston – which was not easy because Neville had given me the wrong number for the colonel who was supposed to help me – I returned to the house where we were staying and had the headstone, still in its packing, placed beneath a chair. I would look at it when I had some privacy later; I didn't want strangers looking at it until I was ready. Neville, who had been out for the day, had come back with his friend and his friend's parents, so that there were a lot of people in the house. I pointed out to Neville that he had given me the wrong number. Suddenly, in front of these strangers, we were having a terrible argument.

It was very upsetting and I thought, Enough is enough. I dislike discussing private matters in front of other people, and it was much worse being drawn into a fight with him, just at the time when we should both have been united. It was not a pleasant start to our time on the island.

The next day, Saturday, was the anniversary of Stephen's burial. All the arrangements were in place for us to go down to his grave and lay the headstone. However, when we opened up the packing in which it had been sent, the oval photograph of Stephen that was meant to be embedded into the granite stone was not there, nor were the dates.

Early on the Saturday morning my stepfather, who had returned to the island a couple of years before, brought food and water in preparation for the drive from Kingston to where Stephen is buried. It was a good two to three hours away, in the heart of the country; there is no piped water on the land, so everything we might need we had to carry with us in the car.

Being there that day was an emotional experience, and the pain of having lost my first-born son was as fresh as ever. I was too upset to speak – upset that the headstone did not have Stephen's picture on it, upset at how Neville was treating me.

Somehow I managed to get through the day. We returned to the house and nothing more was said.

Georgina had always been treated differently by her father, and it had always been obvious that she was his favourite; but now he seemed to have become indifferent even to her. The tension and misery in the house could be felt by anyone who came in.

Usually if things were not right between us I had always been the one who went more than halfway trying to resolving them. This time I had had enough. I saw no point in trying to build any bridges between us while Neville was in this state. And the children's needs had to be taken care of; it made no sense to do nothing with them for the whole time we were there. I decided to arrange days out for the three of us to visit some of the tourist attractions on the island. We went to Bob Marley's museum, to the mineral baths, and we went to the old slave and pirate harbour at Port Royal. It was the same pattern for the rest of our stay: the children and me without Neville.

I felt by the end of that trip that at the age of forty-one, having put up with so much since I was young – put up with being unhappy while staying with my aunt in Jamaica, and being treated so coldly in my mother's household – I had reached a stage when I should not have to endure any more unnecessary pain. I did not want to live like this; and I told Neville so.

I returned to London. He went back to Florida, where he could stay until November 1994 on his six-month visa.

Then I received a letter from him. Stuart himself, for the first time, had told Neville before our return to London that though it was too late for Stephen and for himself, he worried about his father's relationship with Georgina and how Neville was jeopardising even that. That touched me, and I assumed it would have touched Neville, so I was expecting his letter to make some kind of response to Stuart's plea.

At the same time as Neville's letter arrived, the musician Garth Hewitt had released an album called *Stronger than the Storm* on which there was a track about Stephen and he had sent it to me because it was going to be performed at a church in Kidbrooke, near Eltham. I put on the tape while I was reading Neville's letter.

He did not say that he was sorry for anything, or wanted life with his family back, but instead he told me about my uncle coming to visit him, what my uncle said and did not say: banal gossip and family talk. The first emotion I felt was anger. I sat down and wrote him a reply, putting it in no uncertain terms that this was not what I wanted to hear from him. Meanwhile the music was playing and when it finished I thought, I didn't hear any mention of Stephen. A couple of days later I decided to play it again and it was the second track on the tape. The first time I had been so distraught that I had not even heard Stephen's name in the song lyrics.

Neville came back from Florida in November and it was as if I had not written the letter; he carried on a conversation as if nothing had happened or we had seen each other the day before.

I went back to my studies, and finished the course. I got a 2.2, which was not too bad, considering everything. The graduation ceremony was in November that year at the Barbican; Stuart and Georgina were there, and my sister Cheryl, who wanted to see me in my gown and tasselled cap. For me it was such a special day. Since then I have received three honorary doctorates – from the Universities of East Anglia, Bradford and Staffordshire – but nothing can compare to that feeling of achievement, of having completed my first degree in spite of all I had been going through.

11 Reinvestigation

Close to the first anniversary of Stephen's death we met for the first time with the Commissioner of the Metropolitan Police, Paul Condon, and the Deputy Assistant Commissioner, Ian Johnston. We still had not seen the Barker report, only the leaked conclusions. I wasn't looking forward to the meeting, remembering how haughtily Condon had refused to meet us the previous September. We sat in Condon's huge rectangular office, a thickly carpeted room with a big wooden desk and cabinets of awards and memorabilia. A life-size portrait of Sir Robert Peel seemed to take up a large part of one wall. The view out over London was spectacular. Close to the door was a round table, where we were invited to sit. We were made to feel that we should be honoured to have been invited to Scotland Yard. Condon sat there with his fellow officers, big men all dressed in their smart blue uniforms, imposing – the very figures of authority. He had white hair and a square jaw, and from first to last he was totally unsmiling. He used all the right-sounding words – he was sorry about our loss, it grieved him that the murderers had not been caught, and so on – but no depth of feeling came across. He spoke like a machine, I thought. He went on to talk about how hard his officers were working, that they had done this and they had done that, and Stephen's case was not the only one where they had not managed to catch the killers. Take the case of PC Dunne. He had been killed by armed men when he went to investigate a domestic disturbance in Clapham in October 1993, and his killers were still at large . . .

I have found that a lot of people in authority believe that because they are in a position of power you should be in awe of them and not speak out. I was finding out that I am not of that persuasion. And so I challenged the Commissioner.

'Excuse me,' I said, 'when PC Dunne was killed – and I am sorry about what happened to him – but when PC Dunne was killed you had helicopters out and everyone searching for the killers. Within twenty-four hours you had arrested somebody, albeit the wrong man. But you did arrest someone. In Stephen's case none of those things were done, so don't tell me that you did everything you could. Do not compare Stephen's case to that of PC Dunne.'

He began to apologise, saying he did not mean it that way.

'But how can you tell me that you gave all that you could? No, you didn't. You can see the two cases were treated completely differently. Helicopters? Not even a police car went round to search for Stephen's killers, much less a helicopter. It is not the same; they are two completely different cases. You can't compare them.'

Condon apologised again and said he understood how I felt.

'No, you don't,' I said. 'This happened to my son and I expected his murderers to be caught, I expected him to be treated in the way that any other person would be treated.' I said, 'As far as I'm concerned nobody's interested in catching Stephen's murderers.'

He said yes, they were, and that they would do everything they could to catch my son's killers. And he made more promises: that he intended to launch a new investigation into Stephen's murder, and so on. 'We're going to have new officers take over the case and reinvestigate it.'

A couple of weeks later I met Detective Superintendent Brian Weeden for the first time. He had been the senior investigating officer on the case for the past year. The officer put in charge of the reinvestigation was Commander Perry Nove, and we had a further meeting with him and Weeden. I said to Nove that although we had been promised knowledge of what was in the Barker report, we still had no real idea what it contained. I was made uneasy by the way in which all the police officers I met would talk about it as though it was holy writ. Nothing could have been done that was not done: they seemed to take a great deal of comfort from that. We still wanted to know exactly what had happened in the first investigation: why they had not done house-to-house searches and so on.

We were eventually shown parts of the Barker review, not the whole report, while sitting in an office in Eltham police station. Since we were not allowed to take any part of it away with us, Deputy Assistant Commissioner Ian Johnston handed us the 'executive summary', and sat near us while we read it. He said it was to 'put [our] minds at rest'. It is difficult to concentrate on reading a document while facing a person who has presented it to you with the emphasis that they want to put on it, and you are trying to pay attention to the words, and the room is full of interested parties and one of them is sitting near you; so we couldn't read the thing properly, and they would anyway have edited out things they did not want us to see. It confirmed what the newspaper leaks had suggested: the report was a hymn to the wonderful job that the first team of officers had done. Their work could not be improved, despite the terrible pressures being put on them by 'outside' forces – code words, I was beginning to see, for our lawyers and supporters.

To give Commander Nove his due, he began to look at the case quite differently and, unlike the others, he kept us informed. I believe that he genuinely tried to keep his promises. DS Weeden then retired from the force, and was replaced by Detective Superintendent William Mellish.

Their more energetic attitude bore fruit almost straight away. A few weeks after Mellish appeared on the scene, Clifford Norris, the father of David Norris, who many people had named as the chief stabber both of Stephen and of Stacey Benefield, was arrested in Kent. He had been living a comfortable life in a converted oast house, going to the pub, being visited by his wife and son, completely unmolested by the law. He had a couple of pistols and a submachine gun with him in the house when he was arrested.

Throughout this period, and later, we had to rely heavily on our legal advice, and Imran Khan was very good at sorting out the right people for our team. Michael Mansfield attended the inquest in December 1993, and from then on he and Imran worked on the case for nothing; it was never a problem that we could not pay. We met with Mike regularly as the new investigation got under way.

Mike is flamboyant and has an air of immense confidence about him. He knows who he is, as if to say it doesn't matter what anybody says, and he is comfortable with himself. He's intelligent and passionate, a very good barrister but very aware of the failings of the system. When you sit in a meeting with him, he is constantly jotting things down. He never writes in a straight line; he makes little notes and sometimes circles or puts a line underneath them, and he makes points all across his pad, but they are always constructive things. He nails the main points down and then moves on to something else, or he will put a question mark next to something that he'll follow up later.

Imran Khan has always been very serious and focused. Nothing makes him deviate from what he is working on. In the first week he came to our house practically every day, although he was based on the other side of London, and he would stay with us for the whole day, yet the most he would accept from us was a cup of coffee. People kept bringing so much food and I would plead with him to have something to eat. But whatever I offered he would say, 'No, I'm fine. You have enough to worry about.' I would phone Imran in the middle of the night, and he never once said, 'Do you know what time it is?' – unlike some of the police officers on the case. From the start, every time some information came in, we wanted to make sure the police were given it quickly, so Cheryl or Neville or I would phone Imran and tell him that we had received another name or that we had heard some rumour, and calm as ever – I have never known him to raise his voice – Imran would say, 'Give me the name, I'll deal with it.'

We began talking about the possibility of a private prosecution after the Crown Prosecution Service had discontinued in 1993, and indeed the threat of a private prosecution was one of the things that made sure my sister and Imran got a meeting with the Home Office in August 1993.

Christmas was always the worst time, as it still is, and I would often call Imran and pour my heart out about the frustration of our need for justice and about the police. At Christmas in the second year, 1994, I went out for a late-night walk, wandering aimlessly in the cold and thinking about what we should do. After an hour I called Imran from a phone box and said that we should explore the possibility of a prosecution, despite all the risks.

We met at Mike Mansfield's office to discuss the way forward. All the lawyers said that a private prosecution for murder had almost never been tried before, and that it was our last resort. I suppose it was not a promising idea since we knew there was no single piece of evidence that on its own would be enough; we would have to rely on whatever body of evidence we could build up over a period of time. The risk was that if any of the suspects was acquitted of Stephen's murder, the rule of 'double jeopardy' meant that he could not be tried for the same crime again, whatever later evidence might come to light.

The first hurdle was to get those we believed were responsible for Stephen's murder arrested – to get a summons served on them, and to have them charged.

DS Bill Mellish and the new police team worked closely with our legal team. Imran Khan and his colleague Caron Thatcher, along with the barristers Margo Boye-Anawoma, Martin Soorjoo and stephen Kamlish, used to meet them regularly at Shooters Hill police station to go through all the files. Other lawyers also used to come, all giving their time freely. Rumours began to emerge that the new police team could not understand how the first investigation had been so botched. But even then, though our legal team spent days and weekends at Shooters Hill going through files, papers, documents, and video tapes – all the materials the police chose to give us – we had no way of knowing whether we were getting the whole story.

It was now that we discovered the sheer scale of the information that the police had been given from the first hours of the investigation, and the role of Clifford Norris, about whom we had been kept completely in the dark. We heard that he had emerged from hiding when his son was charged with stabbing Stacey Benefield and tried to bribe Stacey into changing his evidence, wrapping up his offer of £5,000 with a threat to shoot the boy if he did not go through with altering his story. Stacey took the £2,000 in cash that Norris pressed on him, because he was so frightened, but then told the police about it and became a protected witness. It may have been after this that Norris tried to interfere with the jury in his son's trial; whatever he did, it worked. We also learned that the uncle of the Acourt brothers, Terry Stuart, was another gangster, and that he too was a drug smuggler.

These boys were no longer just hooligans: they had sinister and dangerous connections. James Grant's role was also a revelation, and all the anonymous letters. The boys themselves had been involved with many other stabbings or assaults. Neil Acourt had been thrown out of the Samuel Montague sports club, to which his friends also belonged, for pulling a knife and holding it to the neck of a black child in the course of a football match – the only boy expelled from the club in over ten years. Jamie Acourt had kicked a black child down the concrete steps of his school and knocked him unconscious. The school refused to treat this as a racist attack and both boys were expelled. In May 1992 David Norris and Jamie Acourt stabbed and beat two boys, the Witham brothers, in Chislehurst town centre. The brother who was stabbed had a deep holiday tan and dark hair, and looked Turkish or Asian. Norris was charged, but the CPS dropped the charge just six weeks before Stephen was killed. (Later I discovered that the CPS never explained to the Witham family why they refused to press on with the case. Had they not dropped it, Stephen might still be here).

The catalogue went on and on. I was outraged by all this, but had to keep quiet since the papers could only be used as part of the prosecution. And it added very much to my sense of fear and vulnerability: the people we were dealing with were dangerous, and had even more dangerous friends, who had been responsible for many murders and attempted murders. The older criminal members of the boys' families had links with even larger and more powerful families. It was around this time that we had cameras installed outside the house and had serious alarms fitted. I was like someone walking through the woods thinking that there might be a dangerous dog on the loose, but completely unaware that there were wolves at large all around me.

A senior police officer, Detective Chief Inspector John Carnt, was in day-to-day charge of the investigation team, supporting our legal team who were looking through the police files. As they saw what was coming out, Carnt especially gave the impression that he could not understand what had gone so wrong in the first investigation, or how the original team had missed so much that was staring them in the face – a whole catalogue of errors was being exposed. We and our legal team felt, right up to the time of the committal and after, that these police officers were genuinely working together with us to bring

Stephen's murderers to justice. One of our lawyers had even wanted everyone to go out for a meal together to thank those police officers who were working so hard with us; I saw nothing wrong with that, but Imran said, no, they were paid to do a job and that was enough, so I respected his view. But the dinner went ahead, and Imran felt obliged to go along. Mr Carnt would later change his mind so radically about what we were all seeing during those weeks in 1995 that I was glad I did not go. He changed his mind so much I wondered where I was – in the real world or in an Alice-in-Wonderland reflection of it. But all that was in the future.

Because of what had happened (or not happened) in the early days – with the suspects dumping and washing clothes, and everything else that they had clearly been tutored to do – it was difficult to produce any forensic evidence. So Commander Nove, who had said he would cooperate with any strategy capable of putting Stephen's killers before a court, decided to set up covert filming of the suspects for three weeks in December 1994. The hope was that they would in some way incriminate themselves or would make a confession, and admit that they had killed Stephen. The surveillance was set up in Gary Dobson's flat in Footscray Road in Eltham. When the film was later viewed it was clear that somehow the boys sensed that someone had been in the flat. As if they had an idea that someone was listening, they were careful about what they said; it seemed they were talking in code, using insinuation, never being explicit about very much. But they did not realise that it was not just an audio recording, that there would also be visual images. Since they were unaware that a camera was watching, their body language was unguarded and all the more shocking.

In the same month the suspects were being observed, Duwayne Brooks was brought to trial for his involvement in the disorder around the BNP building in Welling. The judge threw out the case against him, saying that it had not been in the public interest to bring it in the first place, and that even if Duwayne were found guilty he had no intention of punishing him, given what he had been through already. He was concerned also at the effect on Duwayne's mental state of going through all the events around the murder and the demonstration. Everything we heard about Duwayne indicated that he was in a bad way, confused and depressed.

Starting in April 1995, all the documents and statements were assembled from the new investigation. Because of the police lapses so early in the case, when the five boys could have been picked up and questioned properly, we had to rely on whatever material we could now find. We had the statements of witnesses who saw the attack, but Duwayne Brooks was the principal witness to the actual stabbing, since Royston Westbrook, a young man who had been passing on a bus, and Joey Shepherd had not picked out any of the suspects at the identification parades, and Joey had stopped cooperating with the police. The police had alienated him, and he claimed had put him in danger, by naming him in the hearing of everyone at the Jamie Acourt identification parade on the evening of the arrests; he was in fear of his own and his girlfriend's lives. We will never know how much he really saw. But together with the film from the surveillance camera, we had enough to get past the first hurdle. I had seen some of the transcripts of the surveillance, and they made nauseating reading. I could not deal with it then, but knew that I would have to watch the films themselves during the court hearing.

One of the most shocking revelations from the papers we saw during these weeks was the record of the conversation that was supposed to have taken place on 13 May 1993, three weeks after the murder, at Southwark police station. It was one of the factors that so weakened the case, according to the CPS, that they decided to drop it. This was when Duwayne picked out Luke Knight from an identification parade. He had already picked out Neil Acourt at an earlier parade. By all accounts Duwayne was in a bad way by then, afraid and disoriented, and very vulnerable. After he had identified Knight, a Sergeant Crowley, who was not connected to the investigating team, and who had driven Duwayne from home, was supposed to drive him back again. He claimed that he fell into conversation with Duwayne, and that Duwayne talked a lot. He told this policeman he had never met before that he had not seen the faces of the attackers, only their build and their hair. He claimed that he had been told he would recognise one of the five boys by the fact that they were wearing tracksuit bottoms, having spent the night in police cells. He confided in him that he had been coached by friends about the appearance of the Acourt brothers so that he could pick them out. And Crowley said that Duwayne admitted he was 'totally anti-police', and wanted revenge for Stephen's murder outside the law.

Duwayne didn't deny disliking the police, and his treatment on the evening of the murder had not made him feel any better about them. But he denied Crowley's claim that he'd been coached. He said that when he had seen Acourt at the parade his memory of his appearance, which until then had been about hair and what his body looked like, came back to him. It was his word against the policeman's, and the CPS accepted Sergeant Crowley's – as did Sir William Macpherson years later during the inquiry into all these things. Yet I can't help agreeing with Sir William that 'there are features of DS Crowley's evidence which are strange'. They had given no hint to us at the time of the existence of this extraordinary story. I was astonished at the attention and pressure that was being placed on Duwayne, who was in many ways without a friend in the world, by the Metropolitan Police. He was being discredited at every turn, and he was not helping himself. He would prove to be a terrible burden to our case later.

On Saturday 22 April 1995, the second anniversary of my

son's death, at Greenwich Magistrates Court, 'informations were laid' against five suspects for the murder of Stephen Lawrence on the night of 22 April 1993. In each case, Michael Mansfield said that we had information that the named individuals had murdered Stephen Lawrence, and the judge said that he would there and then issue summonses and warrants to arrest.

David Norris, Neil Acourt and Luke Knight were arrested immediately; Gary Dobson was brought in later. They had all been under police surveillance, so there was no trouble finding them. Jamie Acourt was already in custody for the stabbing of a young man in a Greenwich nightclub. His knife had penetrated the heart of a young man called Darren Giles, who almost died.

That Monday, when they were brought to court, I saw the five of them for the first time. I felt very tense; I was frightened to be in the same room as them. For the previous two years they had known what we looked like and I felt that we could have been attacked at any time, yet they had walked around safe in the knowledge that we had no clue about their appearance. Now here they were.

When they came into the dock, wearing neat dark suits, their hair washed and gelled, they nearly all had grins on their faces. Only Luke Knight showed any solemnity; occasionally the others said something to make him grin, but he was the only one who ever had a serious expression, the others smirked all the time, as if to say, 'So what?' Even though I was so nervous, I kept staring at them, and at their parents. I had difficulty putting faces to names since they were all together when their names were read out.

They displayed such confidence, and I could not take my eyes off them. And though I might have expected to see evil-looking monsters, these seemed such ordinary young men – cocky, self-assured, threatening, certainly, but those were things that could be said of many young men on the street. Jamie Acourt was brought to the court from prison, so his mother had not seen him for a while. As he came through the door she rushed toward him, clambering to put her arms around him and kiss him, saying out loud, 'We're here for you, son.' If that had been one of my children, I am sure I would be there for him too, but at the same time I would make sure he knew that he had done wrong. She was behaving as if we were slandering her innocent boy, who was a disgrace long before that night two years before. As the brief hearing went on I found their smug arrogance unbearable. I felt I was being insulted in the most public way possible.

The boys did not stare at me, though their mothers did. I was determined not to let them get the better of me. The worst thing about it was that we were sitting only feet apart from them, because the courtroom was so small. As they were leaving the dock, Jamie Acourt's mother again jumped up and grabbed him round the neck to give him another kiss before he was led out. After Greenwich, other family members turned up to support the Acourt brothers but I did not see the mother again, unless she was too far in the background to be noticed. She was very short and dark, in fact she appeared to have mixed blood in her. That would be ironic, considering how racist these people are. We're all mixed somewhere along the line, but to feel shame over it, as that family obviously would, is incomprehensible to me. The nature of their bigotry became clearer to me when I watched their son, as I would soon have to do, behaving 'normally' when he thought no one was watching him.

I thanked God that they were not bailed that day but were taken back to prison.

The next stage – the committal proceedings – began four months later, on Wednesday, 23 August 1995, when we had to go to Belmarsh Magistrates' Court in Thamesmead to present our case, to determine whether or not the suspects could be committed to the Old Bailey for our private prosecution. The presiding magistrate was called David Cooper. Four of the boys were in the dock at Belmarsh. Gary Dobson was brought later.

I cannot forget the contempt with which the mothers of the accused youths looked at me that day. I stared them out. They were on the opposite side of the courtroom, of course, and we were kept separated from them, so we never actually met, and never spoke. They were strange to me, these parents who had brought up children to have so much hate inside them.

Somehow we never even passed them in the corridor. Unconsciously we seemed to leave the court at different times, delaying long enough to avoid standing next to them in doorways or the halls. Only once did I come face to face with Luke Knight's mother in a toilet. We stared at each other in shock as though we had both seen ghosts. Then we both looked away and she left the room. She did not seem to radiate anger towards me; she looked worn down and I imagined that she was concerned only with her son and the depths to which his friends had sunk him.

David Norris's mother was another story. She was especially venomous towards us. She exuded hostility: it burned in her eyes as she looked at me. One day in court when she noticed someone, not me, looking at her, she snarled viciously: 'What you looking at?' This was the kind of thing her son used to shout at people before beating them, and what he was supposed to have shouted at Stacey Benefield before stabbing him, the language of the street tough looking for an excuse for violence.

Once I saw her in Marks & Spencer in Bromley. I was with Georgina; we had been walking around together and then she wandered off a little way, and as I turned I came face to face with this woman. We stopped and stared at one another and then she passed in front of me, glaring at me. She was taller than me, in her forties, tanned with blonde hair, maybe out of a bottle. I would not call her attractive, but she was well groomed and well dressed. She obviously had the resources to look smarter than the others, because of her husband's wealth; they lived in a big house behind gates in Chislehurst, and we heard later at the public inquiry that the police had been inhibited by the wealth around them from ripping up carpets and floorboards to look for the knife that had killed Stephen.

The Norris and Acourt families had known from the start what I looked like; before 1995, I could have stood next to them at a bus stop and had no idea who they were. That day in the shop in Bromley I wanted to shout out: 'This is the mother of one of those who murdered my son!' But if I'd said anything, the commotion would have brought Georgina to my side and then this woman would have known what she looked like. I did not want to jeopardise the lives of any more of my children and I wanted them to be able to walk about unrecognised.

Seeing those boys in court at the committal hearing brought the reality of their lives and their capacity for violence home to me. These were the white people of my nightmares. But there was a feeling that at last something was happening, and that they would go down. There was a feeling of triumph that we were doing this when the state had not dared to do it, that we had managed to get this far, that Michael Mansfield had done his job and got them arrested and that at least they were now locked up.

There were still moments of hurt and anger. The five applied for bail, of course, and Neville and I came to court for the hearing, which was taking place in a room that we had not been in before. We were obviously lost, standing around looking at the signs. One of the defence lawyers came down and saw us, then walked by, completely ignoring us although we clearly did not know where to go. Her manner was cool and hostile. And when the five were given bail, I could not believe it. By that time Norris's girlfriend had had a baby and his mother brought photographs to court to show the judge, and we had to sit and listen to her pleading with him, 'My son hasn't seen his baby – he's missing his child growing up.' But at least he could see his child, at some point; Stephen would never have a chance to do that, never look at even a photograph of a baby he had fathered. They seemed to expect compassion as a right. The judge gave them bail.

Those days at the committal hearings were hard. That was when I think I felt most alone. It was at the committal that we learned for the first time the full details of how Stephen had died. All that time, incredibly, we had not known; on the night of his murder we were told so little, and the police had not told us much more later. As the pathologist Dr Richard Shepherd, who performed the post-mortem, was giving his report, which included very graphic descriptions of Stephen's wounds, I just could not bear to listen. I heard now in very clinical detail how Stephen had run 250 yards before collapsing, despite the severing of a major artery. It seemed incredible that he could do this with such a fatal wound, and the thought of my son summoning up that last burst of energy, his life's blood leaving him, was too much for me. I had seen the wounds and knew roughly what they were; I'd stood on the roadway in Eltham many times by then and could see the length of ground he had run; but Dr Shepherd's description forced me to realise exactly what had been done to Stephen. I left the room. There were benches outside, where I sat down. Neville came out too and joined me on a bench near a window, looking out, but then he more or less turned his back to me.

I asked, 'Why are you sitting with your back to me?'

He looked at me and said, 'If it's a divorce you want . . .'

Nothing more was said, but from then on the distance between us grew big and cold.

Michael Mansfield outlined in detail the evidence against the suspects. It was also at the Belmarsh committal hearings that I saw for the first time the surveillance videotape featuring Neil Acourt, David Norris, Gary Dobson and Luke Knight.

It was like watching some disturbing drama meant to caricature racist attitudes, but this was not artistic licence, this was real. It was deeply shocking that such young people – they were teenagers, younger than Stephen at the time they killed him – could glory in such bigotry. They had their lives in front of them. They should have been thinking about going to college and making something of themselves; instead their only topics of conversation were violence and beating and weapons. And the racism – they could not watch a football match or a sports-personality-of-the-year award without degrading themselves, snarling if a black sportsman did well or an African team looked as though it might rise in the rankings. They were obsessed. When an advertisement on television showed happy black people in the Caribbean, contrasted with the cold and misery of an English winter, Gary Dobson told his friends that this was racist, that it was meant to show white people in a bad light. Every message they got from the outside world seemed to have racial meaning for them.

How do you produce children who think and behave like that? They talked endlessly and mindlessly about what they would like to do to black people – saying, for example, that every black person should be chopped up and left with nothing but stumps; and, not realising they were being filmed, they acted out their fantasies.

Neil Acourt, the elder brother, the leader of the pack, played and acted with his knife all the time. On the film he looked thick-set, tough and bullying. In his striped shirt he would stand and practise a strange overarm stabbing motion, over and down, exactly the way Duwayne described Stephen being struck and exactly the kind of blow with a knife that Dr Shepherd had described – from above, down into his chest. Acourt ran up towards his imaginary victim like a bowler and swung his arm, putting all his weight behind the action as the knife came down. There was something horribly intent and practised about the way he moved. He did it again and again, as though he were in training. His knife was about a foot long, and he was constantly waving it, sweeping it in front of the bodies of his friends, intimidating them, tossing it one-handed and catching it by the handle, stabbing the arm of the chair that Luke Knight was sitting in. He would thrust the knife at one of them, once mock-stabbing Knight and stopping the knife an inch from his stomach.

I had to leave the room several times during this obscene performance. These were things that I just could not face watching in public and there could be no private moments in that open courtroom. It was truly impossible to comprehend how these boys' parents could watch that video without showing any sign of shame. I had to assume that their children got their views from them.

Each time they left the flat, the boys were armed with knives. At one point the transcript records:

NEIL ACOURT WITH COAT ON HAVING LOOKED OUT
OF WINDOW RETURNS TO WINDOW LEDGE WHERE HE
PICKS UP KNIFE AND PLACES IT INSIDE HIS COAT –
SUBSEQUENTLY LEAVES FLAT.

In fact Acourt put the knife down his waistband. This was obviously part of his normal dress. I found it amazing that their reputation for carrying knives was so notorious on the Brook Estate, and here we were seeing it confirmed nearly two years after the murder (the surveillance was put in place in December 1994), and yet most of them had never been charged with carrying offensive weapons, and if they had they had managed to beat the charges. I understood that Superintendent Mellish wanted to charge them with murder, but it still seems incredible to me that they were never caught before Stephen's death and never later with deadly weapons hidden in their clothes.

But the worst, the very worst thing was listening to them –

especially Neil Acourt – mock and jeer the listeners they knew they had, because they had tumbled very quickly to the fact that the new plugs their landlord had put in were in fact listening devices. They were as wise to all this as only boys connected with experienced criminals could be, and I wondered which of their parents now in court had taught them about such things instead of teaching them basic tolerance and respect. Neil Acourt said in a sneering tone of voice, taunting anyone who could hear him: 'And they ain't got nothing still. We ain't done nothing that's what I mean, there's none of us done fuck all. But the thing that makes me laugh, Dave, they're gonna be doing it for the rest of our lives mate and I'm just gonna be laughing all the way to the Leeds.' As though he cared so little that he couldn't even be bothered to keep up the pretence of lying.

Later in the same conversation with David Norris he says, referring to Stephen's death:

'I fancy they've had a crack deal meself.'

Norris says: 'Yeah they probably did, they probably had. Probably had a bit of a toot or something or had a bit of crack, it's all gone wrong, the coon's got knackered up and all of a sudden four innocent people are getting done for it.'

'Yeah that's what I fancy has happened.'

'That's definitely what happened, Neil. Every time it comes on the news. The real people are sitting laughing their nuts off.'

'What, the real people?'

'Yeah, the real people are sitting laughing their nuts off.'

Then, not realising that he is sitting looking straight into the hidden camera, Acourt laughs and says: 'Oh yeah, they're definitely doing that.'

The look of gloating triumph on his face as he said that will live with me for the rest of my life.

The hearing was also distressing because of the attitude of those who were defending them. It seemed like an abstract exercise to the defence lawyers. Knowing what they were defending their clients against, they didn't have to enjoy it, but it was as if they revelled in their role. Our pain was irrelevant to them. I know that the law has to be neutral and that each side has to be represented, but at the time I had no experience of court hearings and the ways of barristers and QCs and the rest of them, I found it shocking how they seemed totally to disregard Stephen as a person or our feelings. There was no hint of compassion in them. The barristers who represented the boys were bent only on proving that we were wrong. These barristers had been paid for by legal aid, yet we had at that time no public support. Imran and everyone else on our team worked for nothing until after the committal, when the magistrate let them apply for money from the public purse. We were raising as much as we could through the campaign for the money that we would need if costs were awarded against us.

In court, Duwayne Brooks was questioned relentlessly about what he had seen of the murder, but because of discrepancies in his descriptions of what he remembered seeing, and who had actually done the stabbing, Jamie Acourt had to be discharged, as did David Norris, who had never been picked out in an identity parade by any of the witnesses. It was while Duwayne was being questioned by Neil Acourt's lawyer, who was very aggressively trying to pick holes in his various statements that we heard a quote from Duwayne's original statement. In it Duwayne said that Stephen had screamed 'high-pitched and loud' when he was stabbed. Duwayne had never told us this at the time, and it was a terrible thing to think of my child crying out in pain. I suppose I had always hoped that he would not have felt much, that his nerves would have been cut so quickly that the pain would have been dulled, but the sound of his scream was now in my head. Neville was so upset that he got up from his seat and went outside again. He suddenly cried out and collapsed. For a long few minutes it felt as though the boys in that courtroom might have claimed another victim, but then the ambulance came and by the time he got to hospital it was clear that he had not had a heart attack.

The magistrate ruled in the end that there was a case to answer against Neil Acourt and Luke Knight, and they were sent for trial. The same magistrate agreed later in the year that Gary Dobson should also be tried. The case against Jamie Acourt, because of confusions in Duwayne's statements about him – he thought he had seen him after the murder at a café and pub in the area of the killing, and had given differing descriptions of him, and this allowed Jamie's lawyers to sow further confusion about identification evidence – had to be withdrawn. And Norris was also let go. The person known as Witness B, who had caught a glimpse of the attack from a bus, failed to pick him out on an identity parade. This made me sick, but we had no choice. The evidence was technically just not strong enough. Morally, it was a different matter. Jamie Acourt and Norris had been charged after beating and stabbing the Witham brothers back in 1992; that case had been dropped by the CPS because Norris claimed self-defence. Norris had got off in the Benefield case, despite outrageous evidence of bribery, jury nobbling and intimidation. And before the committal hearing, Jamie Acourt had been acquitted in the case of the young man he had stabbed in Stars, the Greenwich nightclub. Again, a plea of self-defence had been accepted. It seemed that nothing could stick to them.

By the end of 1995, at least we could tell ourselves that three of the five boys suspected of inflicting those terrible wounds on Stephen had been committed for trial and were now ready to appear at the Old Bailey. The immunity of the perpetrators surely had to have limits.

I released a statement after the committal hearings that I still stand by:

It has been two years now since the Crown Prosecution

dropped charges against two men for the murder of our son, without even caring to consult or advise us of their decision. It was an act as hurtful and as painful in its effect as the news that Stephen had been killed. Since that time we have fought against tremendous obstacles to reach this stage. These obstacles have been overcome by our own private efforts, with the help of our family and many supporters who have joined us along the way, and at great financial risk . . . No family should ever experience the last two years of our lives. This is the worst kind of fame. We have been brought into the public spotlight not by our own acts, but by the failure of others who were under a public duty to act. The decision of the court today stands as the first clear indictment of that failure.

I was speaking then with some confidence and hope. I thought, *We are finally getting somewhere.* I really believed that at long last we were on our way to justice for Stephen. All it needed, I thought, was for a jury to hear our case and look at those young men and hear and watch that film. I had faith in the jury system. Unfortunately, my confidence in the wider judicial system was about to take another very severe blow.

On 17 April 1996, in the house we had moved to in Ladywell, in Lewisham, I dressed in preparation for going to the Old Bailey. We were about to do something that no one else had done for a century and a half: to bring a private prosecution for murder. A cab came to take us to the Old Bailey. I felt very calm and determined, but my whole body was a knot of tension. I had never known what is meant by a hunger for justice before, but I wanted this reparation so much that I could not eat or sleep.

I was nervous as I walked into the old building that morning. An official showed us into a small inner room which she said was there for us to go to whenever we wished to leave the courtroom and to discuss anything with our legal team.

It was quite overwhelming to walk into Court No. 1 with its austere wooden panelling and see all the court officials in their places, wearing their robes and wigs and looking very stern. Nobody smiled or showed any other reaction. We could have been invisible to them.

We knew we did not have one single piece of evidence strong enough alone to carry the trial, but with a combination of the video and all the pieces of evidence that the team intended to present, we were optimistic that if the jury heard everything, the jury would convict. It just needed to be put together, and surely any reasonable person would draw the right conclusions. However, during the very first day of the trial, we realised that the judge had a different view of the case.

I felt that this judge, Justice Curtis, a former Recorder of Birmingham, was unsympathetic to us and that he disapproved of the very idea of the private prosecution. I thought that there was an iciness about his manner and an undercurrent of impatience with our legal team, Michael Mansfield especially. He never made eye contact with us throughout the trial. His voice was so soft you could barely hear it; I found it made my flesh crawl trying to follow his whispered comments.

The first morning in court, we were told that there were legal arguments before the case could actually start. The defence lawyers said that they intended to challenge whether Duwayne's evidence was admissible at all. The judge then ruled that our lawyers could not mention it in their opening statement. No further reason was given. People were astounded. That was not the usual process and Michael Mansfield had never known it to happen. Normally, the prosecution would have put its case to the jury, before any relevant legal arguments. Michael was not being allowed to do that. He said that if Duwayne's testimony could not be mentioned, he would not have very much to say in his opening address. Mr Justice Curtis replied wearily: 'You are a much better advocate than I ever was. Can we get on?' Throughout all this back and forth, the suspects and their families stared at us. The hard faces of the three boys looked three years older and harder now.

The jury was sworn in. Each potential juror stepped up, and the judge asked them questions about how long they could serve on the jury and so on until twelve were chosen. I was so traumatised by the whole thing that I must have blocked out parts of what happened that morning. I remember nothing about what the individual jurors looked like; all the members that were chosen were white, but this did not worry me unduly. I had faith that anyone would see what we had to put before them and make a common-sense judgement about it. My whole attention was focused on the judge. We had begun wearing orange ribbons as a way of remembering Stephen – I chose that colour because it seemed to me to reflect his vibrant spirit; I remember a favourite T-shirt his friend Elvin designed for him which had a lot of orange in it. A number of people were wearing them, even some members of the press. We his parents could not be prevented from wearing the ribbons, but the judge banned others from displaying it, as though the ribbon was a threat to order in his court.

Michael Mansfield and the other lawyers did their best to keep us informed and to explain the often obscure procedures. Whenever there was a break in the hearing we went to the room allocated to our family; no one was allowed in unless we invited them, so we had our legal team of Michael and Imran, Martin and Margo, Caron Thatcher and Stephen Kamlish, and a few campaign workers would join us there, and my sister too. It took me nearly a week to fully realise what was happening, although very early on, on that first day, a few doubts had been planted. Faint alarm bells were ringing, but I was still focusing on the evidence we had accumulated and looking forward to seeing it presented to the jury.

The first people to take the stand could be thought of as uncontroversial witnesses: there was a French woman, Alexandra Marie, who used an interpreter, and a man called Royston Westbrook, who had both been waiting at the same bus stop as Stephen and Duwayne on Well Hall Road. Their input was minimal because although they had been at the scene and they saw the boys surround Stephen, they were too far away to describe what had actually happened, and could not positively identify the killers, especially as it was dark and they had immediately boarded a bus.

Then it was Duwayne's turn to be cross-examined. A great deal rested on his ability to be a credible witness about whom and what he had seen. Michael Mansfield gradually took him through his story, from the time he and Stephen got to the bus stop, up to the actual stabbing. Then there was a pause before Duwayne reached the disputed part of his evidence, concerning his identification of the boys and which of them stabbed Stephen. The jury were asked to leave the courtroom before the questioning continued.

The problem with Duwayne's testimony was that the details did not match in various statements he had made, so he appeared to have changed his story – he had talked about a man with long frizzy blondish hair, 'like curtains', and at other times stated that the attacker had short dark hair, like Knight, the Acourts or Norris. Imran Khan was also questioned about what Duwayne had told him at meetings after the murder. Later, of course, Duwayne had picked out Neil Acourt and Luke Knight at identity parades. Duwayne was under a lot of pressure and really did not help himself. I heard afterwards that it is normal for a witness in his position to have the chance to review his written evidence before he comes into court, so that he does not forget or become confused about things in the glare and intimidating formality of the courtroom. But Duwayne was never given this chance, for reasons that are still not clear to me; he came in cold, and was obviously very nervous and upset. The defence spent a lot of time trying to discredit him, and they did a good job. He had made differing statements to the police, and he was cross-examined closely about the identity parades that he attended to pick out the suspects. He was hit again with the statement of Sergeant Crowley, that he had been coached by friends to know what the Acourts looked like. This was very damaging to us. He was in the dock being closely interrogated for hours while his evidence was dissected. Under this kind of pressure he became sullen and childish, taking refuge in mono-syllabic answers.

Neil Acourt's lawyer, Stephen Batten, seemed to delight in tearing him apart. He got Duwayne to admit that the man he had picked out on the parade, Neil Acourt, could not be the same man he had seen outside the burger bar and who Duwayne then thought was the stabber. Duwayne had agreed at the time with the police that this was not the same man he had seen at the identity parade. If, of course, the two men were different then Neil Acourt could not be the stabber.

They used the psychiatric reports from his prosecution for violent disorder at Welling to claim that he was suffering from post-traumatic stress disorder and that he had a kind of amnesia. They produced police statements from the officers who had dealings with him after the murder to the effect that he was aggressive, unstable and hostile to the police. As ever, the Metropolitan Police's contribution to our case was a negative one.

What all this ignored, of course, was that Duwayne's statements had been made under terrible conditions and that like many traumatised people he did not remember everything that had happened to him at once. Sometimes, as Michael Mansfield pointed out in his argument, people in such violent situations see a face that they store inside their minds for a long time, and it is only later that the face or other memory flashes back. Sometimes they need to see the face again to remember it – indeed many of us do, in less fraught situations. It was not surprising, then, that Duwayne only fixed on Neil Acourt at the identity parade. And the finicking arguments over which of the boys actually stabbed Stephen were beside the point – they were all there and had all attacked, and they were all responsible. But the case was now bogged down in an argument over the admissibility of Duwayne's evidence – a trial within the trial, as Michael called it.

Towards the beginning of the second week of the trial, Michael came into the room we were using for private discussions and said to us, 'They're going to throw the case out.' Reading what was happening, he felt that the judge was going to stop the proceedings. It was a Tuesday, less than a week after the trial opened. By the time that Mike told me, I felt exhausted and in turmoil, having had to sit quietly in court every day watching the faces of those three boys, hearing the mounting tension of the arguments and running the gauntlet of the press outside. And he was right. Justice Curtis declared that afternoon that it was 'a fleeting glimpse case', meaning that the witness was unreliable because he had only snatched a quick look at the person and that it would be unfair to convict on that basis. Devastatingly, Mr Justice Curtis concluded his ruling:

> I have heard Brooks's evidence and seen him. I am entirely satisfied that where recognition or identification is concerned he simply does not know, in ordinary parlance, whether he is on his head or his heels. This, I hasten to add, is understandable: he was undoubtedly shocked at the terrible events I shortly described at the beginning. Second, he only had a snap look at one and no more than one of his friend's attackers. Third, since then by many people and at many times he has been asked about identification matters. Next, nearly three years further on in effect he has identified three if not four people as the stabber . . .
>
> The perils of misidentification are well known, and an Act of Parliament and the established cases require the trial judge to act as a screen to see that the material to go before the jury is material on which they can properly convict according to law . . .
>
> I shall direct that Brooks's identification of each of these defendants [Jamie Acourt and Luke Knight] does not go before the jury; to do so would amount to an injustice. Adding one injustice to another does not cure the first injustice done to the Lawrence family.
>
> I so rule for the reasons that I have given.

That was when, for the very first time, I physically collapsed in public. I have always had difficulty in showing emotion in public but I was going through hell, and my body just gave out. They had to bring me out of the Old Bailey through the back in a wheelchair. I felt that I just couldn't take this any more. Why wouldn't the judge listen? Why wouldn't he let the jury hear the evidence we had? They had led us on, giving us a false sense of security that we were getting somewhere. It was like taking us halfway up a mountain and then pushing us off the edge rather than letting us finish the climb. That is how it felt. When I got home, a doctor was called to give me a sedative.

But the legal system was not finished with us yet. The following morning I was too shocked to attend court. Our case had effectively collapsed, but I do not think even Mike Mansfield realised what the judge was about to do next. He brought back the jury, who had not even been in court for much of the argument over Duwayne, and told them that it was their duty to answer 'not guilty' when they were asked if they so found 'on the direction of the judge'. The jury, who had never seen the videotapes or any of the other evidence, retired and came back after a short break and did as they were told. Neil Acourt, the racist knifeman in the film, and his friends Luke Knight and Gary Dobson, were found not guilty of the murder of my son. Once that was done, any chance of ever trying those boys again was lost, under the double jeopardy rule. I am sure they gloated, and I was glad I was not there to see that.

What Curtis could have done instead was to say that this evidence was not admissible, but still allowed us to put all the supporting evidence to the jury, and ask the jury to decide on the whole picture of the defendants. Until the day before that 'not guilty' verdict was announced, I had tried so hard to put on a brave face, still focusing only on us getting a conviction. To know that could never happen now, that these people were home free, was crushing. I still believe that if Duwayne's evidence had not been seriously undermined from the start by police incompetence and hostility, and if he had not been so unstable in himself, he would have stated what he saw and the jury could have decided whether he was telling the truth or not. The video evidence was so compelling about the boys' pathological state of mind and their addiction to violence that the jury would have come to a reasonable conclusion. I believe in the English jury system, but here it was never given a chance to work.

Only later did I start to analyse the implications: bringing a private prosecution was a very rare event, yet here was a black family doing just that, in a case that threatened to show up the Conservative government, show up the Crown Prosecution Service, show up the Metropolitan Police force, show up the entire justice system – the enormous odds against us winning had not dawned on me before. In my mind's eye, I had believed that in the end right was on our side, but the forces lined up against us were too great. I may be wrong; but I know I was naive to think we could succeed.

What we did not realise at the time, which we now know as a result of the public inquiry, was that the police were massively incompetent in the way that they handled the first investigation. Clifford Norris was a well-known and influential criminal, who had tried in the past to put pressure on the police. It may never be possible to investigate exactly how far that influence reached. Besides, the police themselves would be the only ones with the resources and experience to conduct that type of investigation. So we have only our own suspicions about what other elements hindered our ability to gather evidence and present our case, but I hope that some of the people who played such strange roles in the original investigation may in the end have to give a full account of what they did.

This was the lowest point for me since Stephen's murder. I retreated into myself again after that. There were days once more when I would not leave my room. I managed to get myself to the toilet and that was about all. Injustice is like a second bereavement. I would not eat, I would not drink, I would not talk to anyone. I was reduced again to crying helplessly all day.

13   An Ending

The whole family was due to go to Jamaica in 1996 for the filming of a television documentary on our story. It would also be an opportunity for me to put some flowers on Stephen's grave, which I try to do every year now, usually silk flowers so that they will last.

Neville went ahead in July, and the children and I followed, travelling with the film crew, meeting him in Ocho Rios. They were to film us for a week. I hate having cameras on me all the time. The film crew tried their best, but I just did not feel comfortable. They wanted to film on the plane, for example, but I was not prepared to sit there with everyone around me staring at me while I pretended to look unselfconscious. This is the side of being well known that I find most difficult.

When we met up with Neville in Jamaica I realised how much we had all changed, and how much hurt we had sustained because of Stephen's death. As usual, everyone had their different ways of occupying themselves, despite the tensions between us. Elvin Oduro had come with us, so he kept Stuart company. Neville was always with the camera team, and of an evening Georgina would have her meal with us in the restaurant, but she never liked to stay around afterwards. She was only twelve and she wanted to go back to her room where she could watch TV. I would see her to her room because I did not want her walking on her own at night; the room was quite a distance from the restaurant, reached through an old botanical garden. Usually I would feel too tired to go back and in any case I did not want to leave her in her room in a strange place, so I would stay with her and so I missed out on the social part of the evening. Not having that interaction with people made me feel even more isolated

Here in Jamaica Neville was behaving as he had been since returning to London at the end of 1994: sociable with others, distant from us. Something was dead. The children and I stayed on the island until August; Neville decided not to return to London with us. I was working at the university by then so I had to get back in time for the new term, Georgina had school and Stuart was at college. It felt like a parting of the ways when we said goodbye at the airport.

Neville called his cousin to say that he was going to America. For a whole year, which he spent partly in Florida and partly in Jamaica, we didn't hear from him. I was on my own and it was a struggle. I worked, paid the bills, looked after my kids, and studied.

In 1997 the Churches' Commission for Racial Justice funded Georgina, Stuart and me so that we could go to Florida to meet Neville. I was still keeping an open mind about our relationship, though I knew the outlook was not good. I rang my aunt to say I would be coming. Before we left London I spoke to both Stuart and Georgina about us going, and told them to be honest about how they felt, and to talk to their father rather than give me a hard time about him.

Neville was staying down in Miami and my aunt lives near a place called Melbourne, as far away from Miami as London is from Manchester. My aunt said it would be best if I stayed with her and that the meeting could take place at her house: 'At least you'll have support here,' she said. So that is what I did, and Neville came up for the weekend. He arrived on the Friday night. My aunt had gone to work, and her husband and I went out on the Saturday morning. I thought that this would give Neville and the children a chance to talk.

When I came back, Georgina was upstairs, Stuart was in the living room watching television and Neville was outside on the porch. It was clear from the atmosphere that the reunion had not gone well. I was angry, and that prompted a massive argument between us, and Stuart became involved, taking his father's side. All of us seemed to be sinking into bitterness and strife. I felt that I'd protected Stuart for years and sheltered him from my problems with Neville, and his accusations hurt.

I went for a walk. I thought, If I stay here any longer I'll say more things that I will regret. Neville stayed till the Sunday, and then he went back to the Miami area where he was staying. He came up once more, and still nothing was resolved. In the end we returned to the UK, leaving him there in the United States.

It was not until late June 1997 – almost a year since he had left London – that he eventually came home. This was after the inquest, which I had faced – that and everything else – on my own. Neville had disappeared into his own depression and his desire to escape from England, from the place where his son had been killed and from me.

When he came to the house I knew that there was no point in going on, and Neville realised that I was serious. Perhaps he thought I would not be able to cope in the long run without him. I had not chosen to be on my own; but now I was, and I found that there was no going back. I remember that I said to him as calmly as I could, as if there was still one more chance for us, 'Neville, if you have a choice now, what is it that you want?'

He could not answer. Sadly, he did not say what I really wanted him to say – as a man, a husband and a father – which was that he wanted his family. But he stayed until the following July, sleeping in the living room. He still was not working, and he was restless and unhappy. This was not a good time for any of us.

When the children later rebelled, as all children do, against me especially, I think they were taking their anger with Neville out on me. Whenever they complained about their dad, I would urge them to talk to him, to tell him what they felt. But they never did. They never let him see how angry they were. Maybe they felt safer with me; they knew that I was not going anywhere. With their father there remained this wall that couldn't be climbed.

Nevilleand I finally parted in July 1998. Our marriage had become another casualty of the events set in train by the murder of the son we both loved so much. When he left I was beyond feeling sadness: it was a relief.

The inquest, meanwhile, had finally taken place in February 1997 at Southwark Coroner's Court. It could not happen before in case anything *sub judice* came out that we could not then have used in a court of law, but the private prosecution was now over and there could be a formal judgement about how Stephen had died. It felt weird to me that we should be going back to establish such basic facts after all that had happened, with police investigations botched, cases dropped, suspects charged and walking free. But the law ground on in its own slow way. The coroner, Sir Montagu Levine, who was presiding over his last inquest before he retired, was very supportive to me. I had to take the stand to answer questions, but I was given the opportunity to read out a statement in court, in which I criticised the police and the CPS, the government and the judicial system. I was grateful for the opportunity. After the collapse of the Old Bailey trial, I was more determined than ever to hold the police accountable for their actions, and it became clear to me from reading the documents that we obtained during the pre-trial period that there was much more to come out – about police mistakes, and about Clifford Norris's links to individual policemen who knew some of the officers involved in the case. There was such a pattern of error and incompetence that simple stupidity could not explain it – not to me or anyone who had taken the trouble to look at the evidence.

In my statement, I said in part:

My son was murdered nearly four years ago. His killers are still walking the streets. When my son was murdered the police said my son was a criminal belonging to a gang. My son was stereotyped by the police – he was black then he must be a criminal – and they set about investigating him and us. The investigation lasted two weeks. That allowed vital evidence to be lost.

My son's crime is that he was walking down the road, looking for a bus that would take him home. Our crime is living in a country where the justice system supports racist murderers against innocent people.

. . . In my opinion what happened in the Crown Court last year was staged. It was decided long before we entered the courtroom what would happen – that the judge would not allow the evidence to be presented to the jury. In my opinion what happened was the way of the judicial system making a clear statement, saying to the black community that their lives are worth nothing and the justice system will support anyone, any white person who wishes to commit a crime or even murder, against a black person. You will be protected. You will be supported by the British system. To the black community: your lives are nothing. You do not have any rights to the law in this country. That is only here to protect the white man and his family, not you . . . I hope our family will be the last – even though there is no sign of it to date – the last to be put through this nightmare, which it has been for us. There need to be changes for the future. The Establishment needs to have in place a system that will allow all crimes to be treated in the same way and to be investigated in the same way regardless of who is the victim, of who the perpetrators might be, not to have one rule for the white and another for the black people.

When I was questioned about the piece of paper with the names of suspects that I had given to Ilsley, which he folded up so tightly, the coroner himself took the page and folded it over and over in the way the policeman had done. The folds were still creased into the paper after four years, and he followed them exactly. He held it up and said publicly that I was right, that Ilsley had folded it 'into something the size of a postage stamp'. The public at the inquest burst into applause – they could not help themselves.

The five young men – Neil and Jamie Acourt, David Norris, Gary Dobson and Luke Knight – came in swaggering like a gang of football hooligans, bristling with aggression and defiance. Older, but no wiser. They literally strutted. One by one they took that witness stand, and all they would say was 'I'm claiming privilege.' They chose to hide behind their right not to incriminate themselves, but they did this for every question, even the simplest. They would not even acknowledge their names. 'Are you called Mr Norris?' 'I'm claiming privilege.' 'Can you shed any light on the murder of Stephen Lawrence?' 'I'm claiming privilege.' And each time they answered it was with a lazy, sullen sneer. Obviously their lawyers had advised them that by giving only that response they could not trip themselves up. It was a farce; they saw it as a game.

At the inquest still more evidence was brought to my attention that I had not heard about before. For the first time I learned there had been no attempt to apply First Aid by the roadside that night and realised that nobody had put Stephen in the recovery position: he had fallen into what looked like that position, but no police officers present at the scene actually attended to Stephen's injuries, gave him the kiss of life or checked to ensure he could breathe properly. Whether or not anything could have saved his life, and the doctors said that nothing could, the police did not even look to see if he was seriously hurt; perhaps they did not want to touch Stephen because he was black and young and they assumed he was a criminal.

John Carnt, the senior policeman who had helped us back in 1995 and who had been so sympathetic to us during the private prosecution, now pulled a rabbit out of the hat. When he was called to give evidence at the inquest and was questioned about the original investigation, he said in effect that he saw nothing wrong with it, that the only difficulty had been between the liaison officers and the family. He told a story of great efforts: over 1,600 people seen, hundreds of lines of enquiry, of statements, of witnesses. He gave the impression that fear had intimidated witnesses, which was true, but not that there was much wrong with the way they had been handled by the police. This was the Barker line: the first investigation was a professional triumph and it was only the troublesome family and their 'political' pressure that had caused problems for the police. All that mattered was their resentment at our 'interference'.

I sat there amazed; I just could not believe what was coming out of his mouth. If I had not been part of it all along, having had leisurely and apparently friendly meetings with these people, I might not have felt so astounded by the fact that he said things that he surely could not believe.

Everyone saw how angry I was. I thought we all knew, that everyone involved knew the truth about the first investigation. I was sitting on the bench across from Carnt. I looked straight at him and he did not even react. There was something chilling about it, as though he'd been brainwashed or had all along been acting a part with us.

I now began to think that the second investigation, rather than coming up with information that would help us, might almost have been a hindrance. We had only been shown what the police wanted us to see. We could not have had full access to the material, even though they said that we did.

That John Carnt spoke in such a bland evasive way was the last straw for me. Nothing was going to come out of that inquest, had it not been for that question to Carnt and his answer. I was from that moment determined that something more and something radical must be done. Had he behaved differently, I'd probably have let it go and walked away: we had tried a private prosecution and got nowhere, and at times I felt that my strength was exhausted. Those boys had been shown to be evil, but there was still no justice. There was only so much that I could do. Perhaps I should just become a private person again, and stop being obsessed with the search for the truth. Now I felt that if Carnt could invert reality with a straight face, what else was being covered up?

Ian Johnston, the Deputy Assistant Commissioner at the time, came down on the last day of the inquest. I'm a lot calmer than I used to be – in those days I was so mad I did not care who I was speaking to or how I said it. I was not rude, and I never swore at anyone; I just told it as I saw it, whoever they were – titles did not impress me. Johnston was trying to apologise, but I cannot tell you what he said because I was not listening. His very presence offended me. I presume he was trying to tell me that it was not what Carnt *really* meant. At that point I did not need to hear any more.

Unfortunately for the police, the political climate was changing. It was obvious that eighteen years of Conservative government, with its unthinking backing of the police no matter what they did, was coming to an end.

At least the jurors' unanimous verdict rang out clearly, an indication of what might have happened if we had been allowed to put our case to a jury in 1996: 'Stephen Lawrence was unlawfully killed in a completely unprovoked racist attack by five white youths.' It was significant that rather than just concluding that it was an 'unlawful killing' they added those extra words; they had seen – and it was plain for everyone to see – how appallingly those five young men behaved. It was unusual at the time for inquest juries to give a 'narrative' verdict, to say who had done the unlawful killing. No one could be under any illusion as to what kind of boys these really were.

A measure of my anger at John Carnt's refusal to face the truth about the police investigation was my statement after the inquest about the failure to give my son any medical help where he lay dying. They just stood there, I said, while my son bled to death. I asked the question, was it because they did not want to get their hands dirty with a black man's blood? That is how I felt: the police had not treated him like a fully human being. My statement ended: 'Before yesterday I was beginning to think there might be the odd few police officers who believed in justice for all. Whatever trust that I was beginning to build up again towards the police shattered yesterday. I suppose once a policeman always a policeman who protects their own, and not the black community.'

On Friday, 14 February 1997, the day after the inquest ended, the *Daily Mail* wrote the now famous front-page report with a headline in two-inch high letters: MURDERERS. Over photographs of Gary Dobson, Neil Acourt, Jamie Acourt, Luke Knight and David Norris, it said, 'The *Mail* accuses these men of killing. If we are wrong, let them sue us.' It went on:

> The *Daily Mail* today takes the unprecedented step of naming five young men as murderers. They may not have been convicted in a court of law, but police are sure that David Norris, Neil Acourt, Jamie Acourt, Gary Dobson and Luke Knight are the white youths who killed black teenager Stephen Lawrence. We are naming them because, despite a criminal case, a private prosecution and an inquest, there has still been no justice for Stephen, who was stabbed to death in a racist attack four years ago.
>
> One or more of the five may have a valid defence to the charge which has been repeatedly levelled against them. So far they have steadfastly refused every opportunity to offer such a defence. Four have refused to give any alibi for that night in

April 1993. One initially offered an alibi, but it did not stand up when police checked it out. This week the five refused to answer any questions at the inquest on Stephen, citing their legal right of privilege not to say anything which might incriminate them . . .

If these men are innocent they now have every opportunity to clear their names in legal action against the *Daily Mail*. They would have to give evidence and a jury in possession of all the facts would finally be able to decide.

The paper was careful not to accuse the police of any misconduct in the case, but the naming of five unconvicted men was unheard of, especially from a newspaper with a long history of hostility to immigrants. But anyone who had been in that courtroom and seen how arrogant those boys were would have agreed with what the paper was saying; and if they did sue, they would have to go to court. They would have to answer questions, which they clearly hated worse than poison. I felt some small satisfaction when I saw the headline, knowing that unless they sued they would be tainted for the rest of their lives as killers. None of the five has ever sued the *Mail* for libel. Their silence is more eloquent than any denial.

15   A New Regime

The smokescreen thrown up by John Carnt at the inquest set in motion a new train of events. I was now more committed than I had ever been to making the police accountable for all that they had failed to do, and I was willing to use every lever I could find to topple the whole house of cards they had built to protect themselves. Just as we had felt ourselves drowning in the waves of corruption that seemed to centre on Stephen's murder, now the police service was feeling itself undermined by the ripples that the scandal sent out. We thought we were dealing with the brutal killing of our son, which was bad enough, and found ourselves facing a network of criminal families, investigative incompetence and general corruption throughout the police in south-east London, as well as pervasive racism. The Met now had to deal with accusations that threatened their closed world and their whole method of policing, especially of black people.

Imran Khan wrote a formal letter on our behalf to the Police Complaints Authority (PCA) about our dissatisfaction with the way the investigation had been conducted. Ian Johnston had come to see me after the inquest, trying in vain to allay our fears about the police commitment to the continuing search for evidence with which to convict the remaining two suspects, David Norris and Jamie Acourt, who had not been tried at the Old Bailey. I felt that Mr Johnston and his senior colleagues realised that a terrible mistake had been made in trying to whitewash the affair at the inquest, and that they felt the wind of change on their necks. Now they were trying to contain the damage.

They decided to bring in a police team from outside London to go through the evidence that the Metropolitan Police had collected, and the Kent constabulary was chosen for the task.

In September 1997 I was invited down to the Kent headquarters, a rather grand house surrounded by empty fields, where Chief Superintendent Ayling and his men did a presentation of their findings. There I heard for the first time that within twenty-four hours of Stephen's murder, the police had information that could have led to the arrest of the boys we believe killed Stephen, yet they did not act upon it. I had heard about James Grant before, but not realised that he walked into a police station the day after the murder and told them which house the killers were in and who they were. And it was now I learned that he had been treated aggressively and given the run-around by policemen who were either disbelieving or had no wish to find the truth. In the previous investigation in 1995, as I've said, we were supposedly told everything that was in the files about the case, yet at no time were we ever told, or was our legal team made aware, of that evidence being given to the police so early. It was like peeling an onion: every time we returned to the case new layers of ridiculous malpractice came to light.

The Kent Report, eventually presented in December 1997, found 'significant weaknesses, omissions, and lost opportunities in the conduct of the case'. They mentioned eleven lines of inquiry that should remain open in the search for Stephen's killers. This was a world away from the Barker review. The police were at last admitting that the conduct of the murder inquiry had been woeful, and that we were not the problem – the uppity family and its lawyer had not hindered the investigation in any way.

Now I felt that my persistence was paying off, and I could take some comfort from not stepping back into the shadows where I often longed to be. I knew that many other murders of black people had gone away and never returned to haunt the police. They had refused to call Rolan Adams's death what it was, a racist murder, insisting that it was a 'territorial dispute' – a gang fight. I remembered how they had been tempted to slot Stephen's death into the same category on the night of the murder, neglecting literally to go down the right road because they had assumed my son had been involved in a fight. We had already come a long way.

Not long after the inquest took place we first met Jack Straw, who at the time was shadow Home Secretary. In April 1997, the month before the general election, we met him in his parliamentary office, together with the black MPs Diane Abbott and the late Bernie Grant, and some members of the Stephen Lawrence Family Campaign. Diane Abbott helped to organise the meeting. We talked about what had happened at the inquest. Now people were beginning to see that it was not just some loony blacks complaining that things were not as they should be: there was racism in the justice system. The *Daily Mail*'s front page had helped to open the story up. In fact the press had always been interested, but that report was said to have 'touched Middle England', the feelings of white people who don't normally care much what happens to black youths in inner cities.

I told Jack Straw how I felt about the whole case and the investigation – that I suspected there was conspiracy involved, that there was corruption as well as racism – and about how we had been treated. He listened sympathetically and gave us the assurance that if a Labour government came to power they would look more closely at the case. He did not promise us a public inquiry, but that was what we always wanted – I wanted to know everything that happened on the night Stephen was murdered, and in the weeks and months that followed. All he would say was that if they won the election they would certainly consider holding such an inquiry.

The general election was in May 1997. The Conservatives went down to defeat in a landslide, taking Michael Howard, who had never shown a single ounce of interest or sympathy in our fight for justice, and had always refused even to meet us, along with them. Once the Labour government came to power we had another meeting with Jack Straw, who was now Home Secretary. I heard from people in the party that certain ministers and advisers in the new government were beginning to get a bit nervous about having a public inquiry focusing on Stephen's death.

On 24 June 1997 we met with Jack Straw at the Home Office, this time around a large boardroom table in a huge office attended by squads of aides in well-cut suits. The furniture was massive, the curtains were thick and expensive and everything gleamed. You could not help feeling privileged to be in such grand surroundings, but of course that is what you have to resist. I don't know how many civil servants were there: a minister never meets you on his own, he always has other people with him, junior ministers or advisers, and everything is recorded in writing. I was there with Mike Mansfield, Imran Khan, and a few of the campaign supporters. Neville was in London at the time, and came along to this meeting

There was talk about setting up something similar to the Scarman Report, like a community inquiry of the kind that Lord Scarman conducted after the Brixton riots in 1982; the politicians would have felt comfortable with that, something that would look at general police relations with the black community in south-east London. I could see where this was heading – a benign report talking in generalities about improving race relations, and so on. The argument went round and round the table. I said plainly, 'That's not what I want, that will never give me what I want.' Still the civil servants and politicians argued that they thought it was the best way forward. I said, 'Well, we've had Scarman, and it just sits on the shelf, it does nothing. What really changed after the Scarman Report?'

I was furious, to be honest. I felt that I was being flannelled, even if the atmosphere was so much more positive than it had been under the Tories. At the end of the meeting as we walked down the vast corridor towards the lift, Jack Straw was walking beside me and I said to him again: 'That won't give me the answer I want. What I need to find out is how Stephen was killed and what happened afterwards – what the police did or didn't do, why they didn't catch the killers. What you are planning to do won't give me that information.'

I believe it was that exchange as we walked along the corridor that changed his mind and persuaded him not to go down the line of least resistance. After the meeting, he issued a news release:

I am glad to have been able to meet Mr and Mrs Lawrence today and have been deeply moved listening to the tragic circumstances surrounding the death of their son Stephen.

Whilst in opposition I met Mrs Lawrence and was impressed by her determination and courage in such difficult circumstances. This meeting was my first opportunity to meet Mr and Mrs Lawrence in my capacity as Home Secretary and another chance for me to discuss with them the distressing details of their son's case. We have also had the chance to discuss broader issues, including racially motivated crime and the relationship between the police and ethnic minority communities.

It is not an option to let this matter rest.

I recognise that a strong case has been made by Mrs Lawrence for some form of an inquiry and I am actively considering what she put to me.

I will also carefully consider the other issues that were raised during our meeting and reflect on the best way to address the widespread concern resulting from this case.

I hope to make an announcement soon.

That was just before the summer holiday. It did not take long for them to announce that they were to go ahead with a judicial inquiry. Diane Abbott later confirmed that Straw went into the meeting prejudiced against an inquiry, and came out convinced by our case. Scheduled to begin after the completion of the Kent Report, the inquiry's terms of reference were: 'To inquire into the matters arising from the death of Stephen Lawrence on 22 April 1993 to date, in order particularly to identify the lessons to be learned for the investigation and prosecution of racially motivated crimes.' To head the inquiry they appointed a former High Court judge called Sir William Macpherson of Cluny.

Looking back now, I am sure that if the government had realised all that would come out of the inquiry, they would not have let it take place.

16   The Public Inquiry

Nothing could happen until after the Kent Report was released at the end of 1997, and thoroughly examined. Then there was a preliminary hearing of the public inquiry in Greenwich Public Hall in October 1997, at which the chairman was to outline the procedures that he would follow. I did not attend. I was not pleased that they had appointed Sir William Macpherson because of what I heard about his background, and to attend would have been to endorse the proceedings with my approval. Sir William's record as a judge revealed that he had been very severe on asylum seekers and immigrants. I felt that he was an old-school Conservative who would have made up his mind before he entered the inquiry room. I had the experience of Justice Curtis fresh in my mind, of course, and by this stage I was not ready to give any Establishment figure the benefit of the doubt.

The inquiry proper was due formally to open on Monday, 16 March 1998. The previous day there were reports in the *Observer* suggesting that Macpherson was insensitive on issues of race and there was a lot of indignation in the black press, and I still had my own doubts. Michael Mansfield asked for a week's adjournment in order for us to have an urgent meeting with the Home Secretary.

The next day we had a ninety-minute meeting with Jack Straw at the Home Office. I expressed my unease about Macpherson and my doubts that he would be impartial. If he had a biased view on refugees, how on earth was he going to be open when it came to our case? I did not see him as the right person to head an inquiry that had racism at its heart. Jack Straw did not know what to do, and saw a public relations disaster in the making. He pleaded with us, saying that Macpherson was the only judge available with the time to undertake the inquiry, since he was retired and all the other senior judges had heavy caseloads. In addition, he would be working with advisers, so would not make any decision entirely on his own. Eventually I was persuaded that Macpherson would do a good job and that he was a fair man.

Raising our objections also sent a clear message to Macpherson that we would not tolerate another whitewash. It was important to protest before he started work. I felt I only had one chance and I wanted an investigation centred on Stephen and the mechanisms that had allowed his killers to stay free. I needed to have those questions answered.

I think it's fair to say that this case changed Macpherson himself. He listened and opened his mind and I think he himself was shocked at the level of racism that we had encountered, not just among constables, but also much higher-ranking officers. I can imagine that he did not credit at first what we were saying about how racist the police had been in their treatment of our family, and how they had failed to do their job. Once he heard the evidence, his opinions changed.

When the inquiry resumed, on Tuesday, 24 March, in an office building called Hannibal House above a shopping centre off Elephant and Castle, I started attending each day's hearing. From then on, I missed very few days. It was a grim location, though the atmosphere in the inquiry room was efficient and relaxed and we were made to feel very welcome. I never used the front entrance, which was in the Walworth Road, but went in from the Old Kent Road side. I would park underneath the building and walk up the stairs.

Inside the main room on one side was the gallery where members of the public could sit. At the front were the representatives of the inquiry's legal team – including Edmund Lawson, QC, and Anesta Weekes – as well as our counsel Michael Mansfield and the rest of our legal team, the barristers Stephen Kamlish, Margo Boye-Anawoma and Martin Soorjoo, and of course our solicitors Imran Khan and Caron Thatcher. There must have been a dozen people on those front tables. In the row behind were the lawyers for the Metropolitan Police, the Crown Prosecution Service and the Police Federation. In the third row were Duwayne Brooks's legal team led by Ian Macdonald, QC, and his solicitor Jane Deighton; and the Commission for Racial Equality's barrister Jeffrey Yearwood. Other legal representatives were in the last row. Altogether there were twenty-one barristers, including six QCs. They were dressed, I was relieved to see, in normal suits. There were computer terminals in front of each lawyer, and machines for scanning documents and projecting them onto overhead screens.

Behind them all were the ranks of reporters. Neville and I sat in front alongside Michael Mansfield and Imran Khan. The stenographer sat near the front on one side and the witness box was on the other side, to my right.

Facing the front, sitting on a raised platform alongside Sir William Macpherson, was the panel of advisers who would assist him: Tom Cook (former Deputy Chief Constable of West Yorkshire), Dr Richard Stone, the GP and race relations activist, and the Ugandan-born Right Rev. Dr John Sentamu, Bishop of Stepney, who always sat next to Macpherson.

My lasting impression of Macpherson is of a very thin, fit-looking and elderly white man, with grey hair and a pointed nose supporting half glasses. He looked rather elegant and intellectual. He wore civilian clothes rather than judge's robes, and always tended to have something about him that hinted at his Scottish background, usually a tartan tie. He did show us great respect, for which I respected him in return, and he always addressed us in a very formal way. On the first day, he began by making some opening remarks about how the inquiry would be conducted.

'The procedure of the hearings will be reasonably informal: nobody need stand to ask questions unless they wish to do so,' he said. 'Our hope is that, at the end of the day, we will establish what happened and what may have gone wrong over these last years in connection with the investigation and management of this case. To Mr and Mrs Lawrence, these years must have been dreadful. We hope sincerely that while nothing can alleviate the pain and loss which they have suffered, they may accept that all of us have done our best to establish what was done so that the future may not see repetition of any errors that may be uncovered during our hearings.'

Then Bishop Sentamu spoke: 'In Uganda we have a proverb for every conceivable situation, and the one which adequately suits this inquiry says that, "When two elephants fight, the grass gets hurt." Words, arguments and counter-arguments are going to be vigorously offered throughout this inquiry. Let us not forget in that combat the really hurting ones: Neville and Doreen Lawrence and Stephen's brother and sister, Stuart and Georgina. For five years they have laboured hard to see truth and justice prevail since Stephen was brutally murdered on 22 April 1993.'

Bishop Sentamu concluded: 'Throughout this Inquiry the name of Stephen Lawrence will be used again and again and again. May I ask you to stand in silence to honour his memory to remember him now and always.' He said a prayer and everyone stood for a minute's silence in remembrance of Stephen.

I appreciated that Macpherson allowed the inquiry to be conducted with such dignity and seriousness.

Then Mr Edmund Lawson, Queen's Counsel for the inquiry, made his introductory remarks. He began by reminding everyone of the sort of person Stephen was, quoting a description of Stephen by Barry Ferguson, who had known him at the Cambridge Harriers Athletic Club:

During the period I knew Stephen, I found him to be polite and respectful. He was a dedicated athlete, always reliable. By far the best athlete in my group and although he was very aware of this fact he was never big-headed about it, on the contrary, he appeared embarrassed about his talent. I never saw him display any form of aggression and would describe his temperament as the same as his father, quiet and unassuming. He was of good character, exemplary character. He was a young man who had never come into contact with or to the notice of the police.

Lawson outlined the questions they would seek to have answered in connection with the investigation. He raised the matter of 'jury nobbling' and whether police knowledge of the Norris family should have required further steps to protect witnesses. Given that information about the identity of Stephen's murderers was received within twenty-four hours, on 23 April, he asked, why did the police delay taking any action? I was very struck by his summary of the bizarre episode of the police surveillance in the first week: 'Some of the principal suspects were under surveillance from the 26 April: firstly, the Acourts and then a few days later Norris. Why, if surveillance was thought to be appropriate, was it not started much earlier?' Lawson asked. 'There was a particularly crass failure, as it seems to us provisionally, in these respects. A photographer was put in place to keep surveillance on the Acourts. Before he got his camera set up on the 26 April, he saw somebody leaving their house with what was, appeared to be, or might have been clothing in a bin bag, get into a car and clear off. He actually photographed Neil Acourt doing the same thing the following day. He made no report at the time of either of these events. It is fair to say that he had not been told to do so, and incredibly, even if he had been told to do so, he could not because no one had the brainwave of giving him a telephone, so he had no means of communication. So what was or might have been important evidence was lost, because no one knows where they went or what was in the bags.'

Michael Mansfield set out the position from our point of view:

> Nearly fifty years ago from now, namely in 1948, in the southern states of America there was a black Baptist minister by the name of Dr Vernon Johns and his parish was a Baptist church in Dexter Avenue, Alabama. Following a series of murders of young black men in that town in 1948 and just before by gangs of white men, those murders having gone unchecked, with no sanction, in the face of enormous public disapproval and the risk of violent retribution to him he entitled his last sermon, 'It is safe to murder negroes.' He was detained by the police and forced to leave. He did. His successor was Dr Martin Luther King and hence the birth of the Civil Rights movement in the United States of America.
>
> Dr Johns's point then and our point on behalf of the Lawrences now is this: Stephen's teenage killers and their close friends and relatives all felt safe in what they did and in the knowledge of what they did. We suggest that the Inquiry needs to examine closely how a climate has been created in which such obvious and overt racism can breed and wreak such appalling habit with impunity.
>
> In part there are three answers to this: the first is that it lies with those in our community who continue to applaud and support these attitudes and activities. It also lies with those who remain silent or indifferent and who are not prepared to confront such attitudes at source . . . Thirdly, and perhaps most pertinently for this Inquiry, the climate is created by law enforcement agencies which fail to take speedy and effective and committed action to pursue such illegality.
>
> The magnitude of the failure in this case, we say, cannot be

explained by mere incompetence or a lack of direction by senior officers or a lack of execution and application by junior officers, nor by woeful under-resourcing. So much was missed by so many that deeper causes and forces must be considered. We suggest these forces relate to two main propositions. The first is, dealing with the facts themselves, that the victim was black and there was as a result a racism, both conscious and unconscious, that permeated the investigation; secondly, the fact that the perpetrators were white and were expecting some form of protection . . .

The inordinate and extensive delays and inactions, some of which to use the phrase already applied were 'crass', give rise to one plain inference and one plain question which we suggest has to be boldly addressed: was the initial investigation ever intended to result in a successful prosecution?

The process being undertaken by all of us must begin from a clear and unequivocal premise that this was a racist killing . . .The forces that applaud and support and continue to support racism go unabated up to the doors of this inquiry . . .

Among those questioned in the following days were the family liaison officers, John Bevan and Linda Holden. DS Bevan admitted that the search of David Norris's family house had been 'cursory' yet he could not give a convincing explanation as to why that had been. No one could believe what he said next, a mixture of envy and silliness:

BEVAN: It is hard to actually describe why, but the property was a mansion, in short, a very, very expensive property, very expensively decorated, and carpets, for example, were top-quality fitted. I felt and I obviously made a decision at the time that the extent of my search was an adequate one, whether it be for the fact that David used that address on a temporary basis, which might have been indicated due to the fact he wasn't there.

LAWSON: Mr Bevan, forgive me. That might be taken to suggest that if you have a posh house you are not going to be the victim of a proper search whereas if you live in a grubby council flat you will have it torn apart.

Michael Mansfield and Stephen Kamlish challenged all the police witnesses closely about everything that happened, from the night of the murder onwards. Kamlish tackled Bevan about they way he portrayed me in his statements to the Kent investigation, in which he commented that I never smiled.

KAMLISH: You described her in your interview as aggressive, this grieving mother, from day one, did you not?
BEVAN: Mrs Lawrence did adopt an aggressive stance.
KAMLISH: Was it aggressive for somebody whose son had just been killed a day or two earlier in a racist attack, for her not to smile at you and not to talk much to you? Is that aggression? . . . Do you want to take that word back now, with hindsight – that she was aggressive, a day or two after her son had died?

When Stephen Kamlish cross-examined DC Linda Holden a few days later, on 5 May, she tried to insist that she had behaved faultlessly as a family liaison officer, despite everything that was revealed about the insensitive treatment we had in fact received.

KAMLISH: You were patronising. Maybe you didn't intend to be, but you were.
HOLDEN: I am sorry if they took the view that we were patronising, but there was no other way of sometimes speaking to them . . .

DCS William Ilsley was one of a number of senior policemen questioned who claimed not to know at first or not to suspect that David Norris had any connection to Clifford Norris. None of them thought it was worth looking for the father to remove the fear he inspired in witnesses. The first officer in charge of the investigation, DS Ian Crampton, claimed to have made absolutely no connection between David Norris and Clifford Norris – this despite the fact that he was at the time involved in another major case, that of the murder of an informer also called David Norris, who was thought then to be a cousin of Clifford's. I found Crampton incredible. The man who took over from him, DS Brian Weeden, said that he had never heard of Clifford Norris or his family either, at least not until he took over from Crampton on 26 April 1993. Here was a senior policeman in south-east London, who had been in the force for about thirty years, claiming ignorance of one of the most important organised-crime figures in his area. Macpherson later concluded that he was an honest man, but that struck me as a subjective judgement. But Macpherson did not believe Weeden when he said that 'additional matters' had made it a good idea to arrest the suspects on 6 May; in fact, nothing had changed between 26 April and 5 May. They could have been arrested a week earlier. They were arrested because we raised the profile of the case by meeting Mandela.

One after another the police officers were grilled, their evidence being examined minutely and criticised when it did not add up. The reaction of the commissioner Sir Paul Condon was to issue a statement, as the last witnesses were being called, more or less attacking our legal team and complaining about the 'confrontational nature of cross-examination'. He even suggested by implication that Imran Khan was hindering the search for the killers, and claimed to be concerned that the questioning was damaging relations between the police and the black community. What he really objected to was that his officers were being humiliated and made to look stupid. The nightmare of the Metropolitan Police leadership was a failure to 'manage' knowledge of how it worked, and now it was being exposed. This was not some cosy internal review by other police officers, but was taking place in the cold light of day.

I noticed that whenever one of the black barristers was speaking – there was a black lawyer representing the CRE, and on Duwayne's side there was an Asian man – some of the police officers were rude and did not answer properly, as if to say: 'How dare you question me?'

The police lawyers attempted to put pressure on me in particular. I was questioned in the witness box by the Commissioner's QC, Jeremy Gompertz, in June, three months after the inquiry began:

GOMPERTZ: Mrs Lawrence, I want to ask you some questions on behalf of the Commissioner. In doing so can I make it absolutely clear that my purpose is not to criticise you and your husband. Secondly, can I make it clear that I am mindful of the Chairman's ruling that was made a long time ago that counsel who wish to ask you and your husband questions should confine themselves to matters of fact and not opinion?

Can I ask you please to look at your note? Those are the names, are they not, that you wrote on the piece of paper and took with you when you went to see Mr Ilsley?
MRS LAWRENCE: Yes.
GOMPERTZ: You see, the reason I ask you is that if all the names were written on this piece of paper, they did not include the names Norris or Knight, did they?
MRS LAWRENCE: No, people were confused about the names when they came to us.
GOMPERTZ: Can I ask you about something quite different now: your journey home from the hospital on the night in question. You went, did you not, to the Welcome Inn?
MRS LAWRENCE: No.
GOMPERTZ: Where did you go then?

MRS LAWRENCE: Can I ask a question here? Am I on trial
here or something here? I mean, from the time of my son's
murder I have been treated not as a victim. Now I can only
tell you or put into my statements what I know of what
went on that night. And for me to be questioned in this way,
I do not appreciate it.

He obviously meant to suggest that we did not have a clear view
of the road, and to work up to a suggestion that the police were
in fact working away, invisible to us, that night. They may have
been, but I already knew that they had not bothered to send a
search party down Dickson Road, where Duwayne Brooks had
seen the killers running. Gompertz must have known that he
was on very shaky ground, but he tried anyway. Macpherson
put a stop to this line of questioning, much to my relief, because
I was so angry I could hardly speak.

The public interest generated by the inquiry was underestimated. It was turning into a wake-up call for the justice system.
People would take time off from work to come: there were law
students from the nearby South Bank University, ordinary people of all kinds were turning up. Nothing like it had ever taken
place before, a black family questioning the Establishment and
the Establishment in the shape of Sir William questioning itself.
The police had always gone about their business and done what
they liked, a law unto themselves, even though they are as falli-
ble as any other human beings. We in the black community
knew this very well, but the white world was often in denial: the
police were fair and they were law-abiding. Now the wider society could actually see how the police behaved in detail in a single case, and it was a shock.

Towards the end of May, Michael Mansfield cross-examined
Brian Weeden. Weeden admitted that there had been errors and
omissions over the fourteen-month period when he was in
charge. He accepted without reservation that there were reason-

able grounds for making arrests at a much earlier stage. The most astonishing thing Weeden said was that in 1993 he believed that he did not have the power of arrest until he had absolutely firm evidence, as opposed to reasonable grounds for suspicion – and he had been a serving officer for nearly thirty years. By his own admission he did not know what Mike Mansfield called 'a basic tenet of criminal law'.

I would still like to know what it was about these suspects that gave the police such difficulty, though the answers that some other officers gave provided some clues. Sergeant Davidson, for example, who had not registered the witness 'James Grant' as an informant, refused to recognise the murder as a racist attack. Never mind that one of them had called out 'What, what nigger?' before they closed in on Stephen. Linda Holden denied in her testimony that racism had played any part in Stephen's death. She couldn't say, had no idea what the motivation of the killers was. It looked like a racist attack, sounded like one and it certainly must have felt like it to my son. But this policewoman couldn't see it. Nor could Sergeant Bevan. He also marched out his old dislike of Imran Khan: he still couldn't see why we needed a solicitor, and Imran was 'one more barrier to communication.' Their general attitude made me see why they had been so slow in chasing down those boys. If the attack had nothing to do with race, why go looking for notorious racists in the area?

It was not until I heard Inspector Steven Groves at the inquiry that it really fell into place for me how fixed their attitude had been, right from the very first minutes and hours of the investigation. It had taken me five years to discover this. He had been the most senior officer at the scene in the hour or so after the murder, and he said that he thought there had been a fight, not a racist attack, and he chose to ignore Duwayne's statement that the boys had run off down Dickson Road. Instead, unbelievably, he went off to the nearest pub, the Welcome Inn, trying to see if anybody there had seen a quarrel between black and white youths. He clearly thought that these two young black men were at least partly responsible for what had happened to them.

I won't attempt to describe all the evidence that was aired and the exchanges that took place at the inquiry. One of the most astonishing to me was the discovery that the police officer looking after Duwayne Brooks during the private prosecution – the man who guarded him at night and took him to the court during the day – was a notorious sergeant who used to be in the Flying Squad and who had been filmed years previously by Customs and Excise officers taking thick packages from Clifford Norris in a pub. At the time Norris had been under surveillance in a major drug operation. Immediately after he was observed with this policeman, he fled the country and was not arrested for another six years. And this sergeant had had a reference written for him by DS Crampton, the man who was in charge that first weekend and who made the decision not to arrest David Norris and his friends. If all this was in a crime novel everyone would say it was unbelievable.

It was the Assistant Commissioner, Ian Johnston, who first apologised to us at the inquiry, on behalf of the Commissioner Sir Paul Condon. He was about to give evidence in the witness box, on the forty-fifth day of the inquiry, when he said he would like to make a statement. I was not there that day so he addressed this unprecedented apology to Neville. He asked permission to stand up, I was told, and it was apparently very theatrical:

Mr Lawrence, I wanted to say to you that I am truly sorry that we have let you down. It has been a tragedy for you; you have lost a son, and not seen his killers brought to justice. It has been a tragedy for the Metropolitan Police, who have lost the confidence of a significant section of the community for the way we have handled the case.

I can understand and explain some of what went wrong. I cannot and do not seek to justify it. We are determined to learn lessons from this. A great deal has changed and yet will change. We have tried, over the last four years since the first investigation, to show imagination and determination to prosecute Stephen's killers.

I am very, very sorry and very, very sad that we have let you down. Looking back now, I can see clearly that we could have and we should have done better. I deeply regret that we have not put his killers away.

On behalf of myself, the Commissioner – who specifically asked me to associate himself with these words – and the whole of the Metropolitan Police, I again offer my sincere and deep apologies to you. I do hope that one day you will be able to forgive us.

Finally, I would like to add my own personal apologies for supporting the earlier investigation in ways in which it has now been shown that I was wrong. I hope the reasons for my support will be understood, and I hope that, eventually, you will forgive me for that, as well, Mr Lawrence.

While we accepted Condon's apology at the time, it would have meant more had he apologised four years earlier. It would also have been better if he had come to the inquiry in person to deliver the apology himself. But none of it altered the fact that Stephen's murderers were still enjoying their liberty. We issued a statement that day:

It has taken five years of trauma, heartache and suffering for our family to reach this stage of our struggle. The Commissioner now accepts that the first investigation was flawed and incompetent. What will happen to those officers? Will they be disciplined? Will those now retired lose their pensions? Maybe we need another public inquiry into police corruption for the Commissioner to then accept that these boys were protected in some way. If it hadn't been for this inquiry the Commissioner would still be saying that officers did everything they could to bring our son's killers to justice. Whilst we accept the Commissioner's apology, we do not forget that Stephen's killers are still free.

On 20 July the five suspects took the stand. They had to appear, otherwise they would have been held in contempt. When they entered the building in the morning, two of them wearing sunglasses and looking as usual as though they were out for a night on the town, there were shouts from the crowds outside of 'Scum!' and 'Murderers!' Their arrogance did not falter. David Norris was the worst – his whole attitude expressed bullying defiance and aggression. His mother was there, radiating hostility to the fact that her son was being questioned at all. He kept looking over at her as if he wanted her to signal approval of his answers.

Hundreds of people wanted to get into the public gallery that day but of course there was not room enough for everyone. The Nation of Islam wanted to sit in on the inquiry; the police would not let them go up there, and a scuffle broke out as the police were trying to prevent them entering. The police over-reacted and blamed it on the Nation. CS gas was used on demonstrators and a riot nearly began. The hearing was adjourned for three hours and we had to appeal to the people, using a microphone. I said: 'For the safety of everybody, please could you keep calm . . . The police have this thing that if there's a group of black people there has to be a problem. I'm begging you, don't show that's true.'

I do not believe that the Nation of Islam intended to cause any problem that day. To the white community they may look intimidating but in fact all they do is stand there quietly in their smart dark suits and white shirts; they are clean-shaven and disciplined. If many black youths were to follow their example – not necessarily to join the Nation of Islam, but to learn from their dignified way of presenting themselves – they would not get themselves into half the trouble they do.

The five suspects were completely uncooperative during their questioning. The terms of reference meant that they could not be subjected to a retrial for murder; Macpherson had said at the outset, 'This inquiry is not about finding the killers of Stephen Lawrence; it is about how the subsequent investigation and prosecution was conducted.' But they had to answer questions. They couldn't stonewall here and claim privilege, as they had done at the inquest. Still, they were as nasty as ever – 'arrogant and dismissive, evasive and vague', in Macpherson's words later. None of them could remember anything, until they had to. They had to admit that knives had been found in the houses they lived in, including a long knife that Gary Dobson's girlfriend was keeping for him in her bedroom, and a hammer head on a strap that was one of David Norris's toys. The Acourts had to agree that a sword had been found in their house. It was very frustrating and everyone there was disgusted with the way they dodged even the most straightforward questions and were obviously lying.

When the boys left together at the end of that day, swaggering out to a chorus of boos, there were angry reactions from the waiting crowd. Neil Acourt grinned in his horrible way and made a come-on gesture with his hands, as though he was inviting anyone there to take him on. It was chaos. They were pelted with plastic water bottles and eggs, and they responded aggressively. That was when a picture of David Norris throwing a punch was taken, his face distorted with hatred, the mask of bored insolence stripped away. Their defiant strut crumbled and they began to run in single file, desperate to escape into a waiting van.

A week or so after their public display of their own sickness, their local football club, Charlton Athletic, banned them from attending games. I wish that other institutions in the community

– pubs, restaurants, employers – had also made them feel like outcasts. It would be fitting.

There were also very different witnesses at the inquiry. Mr and Mrs Taaffe, the couple who had been coming out of that handsome Catholic church on Well Hall Road on the night of the murder and gone to see if they could help Stephen, told what they had seen. At first, Mr Taaffe admitted, he thought Duwayne was a mugger when he saw this agitated young black man approaching him. He described how he had later gone over to where Stephen was lying and tried to stem the flow of blood from my son's body, and how he still had the blood on him when he reached home. He had washed his hands and poured the blood and water over a rose tree in his garden.

Most days while the hearings were in London I was there, but between 8 October and 13 November there were public hearings in Southall, Manchester, Tower Hamlets, Bradford, Bristol and Birmingham. As the proceedings moved around the country, I was unable to attend them. Neville could attend all the time, since he was not working; but as the only one supporting our children I had to go out to work and I had difficulty getting time off.

I had begun a part-time job at the university in March 1996, working two and a half days a week. On the days I was not working I could go down to the inquiry and listen and make notes. During holiday time I worked a full week to make up for any days that I had missed. I did that throughout the inquiry, which lasted almost to the end of 1998. I think it was Bishop Sentamu who talked to me about being available when the report came out. Someone must have had a word with the vice-chancellor of the university and wondered why the university was not showing me more support. The stress of the inquiry had been so severe that towards the end I caught a cold and became ill. I felt totally drained and by January 1999 I felt so tired that I did not go to work for a month. I was allowed to take leave so that I could, after all, be around when the inquiry report was published.

In his closing statement to the inquiry, Sir William Macpherson said: 'It seems to me right that we should end as we started, with a minute's silence to remember Stephen Lawrence and to couple with that our congratulations, if that is the right word, on the courage of his parents.'

17   A Landmark?

The day before the Macpherson Report was due to be published in February 1999, we were invited to go and stay in a hotel not far from the Home Office. Some people around me felt we were being isolated from our legal team, from anyone who might influence our response to the report. The only person who came with me was Ros Howells, who in 1993 had been awarded the Order of the British Empire for her work in race relations and community services (and in 1999 became Baroness Howells of St Davids, one of the new Labour life peers appointed by Tony Blair). Our solicitor Imran Khan was not at the hotel. The police had had a problem with Imran from the start because he was so sharp and asked such searching questions; they felt that he was feeding us questions or prompting us about what to say. However, Imran has always been very fair, and if I wrongly challenged something, he would say, 'No, that is the legal procedure and that is the way it's done.' He never hesitated to put me right. They were simply not used to dealing with a victim's family represented by a solicitor. So long as they had the family alone, they could always manipulate the family, and they mistakenly felt Imran to be a barrier. I thank God we appointed him after the murder. Otherwise we would have been told nothing, and we would never have learned the truth.

The evening before the Report was published Neville and I and Imran, but not the rest of our legal team, were at least given the opportunity to read it at the Home Office. When I arrived at the Home Office, there were throngs of photographers and reporters outside and I had to be taken in a back way. I read the main recommendations and skimmed some of the rest, but the report is 330 dense A4 pages, with another few hundred pages of appendices, and I could only take in so much. Imran was reading it quickly, going through the recommendations and, since the other people on the team could not be there, trying to make notes in order that he could report back to them. We left by the front door, and an adviser shoved me in the cab and slammed the door quickly as the cab took off; there was a frenzy of reporters wanting to know what I thought. It was a strenuous time; people's expectations were very high. As the Report was not to be published until the following day, it was still embargoed and we were not allowed to say anything about what we had read. There had already been leaks, we suspected from some Home Office official, and the hostile *Sunday Telegraph* had run a story about it.

From the Home Office we were taken to the hotel. The next morning Jack Straw came to meet us. He knocked on my door – I was sharing a suite with Ros – and then went downstairs to find Neville's room. We were to go to Downing Street and from there to the House of Commons, where the Report would be announced.

I had met Tony Blair before he became Prime Minister in 1997, at Southwark Cathedral when the Anne Frank Trust launched an exhibition that included a panel about Stephen's story. At Downing Street on the day the Report was published he told us how important he believed the inquiry was. For my part, I wanted to thank him, for without his government's willingness to risk a public inquiry we would never have known the full background to Stephen's murder. He was surrounded by aides, of course, and it was difficult to speak to him with so many people in the room and everyone speaking at once.

After Downing Street we were not due at the House of Commons for the announcement until three o'clock in the afternoon, so in that space of time we were given another opportunity to look at the Report – but not to take it away. It was not until just before we got to the House of Commons that our full legal team was allowed in to start reading the Report.

The atmosphere in the Commons was very tense and excited. We sat in the public gallery, knowing that hundreds of MPs and journalists were watching us. Jack Straw stood up. He seemed nervous and a little uncomfortable, but determined to go through with what his body language said was a statement he wished he did not have to deliver. He spoke loudly, with Tony Blair sitting beside him grim-faced, his mouth turned down, not reacting to anything that Straw said.

'Madame Speaker, I should like to make a statement about the report of the Inquiry into the death of Stephen Lawrence . . . There is no doubt that there were fundamental errors. The investigation was marred by professional incompetence, by institutional racism, and by a failure of leadership by senior officers.' Towards the end of this statement he said: 'I want this report to serve as a watershed in our attitudes to racism. I want it to act as a catalyst for fundamental and irreversible change across the whole of our society.'

There was a strong feeling that I should ask for Condon's resignation that very day, but at the time I did not see that it was up to me. I felt he should have the integrity within himself to stand down because of how he had supported the indefensible behaviour of his officers. However, he did not want to blot his copybook and affect his chances of a peerage, and to the House of Lords he duly went. (I remembered this when in 2004 David Blunkett asked for the resignation of the chief constable of Humberside police over the handling of the Soham murders). Looking back, I think I should have made the demand.

I know the police were nervous in case I did ask for Condon's resignation, but my agenda was not to look for scapegoats; it was to find out what happened in Stephen's case and make sure that nothing like it ever happened again, and to see that those boys went behind bars for my son's murder. Anything else that came out of it was a bonus.

When the Report came out, it was regarded as a defining moment in British race relations. We felt vindicated in our criticisms of the Metropolitan Police, who were found by the inquiry to suffer from 'institutional racism'. This was defined as: 'the collective failure of an organisation to provide an appropriate and professional service to people because of their colour, culture or ethnic origin'.

The Report made seventy recommendations aimed at improving police attitudes and encouraging recruitment from the black and Asian communities. There were proposals dealing with openness and accountability, with the definition of racist incidents and crimes, with the treatment of victims and witnesses, changes to the complaints procedure, with training in First Aid, racism awareness and cultural diversity, and the role of education in preventing racism. Among the suggested changes to the law was an amendment to strengthen the Race Relations Act and make it applicable to the police. This was a revolutionary change, given the immunity from scrutiny the police had enjoyed for so long. We were hopeful that real change was going to come about, even if we had only scratched the surface.

There were some truly substantial changes, in the end. The Race Relations Act was extended to cover the police service and all central government bodies – the immigration service, the prisons and so on. And that has made a difference. Back in 1993, I would never have dreamed that an ordinary black couple could challenge the police and the government and end up changing the way they conduct themselves.

As if to demonstrate that the underlying problem had not gone away with the publication of the report, there was a sudden panic after it came out. Somehow, the addresses of certain witnesses were published in one of the report's appendices, which was amazingly irresponsible. That version of the report had to be withdrawn and burned. A lot of money had to be spent moving and rehousing these witnesses.

I was still worried about my own security, and my children's. When we had moved years before, we had to pay for an alarm to be fitted at the new house; then, after the inquiry, protection officers came to check, and discovered that the alarm bell was not actually connected to anything, despite the fact that I had paid Mack Alarms a service charge for years. All that time I had believed I was safe.

The five suspects were still free, meanwhile, to appear on television. In contrast to their tight-lipped behaviour at the public hearings, they agreed to be interviewed by Martin Bashir, the man who had interviewed Princess Diana and allowed her to put her side of her marital story. Perhaps they thought that this was their chance to rehabilitate themselves under soft questioning – 'their side' of a history of gang violence and knifings. They made a mess of it, and in the process contradicted their earlier stories and each other. Norris now said he was with his girlfriend that night, within half a mile of the murder, not at home with his mother. They did not have their stories straight about when they heard of the killing: they always claimed to have heard the following day, and Jamie Acourt now said that it was the same night. Even in the spotlight of television they could not disguise their racism, Norris admitting that 'some people would call you [Bashir] a Paki'. We called for action to be taken in the light of their new admissions, but it was like crying into the wind.

After the Report only one of the officers had to face a disciplinary tribunal in connection with the conduct of the first investigation. Detective Chief Inspector Benjamin Bullock was the only senior officer still serving who had been involved in the original investigation, as deputy investigating officer. He had never even read the manual describing what his job involved. He did not know how to operate the police computer system for major crimes. He had not seen the first anonymous message naming the killers until a day after it came in, and his attitude was at best 'laissez-faire', as the inquiry put it. He was in charge of the unbelievable mess they made of the surveillance operation, which did not even start until four days after the murder and which allowed the suspects to walk out of the Acourt house with stained clothes without following them.

They never have any outsiders present at such tribunals. I don't know how we got them to agree to us being there, but Neville and I found ourselves in a room full of uniformed police officers in a foul mood. We wanted Imran to be with us, and they said no, he was our lawyer and we could only have a friend. I said, 'Well, Imran is our friend,' which was no lie. There was a long negotiation. We not only wanted someone there to support us but somebody with a legal training who could explain to us what was going on. They conceded, reluctantly. On the third day Imran could not be there and so we brought his colleague Caron Thatcher, whom we see in the same light, as both a friend and a solicitor. For having her there we were ticked off in front of everybody present.

Mr Bullock was unwell during the tribunal, and there was much solicitude shown to him for turning up while he was on sick leave. My sympathy was a bit more tempered. I could not help remembering what the inquiry had concluded about the police's initial response in the hours after Stephen's death, of which response Bullock was very much a part:

We were astonished at the lack of direction and organisation during the vital first hours after the murder. Almost total lack of proper documentation makes reconstruction of what happened during those hours difficult . . . properly co-ordinated action and planning which might have led to the discovery and arrest of suspects was conspicuous by its absence. No officers early on the scene took any proper steps at once to pursue the suspects. There were large numbers of police officers available, but inadequate measures were taken to use them actively and properly. This was due to failure of direction by senior officers, many of whom attended the scene, who seem simply to have accepted that everything was being done satisfactorily by somebody else.

To show how leads were not followed up, one officer, DC Budgen, described how he was there when James Grant came in to give the information within twenty-four hours about who had done it and where they lived. The officer ran upstairs to tell Bullock, and Bullock more or less told the officer to go away, they weren't interested, telling him to put it down on a form. He never saw Grant himself. Apparently Bullock disliked Budgen, but that was no excuse for sending away such a crucial witness. Why did he do so, really? The Macpherson Report insisted that there was no evidence that Bullock deliberately bungled the surveillance of the suspects. I would prefer to think that, as with so much surrounding my son's death, there is no evidence that we can put our hands on. The smell lingers. The police accused the community for a long of time of a wall of silence, but there was no wall of silence: people were falling over themselves to offer information. The only walls of silence were around officers' ears.

Bullock took early retirement and a slap on the wrist. Of all the senior officers, he was the only one who was left in the frame, as a sort of scapegoat, and in the words of John Stevens, Condon's successor as Commissioner, he was 'cleared of all charges of neglect of duty, and escaped any serious reprimand'. I have never known that happen to any officer, even one involved in the death in custody of a black person. They always seem either to be promoted or retired.

The Bullock affair was a waste of taxpayers' money; they already knew what they were going to do. The police have changed, but I wonder how fundamental that change is. They are better now at PR, and they know how to come across to the public in different contexts. At any function or public meeting they have the right person there to say the right things. I believe that the police forces need new people who have been brought up to have a completely different perspective on life. Racism is ingrained in the older ones. The BBC documentary film *The Secret Policeman*, which showed how new recruits at a police training depot talked about blacks and Asians, was a revelation of how deeply rooted racist attitudes are in the kind of young men who are presently attracted to the police. It reminded me of watching Norris and Acourt and their friends venting their hatred of people different from themselves. Such people soak up racism like a sponge, and if they become police officers we the public have to endure it, since they have the power.

I sometimes still think about John Carnt, who rose high at the Yard and after retirement became managing director of a security company. All the money the police and the government spent on the inquiry was down to him: if he had given a truer picture of the police investigation at the inquest, we might never have had an inquiry. It was our word against his. The inquiry proved that we were right in everything we said about what had gone wrong in the early stages of the first investigation, about the Barker review and the whole defensive wall thrown up by the police. None of this is any consolation: I can't take satisfaction in having the last word. My son is dead and his killers are still at liberty.

In the years since the inquiry my life has revolved around the Stephen Lawrence Trust, which we set up in 1998, and around the continuing failure of the justice system to deliver justice for Stephen. All the trails run cold in the end, and there is still no reparation.

The further police investigation, looking at those eleven lines of inquiry described by the Kent police, began as the public inquiry finished towards the end of 1998. It was given a different momentum when Deputy Assistant Commissioner John Grieve, who had been the head of the Anti-Terrorist Branch and had worked in Northern Ireland and had achieved some good results on unsolved cases, was put in charge in January 1999. Grieve is a man who took on board the judgement of the Macpherson Report that his organisation was institutionally racist, and who had come to see that a force with less than a thousand employees from ethnic minorities – 3 per cent of all officers – could not claim to reflect the reality of London life. He openly admitted that he had been an overt racist, like most of his colleagues, in the 1960s when he joined the Met. He set out to target hate crime and took on a panel of lay advisers, many of them black. He seemed personally sincere, and was very energetic. Three times more people were charged with hate crimes in the year after Macpherson reported than ever before.

There was still evidence that changing the culture of the police would take a lot more than goodwill and sound bites. In January 1997 Michael Menson, a gifted musician who became a schizophrenic, was attacked by a group of sadistic bullies in the early morning on a street in Edmonton. They poured fuel into his coat and set it alight. He was taken to hospital, very badly burned, where the police refused even to take a statement from him. The crime scene was not secured. He died after sixteen days in pain. The police wrote him off as a mad black man who had tried to kill himself, but his family, perhaps encouraged by ours, would not give up and found experts who insisted that Michael could not have done it. There was that now familiar formal apology to the family, issued in late 1998 just before the Macpherson Report. The Mensons eventually had the satisfaction, if that is the word, of seeing three of Michael's killers convicted.

I had some indication of how tough it would be to change attitudes when Neville and I appeared on a television debate chaired by Jonathan Dimbleby soon after the inquiry reported. There was a large studio audience, several panellists, and a very excited atmosphere. Everyone seemed very sympathetic to us, but after Dimbleby's presentation of the report Glen Smyth of the Police Federation said, 'The report had a lot more balance than we've heard today [sic] . . . overt racism did not play a part in the failed first investigation, corruption and collusion did not play a part, some of the officers in the first enquiry did particularly well; and of course individuals in the MPS are not racist.' This was like saying that the makers of the *Titanic* should have congratulated themselves because the ship got halfway across the ocean before sinking. When it comes to self-regard, the police glass is always half full, never half empty.

And a backlash against us and Macpherson soon started among the police and their political friends. Writing in 2000, Simon Heffer in the *Daily Mail* called the Lawrence report 'stupid and meaningless', especially its charge of institutional racism. I felt that as the election approached in 2001 the Labour and Conservative parties were trying to outdo each other when it came to being harder on law and order, immigration and asylum, and the Macpherson Report was becoming the symbol of 'political correctness', opposition to which has become a polite way of saying that you wish you could say vicious things about people of other races without being picked up on it.

Six months before the 2001 election John Stevens, Condon's successor as Commissioner of the Metropolitan Police, said in a front-page interview with the *Telegraph* that his force was in crisis because of the Macpherson Report. (In a book he published in 2005, after retiring, he wrote that the report 'put the force into a state of shock'.) William Hague, the Conservative leader, attacked the report for causing a crisis in law and order, and said that it was a weapon of the 'liberal elite' with which to beat the police. (The idea that I was a member of the liberal elite almost made me laugh.) Rank-and-file police complained that they could not do their job since the inquiry had branded them institutionally racist and they could no longer stop any black man on the street. I said in a speech in 2002 that no one was asking them to stop doing their job, what people ask the police to do is to respect them, nothing more. I felt that large parts of the police were biding their time, just waiting to revert back to what they used to be, and that we had to remain vigilant.

In the new investigation into Stephen's death, we were led to believe that the police had a witness they had not interviewed before, who could place the boys at the scene in Well Hall Road, and that what this witness said stacked up. We had about six meetings with the police team over the next five years. At one of the first meetings they did a big PowerPoint presentation for us, going through a whole list of scenarios and how the information gathered by the police had been passed over to the CPS and the CPS would make their decision and seek to charge these people. I was very sceptical. I could tell that this formula of kicking the evidence back to the CPS was tried and tested. If there is the slightest doubt the CPS, as I learned through bitter experience, will not dare to prosecute, and they will not give their reasons. I have still not found out the reasoning that led them to drop the various cases over the years.

Yet because the police were so upbeat I allowed myself to become optimistic. At the end of it all, in spring 2004, I had a call from Imran's office to say that the CPS wanted a meeting. The date chosen was a couple of weeks later, the time was fixed and I did not give it much more thought. I had not prepared myself or my children.

That Wednesday morning, 5 May, I travelled up to their office, taking the overhead train so I could pick up any calls on my mobile. Imran and I were to meet at 9.15 and I got there early. I went into a coffee shop to kill time, and sat reading my paper like the other people sitting there on an ordinary day. Then Imran came up and we walked over to the CPS headquarters together.

I had not seen him for months, though we had spoken on the phone. He works far too hard and he looked tired. He said his phone had not stopped ringing since the night before, reporters and others calling about Stephen's case. His phone started ringing again as we walked and he was constantly saying, 'Yes . . . I'll let you know after eleven, I'll let you know.'

Before I actually entered the building the whole experience might have been happening to someone else. I knew where I was going and why I was going but I didn't feel connected to it. It was not until Imran and I went inside that something washed over me and I felt a sinking feeling in the pit of my stomach. I was on edge, couldn't sit properly; I was so uncomfortable. Part of me just wanted it to be over and done with. I did not want to have to see these lawyers with their tense faces and careful poses – I knew now what they were going to tell me. Yet I still hoped that I was wrong and that Stephen's murderers would be prosecuted, that some brilliant young lawyer would say, 'We've got some fantastic new information from this excellent witness that we're going to use, someone has talked at last and we're confident that we will get the killers and they will be sentenced . . .'

An assistant, polite and formal, came to take us upstairs. We were ushered into a room. Then a black police officer came in. I had seen her before. I did not want to be rude but I said, 'Why are you here?' She said she had been asked to be there, but did not know why. I said that I couldn't see any reason for her to be there, and she had to agree. Her presence reeked of tokenism, since she had nothing to do with the case. I was so wound up, waiting for them all to come in.

Then Dru Sharpling, the woman who was the chief prosecutor, entered and said: 'Before we go on I want to let you know how deeply sorry I am about your son and how this case has touched me . . .' I felt as if I was being softened up, covered in soap. We were escorted into another room where I saw all these faces: Commander Cressida Dick, Detective Superintendent Mike Jones, and others from the CPS. I guessed what they were going to say, and had a sick feeling of disappointment just watching them sitting there. Their postures said it all. But then they surprised me. Instead of making a statement, they handed me an envelope.

'We have a letter here we would like you to read and a copy for Mr Khan. Would you prefer us to stay in the room while you read it or shall we wait outside until you call us in?'

I sat there for a moment, thinking, *Something for me to read* . . . I took the envelope. I looked at it. I was wondering why would they do something like that, when I was ready for them to tell me what they had to say face to face. Imran asked me if I wanted them to stay. I said that they might as well go; I could not read it with them sitting there staring at me.

'When you're ready, let us know and if you have any questions we'll be happy to answer them.' The whole troop of police and lawyers left the room.

The letter was about two and a half pages long. I am a slow reader; it takes me time to digest, and as I was going through the letter I could see Imran flipping his pages over. He had already read the first page and was moving on. Then he began saying, 'Oh, God!'

By then I had glanced down the first page, and in the second paragraph I saw the word 'regrettably'. I did not need to read any more. All I wanted to do was leave. Anything else now would be a waste of time.

Imran had not finished reading but I said, 'I want to go.' 'Whatever you want to do, we'll do,' he said. 'There are a few questions I would like to ask, but it's up to you.'

I said, 'I need to go now. I don't want to talk to these people. I have nothing to say to them.' I felt angry that they had made me go all the way there just to give me a letter – why not post it? If they bring me in, at least let them talk to me and have the courage to stand up for their decisions.

Imran went out to tell them that I wished to leave and they came back again. They seemed shocked; I presume they thought that we would have lots of questions for them. But at that moment there was nothing to ask.

Back in January 2004 there had been an article in the *News of the World* saying that the CPS had decided not to take any further action, but when Imran rang the CPS about it they said that no decision had yet been made. It seemed to me that they had already made their minds up five years ago and that all the activity in the meantime had been like marching an army on the spot – the appearance of movement without the real thing. No doubt the expenditure of time would convince the public that they had done as much as they could.

They offered me a car, but I said that I would prefer to go where I was going on my own. I am not so seasoned and hardened that whatever is thrown at me will have no effect. I wanted out of that room and out of that building. So we left, though I knew Imran would eventually need to go back and speak to them. We hailed a taxi and sat there in silence.

That Wednesday, 5 May 2004, was not a good day. My concern was that I had not spoken to Stuart or Georgina beforehand and that they might hear about it on the radio, see it on the television, and say, 'Mum, why didn't you tell us? But all Georgina said was, 'Are you all right, Mum?' She was young when her brother was killed, so she has grown up with that knowledge for most of her life and seems more adapted than I am to hearing now that no one will be charged with his murder.

As usual, there were leaks to the press. The *Daily Mail* reported that we were meeting and even mentioned the outcome. The leaks had to be coming from someone in the police or the CPS. The agendas of the press, the right-wing section of it at least, and the police seemed to coincide in this demonstration of how much they had done, bent over backwards, left no stone unturned, and all the rest of it.

We cannot, of course, force the police to charge the suspects, and they do need evidence. The question is how efficiently they are looking for it, and what other things might come out in court if and when those men are charged – about the links between their relatives and police officers, for example. There are still unanswered questions. The police say they are supporting us and helping us to get justice, but I cannot help feeling that had we succeeded in the private prosecution we would have showed up their complete incompetence, and we would have showed up the justice system for failing to prosecute those boys. The police support for us during that period was like giving you enough rope to hang yourself. We citizens don't have the power to conduct investigations, and we in the black community have very little influence on those who have the power in this society. Now that the CPS has said finally that it cannot prosecute, all we can do is talk about it. But I will never give up the fight for justice in my son's name.

The only miracle that could yet happen would be for one these boys to confess. That would require a radical change of heart, a real awakening of conscience on the part of one of those young men, who are now in their late twenties. I have never understood how even men as brutalised as they undoubtedly are can sleep at night. They must live with such constant anger and hatred and self-justification, perhaps with some kind of guilt, even if they do not acknowledge it as such. I don't live in hope, but I know that the truth will, eventually, come out. It has a way of doing so.

The truth did emerge, as I was finishing this book, in the case of PC Patrick Dunne, the policeman shot down in Cato Road, Clapham, in October 1993. Paul Condon had mentioned the case when we met him in 1994 as an example of a case other than Stephen's that the police had been unable to solve. His killer, Gary Nelson, was sentenced to life in February 2006. I found the case interesting because the police had clearly been determined to convict Nelson, and they eventually did so, despite the fact that (as the *Guardian* put it) 'there was no definite forensic evidence and Nelson was never picked out at an identity parade'. The prosecution built its case on thirteen 'planks' of circumstantial evidence, and convinced the jury that Nelson was in Cato Road and that the gun he owned was in his hand when Patrick Dunne was shot. It shows what might have been done in our case.

The police say they know who Stephen's murderers are. The former Metropolitan Police Commissioner Sir John Stevens himself said in a BBC interview in July 2001 that the police know who murdered Stephen. On the Nicky Campbell programme on Radio 5 Live he was directly asked if he knew who killed Stephen Lawrence and Sir John replied without hesitation: 'Yes.' He spoke as if it was only a matter of time before the killers were caught; it would definitely happen. Yet after we heard from the CPS that no charges were to be brought, he made no statement at all about it, as might have been appropriate. Everyone senior in the police force kept quiet. It is as if for them Stephen's murder was just an embarrassing event in their history, and now it was time to move on. As far as I am concerned, as any mother will understand, Stephen's murder will always be an issue. Eleven long years between the murder and the CPS's final decision was not a long time when for each and every second of those years Stephen had not left my thoughts, as he still does not.

Over the years all the officers involved with Stephen's case have either retired or got promotion (apart from one, Brian Perris, a decent man who became very depressed by the case and ended up in hospital; he is suing the Met, as I understand it, for their lack of support). I said this once, in no uncertain terms, at a meeting with the police. Mike Jones, an officer who had been in day-to-day charge of the last investigation, was about to retire and he was really upset by my words. He had worked extremely hard and felt that nothing would have been better than to have had someone convicted for Stephen's murder. I was not casting aspersions on him personally; he had not been there at the start anyway, and I knew that he was trying to make the best of the bad situation he found himself in afterwards. He told me how genuinely sorry he was – saying that he was retiring because it was his time for retirement and for no other reason. But I was not suggesting that he was personally at fault in any way, merely that the pattern of evasion of responsibility by officers less conscientious than Mike looked depressing to me. Even John Carnt, who brought a world of grief onto the Metropolitan Police, was promoted and has prospered in retirement.

The wider issue of links between the police and organised crime, in south-east London in particular, was not addressed in any detail in the Macpherson Report. There is so much that has not been properly explained – the mysterious 'strategic' decision not to arrest the suspects for over two weeks, the mad lapses in the surveillance operation, all the failings and blind spots.

The world of the police in south-east London at that time was a strange one. For example, Commander Raymond Adams wrote to Imran Khan's then law firm in April 1993 in an apparent attempt to deflect Imran from writing to DS Weeden asking him for information, suggesting that Imran liaise instead with him, Adams, or another more senior officer. Adams was a very senior officer at the time, and I was told that he would not normally have got involved at this level at all. So why did he?

Adams doggedly denied ever having heard of Clifford Norris at the time, and said he had no idea that David Norris was the son of a gangster. The number of policemen in that area who had not heard of Clifford Norris was amazing. Sir William Macpherson gave Mr Adams the benefit of the doubt, concluding that there was no evidence of improper behaviour on his part, though Macpherson said there were 'strange features' to his evidence and that he was 'defensive' in the witness box.

But Stephen's murder is not the only unsolved killing in south-east London around that time. The Morgan family have written to me about their case, for example. Daniel Morgan, a private detective, was murdered with an axe in the car park of a pub in Sydenham in 1987. His family have been fighting for justice even longer than I have, and they are convinced that their son and brother was killed by a man with links to corrupt policemen. According to the journalists Michael Gillard and Laurie Flynn, Morgan used Alan 'Taffy' Holmes, a corrupt police detective involved with the Brinks Mat investigation, as an informant. Holmes had links with other corrupt officers, and with some who were under investigation. Morgan had told friends that he had a major story about the police to sell to a newspaper. Soon after Daniel Morgan's death, Alan Holmes committed suicide because he was close to being exposed as corrupt, having, it is said, taken money from men like Kenneth Noye.

Whatever the truth about Daniel Morgan's murder, there are uncanny parallels with the botched investigation into Stephen's death. I cannot even guess at the reality, but I suspect that there is much more to come out, and the motive of corruption would certainly explain some of the bizarre features of the investigation into my son's murder and that of Mr Morgan. It will take a major self-examination by the Metropolitan Police to get to the bottom of this cloudy well, if it is not too poisoned already.

There are, despite all this, a few police officers I can speak to on a one-to-one basis and feel encouraged that they show some understanding and try to make a difference. But others you can see right through, the ones who abide by the old majority police culture. They don't actually mean what they tell you but are saying what they think you want to hear. I have difficulty with the level of trust that I can give them, knowing that their loyalty lies with their colleagues and in abiding with the Establishment view; their allegiance is more to other officers than to the community, where it should be. If they did their job as they are supposed to, nobody would give them more praise than me. Their perception of me and the people who support me has always been that we were asking for something different. We ask only that they do what they are paid to do.

I do have friends in the Black Police Association, who were sponsors of our programme to commemorate Stephen's life on the tenth anniversary of his murder in 2003. We have also been supported by RESPECT, the Prison Service Ethnic Staff Support Network, which was formed in the wake of the public inquiry to work towards eliminating racism in jails.

I try to hold on to the positive changes that have come about, such as the changes to the way in which the police are trained. We now have what is supposed to be an *independent* Police Complaints Commission to replace the old Police Complaints Authority. The police no longer investigate the police. I don't boast when I say that I doubt if any of these changes would have come about unless we had been willing to stick with our cause. But I do have grave doubts about the real independence of the new complaints body. It is headed, after all, by Roy Clark, who was formerly in charge of Stoke Newington police station at a time when a number of officers there were charged with drug corruption and violence, and who has intimate links with senior police officers. I do know that Clark publicly denounced the 'myths' of police brutality in Hackney, where there were a number of deaths of black people in police custody. But the reality is that we have still only touched the tip of the iceberg in dealing with everything that must happen before people can be confident that the fear of racism in our society is completely gone.

As regards Stephen's case, where else can we go? If we went to the European Court of Human Rights, we would have to rely on the police telling us what evidence they have, and we would not get any automatic access to all the information in their files. When these things become public in fifty years' time, then some researcher will go through the records and write a book to tell people how it was. But that is no use to me. I want the next generation, my children, my grandchildren, to know what I fought for. What I want is quite simple: that someone should pay for the crime. Stephen did not get knocked down by a bus, his death was no accident. Someone deliberately went out of their way to kill him – he was not trespassing at their house, or abusing them drunkenly, or insulting their religion – they just went up to him and murdered him. Usually a person gets charged for a crime like that, and someone is sent away. That seems almost like the natural order of things, but it did not happen that way for my son. The world for me is still out of balance.

Every year I have a small vigil for Stephen on the anniversary of his death. David Cruise, our former minister, always remembers the dates of Stephen's birthday and of his death, and makes an effort to come with me if I need him. We go to the exact place on Well Hall Road where my son died, sometimes just the two of us. Elvin Oduro might come too, and people seeing us standing at the spot and realising why we are there often come and join us. Some people driving past stop their cars and come onto the pavement; some toot their horns in respect. Others can be aggressive, jeering at us as we stand there. I bring flowers to lay on the plaque but I can't stay very long, because I am conscious of being watched and I don't feel safe there. The Brook Estate just opposite, where the Acourts and Gary Dobson lived, is still a bastion of white resentment. Black families do not feel comfortable in those streets, and until recently they were driven out if they went to live there.

The road still has that air of being from the time when King's Cross or Battersea power station was built, when England ruled an empire and thought it could build a green and pleasant land at home. Dickson Road, at the mouth of which Stephen was stabbed and down which the killers ran, looks warm and well planted with trees and shrubs. You could be up in Hampstead, and it is the same right into Phineas Pett Road where Gary Dobson lived. I know that up on Bournbrook Road it feels much rougher, it is on a ridge and the wind is sharper up there on a cold day. The Acourts' house, as it was in April 1993, was a concrete semidetached box. It had no adornment of any kind. They were not people who had any time for making things nice around them; it was all the violent present for them. From Bournbrook Road you can see the old Greenwich Cemetery sloping up to King George's Fields, and beyond that the buildings of what used to be Brook Hospital and its tall water tower, which has been turned into an expensive house. All the ward blocks of the old hospital have been knocked down, including, I assume, the one where Stephen died, but the entrance lodge is still there and the old redbrick administration building.

Stephen's plaque is of plain, grey granite, flush with the pavement and hard to notice if you are walking quickly along the street, and it can look very bare. It is more like a small gravestone than a memorial, and could not be more discreet.

I go down there sometimes on my own and stand by the memorial plaque thinking about him. Standing on that spot I still wonder about how Stephen was feeling after the attack – did he know he was dying, was he calling out for me? What were his last words? Those questions constantly go through my mind and I have no answers, and never will. Was he frightened? He died alone, and it must have felt very far from the people who cared about him. People were around him, but did they hold his hand and comfort him? I was not there to do that. Even those who were charitable towards him, like the Taaffes, were strangers. The police did not even try to ease his last moments. It is not easy to live with that knowledge. Everyone worries about their children being hurt in an accident, but parents of black children also have to worry about them facing racial attack on the streets. My worst nightmare came true. I find myself thinking, did I talk it into happening, by worrying at him so much to be careful?

The first plaque laid down in Well Hall Road was commissioned by black workers in Greenwich, who collected money for the purpose. It was a small tablet and it was vandalised so badly that you could not recognise Stephen's name. A company decided to replace it, and they paid for something the size of a small paving stone. Though it blends in so well with the pavement that you would hardly know it was there, it has been attacked many times: people urinate on it, they spit on it, grind take-away food scraps into it. It kept happening so often that Greenwich Council decided to erect a camera to try to catch anyone causing damage. Just after the report of the public inquiry, a tin of white paint was spilled over the plaque, on the very day that Jack Straw decided to visit the spot, but there was no way of knowing who was responsible because there turned out to be no film in the camera. Now it is the job of the police to monitor the camera, and someone has to check through the film before it can be wiped or taped over again.

I remember the first birthday after Stephen died. It was a Friday night – Stephen was born on a Friday, the 13th September – and we decided to hold a candle-lit vigil. I wanted us to walk past the Brook Estate where those people lived, and then around the Kidbrooke Estate further to the north, down past Sutcliffe Park where Stephen used to go training, and then back up to where he died and say some prayers. It was awful weather that night, pouring with rain. We could not keep the candles lit. We had asked Bishop Wood of Croydon if he would come and take a little service there, but in the end he did not come. What he had wanted was for us to go down to Woolwich, then to walk from there to where Stephen died. I said that would have meant nothing to me. The area where those boys lived seemed a better choice than Woolwich: to show them we did not intend to let them get away, however frightened we actually felt – even if they came out of their houses and confronted us. We had to inform the police of our plans, and as people walked in the road there were big police horses walking alongside. That was frightening enough: our relationship with the police was not very good then. Now it is better; I usually meet senior officers now who know the appropriate things to say, and you can have a civil conversation with them.

We had other, more public and formal ceremonies too. In 1993 we began holding a memorial service for Stephen at Trinity Church. We had a flame burning and one hundred candles were lit. David Cruise spoke, saying that as a result of Stephen's death people had thought much more deeply about the meaning of what it is to be black or white in this country. And in 2003, we marked the tenth anniversary of Stephen's murder with a memorial service in St Martin-in-the-Fields in Trafalgar Square, attended by over 500 people, including members of the Black Police Association and Trevor Phillips, chair of the Commission for Racial Equality. David led the prayers with John Sentamu, who was then Bishop of Birmingham (and is now Archbishop of York). A message from Tony Blair was read out by Barbara Roche, the minister of state for social exclusion and equality. 'One of Britain's great strengths is that it is a country of many races, many cultures and many faiths. The diversity of our society is respected and celebrated,' he said, adding, 'There can be no room for complacency. There is a great deal more to do if we are to build a genuinely fair and inclusive society.'

Every now and then we get letters – never signed – from people saying they are fed up hearing Stephen's name; he is not the only one to have been killed and why are we still constantly talking about it, when people want to move on? Some of them are overtly racist. Every time an article mentions Stephen's name, or an anniversary is publicised, it triggers somebody to send an anonymous abusive letter or do something like defacing the plaque.

Often I'm the only black person on Well Hall Road when I visit the memorial, and I don't feel comfortable. I think, sometimes, that if I wait long enough I will see the killers come driving or walking by. This is not as much a fantasy as it sounds. Five years ago a black man was walking along further down

Well Hall Road, coming from Eltham railway station. It was 11 May 2001. He heard shouts of 'nigger' from a red car and saw two men gesticulating and laughing at him. Then the car accelerated towards him and one of the men threw a drink at him. The pedestrian jumped back and the car sped off, but he was an off-duty police detective and he had recognised the driver as Neil Acourt and David Norris as the passenger. A year later they were sentenced to eighteen months each in jail. They served nine months.

What chilled me to the bone was that they had hired a car and gone cruising around the area where Stephen had died. Were they gloating, reliving the days when they were the terror of the neighbourhood and celebrating the fact that they got away with something unspeakable? And they had not been able to resist threatening and insulting one of the black people, maybe the first black man, that they saw.

At their trial all the reports showed that they behaved just as they had at the inquest and the inquiry, sneering at the court, lounging back on their seats, their families shouting 'We love you, boys' as they were sent down. I could imagine their oafish defiance. The only thing that had changed was that now they talked openly about their 'persecution' at the hands of the police and society. David Norris, I read, has had four children. I wonder does he ever look at them and imagine what it would be like for one of them to die violently, and how he would live with that.

20 Me

I take comfort from the fact that Stephen's name is synonymous with positive change, and is linked everywhere with improving race relations. It is as though he now belongs to everybody and not just to his family. That is something I still have to come to terms with, this loss of my son and myself to the public world. When Jack Straw said in an interview, 'Life will never be the same post-Lawrence', he spoke more truly than he knew. He meant since 1999, when the inquiry reported, but for me life changed in 1993. Sometimes I wonder if I know who I have become.

At the end – the end of the inquiries, the hearings and public speeches, and the end of each day – I still have to live with myself, and it is not easy. I still do not sleep through the night, so I am constantly tired. I go to bed and sleep for a little while but then I am awake again. The only time I feel safe enough to rest properly, without worrying about anyone looking to break in, is when I am out of the country. I would be lying if I said that I was happy, either in my personal or my public life, and I don't know when I will ever feel happy again.

My stress levels for a time rose to the point where I could not lift my arm properly, it was so painful, and I could not cross one leg over the other; I could not turn my head for the severe tension at the back of my neck. I would also get a dreadful anxiety feeling, as if I needed to keep feeding a hunger, yet I was not hungry. Whatever the doctor gave me to relieve the pain upset my stomach – nothing seemed to agree with me, so I just had to suffer. When people say to me, 'You look really well,' I think, If only you knew the half of it. But I had to keep functioning, having two other children to care for. If I was going through the mill, I knew that they were going through it too.

In 1995 I began having therapy. At first, I found it difficult to open up and did not talk about things deeply enough. If I had gone into therapy seriously at that time I felt I would have fallen apart, my emotions would have been left exposed and I would not have been able to focus on all that was happening in the private prosecution and the inquest – and I needed to be able to function rationally and to react to things around me.

I decided to start again in 2003. My mother died in July that year; my grief for her was tinged with the sadness of our past and the bitterness of my childhood. It was also the tenth anniversary of Stephen's murder. My mother had returned to Jamaica in 1998, where she lived in Spanish Town. I went to see her on one of my trips to the island. The old barriers were still there, and relations between us were not much better; she could find no way of surmounting the obstacles, and knew that she needed to say things to me but couldn't. She found it difficult to make reconciling gestures, and I think she was unsure of what she should say when we met, and this lack of communication made a terrible sadness in her, so things were allowed to drift. I felt that danger when Stephen died – I thought about the lost opportunities, the things you would never get a chance to say again. But neither of us could bridge the gap, or work out how to make the first move. Then she was gone. It seemed a good time to explore my own feelings a little more carefully, and to start living for myself as well as others.

Journalists say that they know little about me, and this is true. Apart from my close family and some friends, I am unsure who to trust, so I am very careful about speaking about my own life; and I do not want to come across as if I am constantly mournful or aggressive. There are times when I feel very constrained and restricted, even going shopping. A few months ago I was so upset that I found myself swearing in a shop, something I do not do even in private, much less in public. I was buying something, standing in the queue waiting for a cashier to be free, and someone said, 'Look, that one's free.' I walked up to it but there was no one serving there after all, so I went back to the queue; then I thought another till at the end was free, so I walked over again, but the assistant there was closing down. I swore, not very loudly, but enough. A man began saying: 'Are you Doreen Lawrence?' I thought, Leave me alone. I just want to make my purchases and go. I felt utterly mortified. By then I felt everyone was staring because I looked so stupid and flustered, going from place to place as though trying to push in, when all I wanted to do was to wait my turn and pay.

I don't ever enjoy being recognised. We went to buy something once for the office of the Stephen Lawrence Trust, and as I did not have a company credit card I offered to pay with my own cheque card and showed them a business card with my name on it. The man serving me said, 'Are you the mother?' and it went on from there. 'Where's your husband?' I haven't got one. 'What have you done with him?' Nothing. I tried to smile under the interrogation, but what I really wanted to do was to tell the man to mind his own business, to stop being 'the mother' for a day.

If I go to a supermarket to do my shopping people try to engage me in conversation when I just need space to select my food, so I went through a stage when I hardly went out; I went for groceries maybe once a month, and within an hour I would pick up everything I needed and be home.

I do not want people feeling sorry for me. It is when I get home that I fall apart. The minute my front door closes, I drop my bag and sit down in a chair. Before I know it an hour, two hours have passed and I haven't moved, because nobody is asking anything of me or looking at me. I can just be myself with my children, my family or friends, and sometimes just by myself.

That quietness and intimacy is for me the best kind of escape. Going out is not very relaxing, especially when I am sad and someone says, 'Cheer up.' I enjoy a Chinese or Thai meal on the rare occasions when I go out to eat, and I also like traditional West Indian cooking – chicken and rice and peas, ackee and salt-fish, curried mutton and goat – but Caribbean restaurants in London are few and far between. The cinema is a problem for me, because of the amount of violence that most mainstream films now have in them. I can't abide people getting hurt, even on screen.

I wish I could browse round the shops at weekends but the only time I can do that is when I'm out of the country. Yet a high profile is necessary if the Trust is to succeed, so I have to accept that I'll be more visible than I would like to be for a while yet.

Once I am abroad it is easier, apart from at the airport where people coming in or leaving may recognise me. On one occasion I was flying to Jamaica and the seat next to me was empty. A woman came and sat there and kept chatting away to me, and I was thinking: Please, please leave me alone. I made polite, non-committal responses. Then she said, reading my thoughts, 'You realise you're public property now.' I said, 'Am I?' As we were leaving the airport she asked me for my address. When I said that I was sorry but I couldn't give her that, she was offended. She didn't see me as a stranger, but as someone she knew, and she had a right to part of me.

In 1995, during the committal, there was a little park next to the house where we lived and I remember leaving the house and just walking and sitting in the park thinking about nothing in particular. I sat there for a good two hours. Then I decided to go down to Lewisham, and as I walked in the shopping precinct a white woman suddenly approached me. I nearly jumped out of my skin I was so alarmed. By then I had begun not to trust any white person, in case they might be connected with those who had murdered my son. If I had known them before Stephen's death then that relationship continued, but meeting new people made me very uneasy. It turned out that all that this woman wanted to do was to greet me and wish me well with the case, but she could see that she had terrified me.

That feeling of unease is still there, though not as strongly. When I walk down the road I am very cautious if I hear footsteps behind me. I look around to see who it is, and particularly if it is a white man, hopefully not anyone who would mean me any harm, I am aware of him as I would never have been before. Once it would never have occurred to me to fear total strangers. If anyone at the bus stop talked to me, I would reply and we would have a good short conversation, a passing of the time between strangers, the way it should be in a city. Now if someone says hello I will respond but not get into a discussion. Because I feel so vulnerable I keep praying that the good Lord will keep me safe.

In the last ten years my personality has changed. I argue more with officials than I would have done before; now I weigh up whatever I am told and I do not take authority as gospel as I once might have done. And I have been forced into the arena as a public speaker; even though I try to gravitate back into the shadows, I am still pulled forward. I do public things not because I want to but because I feel I have to, in order to maintain the reforms we achieved after such a long struggle. I feel their fragility more with every passing year. I felt that after the terrorist bombings in London were used to give the police even greater power to arrest and detain people for long periods. When you give the police this power it is hard to ever take it away. So I will keep doing what I do, so long as I seem to have the confidence of the public and can get officials and politicians to take notice.

Many a time I have felt like giving up. There were days, weeks or months when I felt I'd had enough, that I was bashing my head against a brick wall, that no one was listening or taking any notice. It was like going into combat every time I opened my front door, and no one gave an inch. At least now we have the backing of the written law. I wonder, though, whether the legal changes that Stephen's death caused would survive a change in government. Would the party of Michael Howard, who didn't care whether Stephen lived or died, hold the police to the conclusions of the Macpherson Report?

Society may have benefited from the campaign that my family and the people I love have fought, but I have lost my son, I have lost my marriage, my children have lost their brother, and they have also lost a large part of their lives.

For me the loss of my husband and partner has been one of the hardest things to accept. Recently I was watching the television news, a report from Vietnam about a child who had just died from bird flu, and I noticed something about the parents: the mother was crying and her husband was over on the other side of the room, as though her grief did not concern him. Now why were those two, who had both lost their son, not together? It reminded me of Neville and me. I felt that he was always somewhere else, never just there, standing at my side. The worst thing about grief, I have found, is that it cannot easily be shared.

Stephen's murder was such a harsh awakening for all of us. I don't really know Neville any more, as a result of it. He became a different person and now I have almost no contact with him at all. When I see do him, which is very rarely, he doesn't speak to me. The last time I sat on a platform with him was when the *Daily Mirror* gave us a Pride of Britain award in 1998. Neville and I have been divorced since June 1999. I think that he expected me to keep up the front in which people saw only a united family. On the inside it was something else.

When in 2003 we were both awarded OBEs for services to community relations, the thought of us having to stand together and pretend seemed wrong. I told the royal officials that I would prefer to receive my award separately, but they had already thought of that: a date was arranged for Neville to be given his in July and it was in June that my OBE was presented to me at Buckingham Palace by the Queen. It was an honour I was proud to accept in my son's name. At the same time I wished I had not been there, wished I could turn back time, and although I was glad Neville was not there I remembered a time when we were all happy together, when no one knew who we were except our friends and family.

Neville is based in Jamaica now. I have no idea how he lives.

I worry that what our children have had to cope with daily since Stephen's death could yet return to haunt them. I am so proud of them. I worked hard to bring them up and I think they are a shining example. I have watched all that they had to survive, and they have done so well. Yet they never talk to me about their feelings, both because they think they might upset me and also because it is so upsetting for them. I worry that some day all the pressure and heartache they suffered will come out in a negative way, distracting them from what is good in their lives. But they seem happy, at last, and no one has a formula for dealing with the kind of tragedy that they have faced, and they have found their own way of living with its consequences.

Stuart has suffered greatly in that he lost his brother and his father in one brutal night, and that loss is still deep inside him. Neville never had a good relationship with Stuart. As a youngster Stuart was often getting himself into scrapes – no more than any normal child growing up, but Neville had no time or patience for it. Georgina was his favourite; Stuart noticed this and eventually it became obvious to other people how differently Neville treated them. Neville doesn't now have any relationship with Stuart, whereas Georgina will phone her father and they'll talk; recently she spent two weeks in Jamaica with him. Stuart says he doesn't feel bitter, but of course it must hurt him, especially knowing that Neville talks to his sister, though she plays it down so as not to hurt her brother's feelings.

Perhaps Neville resents Stuart being here now that Stephen's gone, which is also hard for me. You hurt any of my children, you are hurting me, and it seems terrible to punish the innocent survivor for your own grief. Sometimes I looked at him and I could see the pain he was feeling, but there was nothing I could do about it. All I could do was to be there for him.

For Stuart, the depression he experienced for a long time was so bad that he developed physical symptoms – lumps on his arm, then on his face. His stress was intensified because he was trying to study, and come to terms with his bad relationship with Neville and the constant media discussion of Stephen's death and his killers. For a time he felt he could not go out with those marks on his face, and he would lock himself in his room and cry. He went through terrible times, and yet he completed his degree and graduated. I felt he needed to be shown how amazing his achievement was after all that had happened, so I had a surprise party for him. He burst into tears as he walked in and saw everyone he knew. He lives with his girlfriend, and is much happier now than he was for years after the murder. After he finished his degree he began training to become a teacher.

Georgina, because she was younger, was in some ways insulated from the worst of the conflict between her parents, and from the aftermath of her brother's death, but of course she was affected by it too. When I went out anywhere I would always rush to get back to her. She would say, 'I'm all right, Mum, I can watch TV and wait,' but I did not feel comfortable leaving her. Until she was sixteen, I would be anxious to be home by nine o'clock. Stuart was at university by then, and I always had the fear that even if she was indoors something could happen to her.

And because she was still at home, she had to see me sometimes descending into the pit. I would lock myself in my room, unable to face the world. I felt sorry for Georgina, guilty for my own sorrow. I would stay in my darkened bedroom all day, while she was downstairs on her own. Looking back now, I feel even more guilty about it. It was a selfish thing to do, and it wasn't fair on her; she was not one of those children who would go out with her friends or constantly have them in. She would be watching TV and every now and again would come up to ask quietly, 'Mum, are you all right?'

It was not a good atmosphere, but at the time I could do no better. Neville was hurting too, I know, and I wish we could have stood together to put a protective arm round the children. At least I was able to insist that photographs of them must not be plastered all over the papers; I did not want to put their lives at risk. Stuart especially, as a young man, needed that protection. Had I not done that, they would have had no privacy and our lives could have been very much worse. They would not have been able to take a bus without being recognised, and Stuart could have become a target for racists.

In all that time anger stopped me from going insane, anger at all the things the police were doing and saying, anger at the judicial system, the lawyers exploiting loopholes for the suspects, the complacent judges bending over backwards and never in our direction. I tried to continue my course work – when I felt that I could not do anything about Stephen's case, I needed the distraction of escaping into my studies. The rest of the time, I was going off to campaign meetings, meetings with police and our lawyers, hoping against hope that we would find a way of making justice prevail.

I am still angry, though I am more mature now and have more experience, so I hope I project myself in a different way. Looking ahead, I hope that with time I will be able to feel more at peace with myself. I would like to be in a place where I can get up in the morning, feel the sun shining inside me, not just on the outside, a place where I can be comfortable within myself.

Reading allows me to imagine that place, and is one of my great pleasures. I can relate to the work of many black women writers. Maya Angelou's memoirs, Terry McMillan's novels, Alice Walker's *The Colour Purple*: these are a great solace to me. I also enjoy the nineteenth-century classics: Elizabeth Gaskell's *North and South* and *Mary Barton* made a great impact on me, because Gaskell's writing made it possible for me to visualise what it was like living and struggling against injustice during the industrial revolution

Black historical work often speaks directly to me, and I feel I am making up for what I wasn't taught at school. I was moved by Paul Crooks's *Ancestors*, about his great-great-great-grand-father being put on a slave ship from West Africa bound for Jamaica. I have learned about the South African struggle from Nelson Mandela's autobiography, *Long Walk to Freedom*, and from books on Steve Biko and Walter Sisulu. I read Malcolm X and Martin Luther King and books on the history of the Civil Rights movement in the United States, as well as a fascinating book called *Black Like Me*, by a white man called John Howard Griffin who took his life into his hands by darkening his skin in order to experience what it was like to be black. I connected with Gary Younge's *No Place Like Home*, a talented black British writer's account of Bush's America. There are still so few meaningful writings about our black British experience; I feel that we are still playing catch-up, and I would love to see more young black writers addressing the realities of our situation in Britain.

Miles of print have been written about Stephen's case, in newspapers and books, and it has provided material for drama, such as Richard Norton-Taylor's play *The Colour of Justice*, and for television films, including *The Murder of Stephen Lawrence* (in which Neville and I were played by Hugh Quarshie and Marianne Jean-Baptiste). It has inspired works of art, such as the painting by Turner prize-winner Chris Ofili called *No Woman No Cry* after the Bob Marley song, depicting a weeping black woman with a tiny portrait of Stephen in each tear. There are two buildings named after my son, the Stephen Lawrence Gallery, at which local artists exhibit their work and which was designed by Tunde Shoderu at the Woolwich campus of Greenwich University, and the Stephen Lawrence building at the Greenwich campus. Benjamin Zephaniah wrote a poem entitled 'What Stephen Lawrence has taught us', in which he says:

> . . . The death of Stephen Lawrence
> Has taught us to love each other
> And never to take the tedious task
> Of waiting for a bus for granted . . .
>
> The death of Stephen Lawrence
> Has taught us
> That we cannot let the illusion of freedom
> Endow us with a false sense of security as we walk
>   the streets,
> The whole world can now watch
> The academics and the super cops
> Struggling to define institutionalised racism
> As we continue to die in custody
> As we continue emptying our pockets on the pavements,
> And we continue to ask ourselves
> Why is it so official
> That black people are so often killed
> Without killers? . . .

What would Stephen be doing if none of this had happened? I often wonder what his life would be like now. I hope that he would have graduated and that he would be practising as an architect, and he probably would have a family of his own. It would have been his thirty-first birthday in 2005.

If only the clock could be rewound, if I could go back in time to that fateful night, if I could place Stephen somewhere else, that chapter of my life could close and I would not miss it. I would be able to sit quietly on the train, I could read and not be embarrassed by anyone coming up to me, and look forward to spending time with all my children and their children. I would be perfectly content to walk down the street with nobody knowing my name.

I try to be careful not to let those feelings overwhelm my life. I do not want to become embittered. I need to stay focused, making sure that I give as much time as I possibly can to my surviving children. Even though I hope I have been there for them all the way along, I daresay they would tell me if they were very frank that there were times when I wasn't there, or was too depressed to give them what they needed. So I want to be able to do that now for them, and for the rest of my life.

It is not just the loss of my eldest son that makes me feel this way. I had such distant relations with both my parents, and that will always be something missing in my life. My biological father, who I met for the first time in the 1960s, went to work in Nigeria for fifteen years, managing a shoe factory and training people to make shoes. He used to come to England twice a year; we saw him during the summer and at Christmas, but I can't say that I ever really knew him well. He was a gentle man and he was always glad to see me. He never showed me anything but love, even when I was bitterly resentful of him for leaving me as a child. When he became ill with Alzheimer's disease I felt desperately sorry for him; he could not understand what was happening to his mind. By that time he had divorced and was living with my half-sisters. They lived in north London, a round trip of at least three hours for me, so I did not see him often, though I went there whenever I could. He had always been such a dapper, well-turned-out man, perfectly dressed and a little vain, dying his hair when it began to go grey, but when I saw him after the disease took hold he was completely grey, weak and confused. He was unhappy, knowing that he was losing his powers, and the worst part was losing his memory. The last time I saw him was unbearable. At first he seemed not to know who I was. I sat there talking to him and all of a sudden he recognised my voice. Then he started singing:

> I've been waiting just for you,
> Why do you treat me like you do?

It was a song he often sang, but he just sang it at the moment when he suddenly realised it was me holding his hand, talking to him and trying to see if he understood me. It was so sad. That was the last time I saw my father alive.

He died in 2001. He took to wandering on the streets and he died one day while outside the house, probably from a heart attack. It was a lonely death, and he deserved better.

I will never accept Stephen's death and while his killers are still free I will never have done enough about getting justice for him, but I am more comfortable with myself than I was ten years ago. I try to feel positive about the changes that I have helped to bring about: new laws, training for the police, and the fact that whenever any big organisation is working on equal opportunities, the first thing they mention is the Stephen Lawrence Report. That 'institutional racism' phrase was never common currency, and now it is spoken about everywhere.

Sometimes language can change the way people see things, and this phrase has been like a spotlight on the way prejudice gets ingrained in organisations. It has taken me a while to acknowledge my part in bringing this about. The very first time I saw my therapist I remember saying that when people recognise me on the street I wanted to cover up and hide. She said I must understand the significance of what has happened; people wanted to acknowledge me for it, yet I was shying away from it. To a certain extent I still do but I am at last beginning to accept the reality, to step up to the role that has been given to me.

This is life, this is my life, and no matter what I do I can't go back to the way it used to be. It is about accepting the changes, and rising to the challenges. I continue to be inspired by Maya Angelou's poem 'Still I Rise', which ends:

> Leaving behind nights of terror and fear
> I rise
> Into a daybreak that's wondrously clear
> I rise
> Bringing the gifts that my ancestors gave,
> I am the dream and the hope of the slave.
> I rise
> I rise
> I rise.

It is ironic not to be able to live up to the name, Joy, that everyone close to me once knew me by, although I am truly joyful about my baby granddaughter Mia. It was a wonderful experience to be there when she was born and to see a new life coming into the world. It is quite a different thing from being involved in the process of giving birth yourself, when you are blinded by pain to the miracle that is happening, that everyone else can see. Everything about her was perfect. Mia is a ray of sunshine. I have been focusing a lot on her and I can't wait for the next time I see her. I want her around me all the time – I do not want to miss a single moment of her. The shock of Stephen's death taught me the importance of life, which I once took for granted. May she grow into a better world.

Afterword

Publishing a book is a strange experience, I found. Suddenly your photograph is staring out from shelves in bookshops and supermarkets, and this story that you've lived with for so long is printed and available to anyone to read. It feels more public, somehow, than reading about yourself in a newspaper or seeing yourself on television. Newspapers are thrown away. People remember something of what they've seen on the TV news, and then it fades, but a book lasts for a long time, gets passed from hand to hand and there's no escaping it.

We threw a party to celebrate the book, and it was good to have so many members of my family and friends, and people who had helped with the campaign, gathered together in one room. My granddaughter Mia came, and for a two-year-old she coped very well with all these adults standing around with drinks in their hands.

Once the book was out in the wider world, I expected it to arouse discussion about the criminal-justice system and Stephen's case in particular. This debate took place, to some extent. The *Voice* and the *Sunday Times* paid attention to the book, and Andrew Billen in *The Times* wrote about me and the book in very favourable terms. Maureen Lipman was also very warm in her praise. I was glad of their support because the book is not just about me but about what black people have suffered and about the damage that an unreformed police service can do. I know that it has had an impact on people from the letters that I've received and the comments strangers have made about it. At events in Brixton and elsewhere, people have bought several copies for their friends. That is some satisfaction.

And although a book seems so permanent, it is never the last word. There was a lot we could not print in the book you've just read. Lawyers spent many hours going over the text, telling me that I couldn't say things that I thought needed to be said or say them the way I wanted to. The libel laws in this country are so unfair that they allow those who've done some terrible things to brazen it out, or to live quiet lives unbothered by public discussion.

One of the things, for example, that concerned the lawyers was the suspects themselves. Could they sue me for suggesting they were guilty? I resent even having to use that word 'suspects', always giving them the benefit of the doubt. I wish they had sued. It would have allowed their stories to be examined in public, under hard questioning, and they could not have stayed silent as they've always preferred to do.

Some people who played a part in the denial of justice to my son have not remained silent. Clifford Norris, the father of David Norris, was the subject of a Sunday newspaper article in August 2006. In it he claimed to be a much misunderstood individual. He had obviously given the journalist an interview in the hope that he would be treated sympathetically. He claimed he was not a violent man; his reputation as a vindictive gangster was a myth. It was just that his drug dealing got out of hand and it all snowballed. And of course he had never interfered with the course of justice in any of the cases involving his violent son. So he'd have the readers of the *Observer* believe. He was living, allegedly in poverty, in a bedsit somewhere in Ashford, Kent. The big house was gone, and with it his marriage. I found it hard to feel any sympathy for him, and harder still to take seriously anything he said.

Though Clifford Norris lost his fortune, the past did not seem to be catching up on any of the people who had behaved so viciously in 1993. Indeed Clifford Norris is now a grandfather, his son having had the child that my son never had the chance to father. The Acourts, Dobson and Knight also live quiet lives. They have families and children, and they still live in Greenwich or nearby. But I have always believed that truth is difficult to suppress, and that in the long run it emerges and stands there asking to be heard.

And in July 2006 the truth took a big step forward out of the shadows. The BBC screened a documentary called *The Boys Who Killed Stephen Lawrence*, and the claims made in the film could not be ignored.

They showed it to me before it was broadcast. It was unbearable to watch. I can think about what happened to my son, but seeing certain things on film forces you to relive them in very painful ways. There were the five of them again, strutting along in their dark glasses as though they were imitating some trendy gangster film, spitting at the crowd outside the inquiry, defiant and gloating. There was Neil Acourt, mock-stabbing Gary Dobson in the police surveillance film. His idea of fun. And there was David Norris as he rested his infant son on his hip, looking affectionately at him as he carries the child to his car.

The BBC recreated the murder. The young actors playing Stephen and Duwayne looked up the road, waiting for their bus, and then there were five white boys charging across the road, the cry of 'What, what, nigger?' and the animal rush towards Stephen. He was surrounded and I could see a stabbing movement with a very long knife. They filmed it mercifully fast so it was all a blur, but they showed them kicking him when he was lying on the ground. What struck me was the way they showed the attackers moving so fast, and of course that is the way it was, over in seconds. They never had to think about it, they saw a black man alone on the street at night in Eltham and just attacked, stabbed and kicked.

It was also terrible listening to Duwayne tell the journalist

Mark Daly: 'He did scream. I've never heard anybody scream like that before.' And Duwayne said that as he ran Stephen was calling out 'Duwayne, tell me what's wrong, tell me what's wrong.' The further he ran the fainter his voice became.

Then the images for which nothing had prepared me. I did not know they were going to show my son's body, and I sat there in shock, unable not to watch. The first picture was taken from above. On his upper chest, just below the shoulder, an L-shaped bandage stood out white against his skin. There was a vivid red spot of blood on his shoulder, which looked so strong – you could see how strong he was even in death. The next photograph was of his sleeping face, which had bloodstains – perhaps they were bruises – beside his right eye and next to his mouth. His head was turned away, as though he had turned in sleep. His eyes were closed, and his mouth slightly open. He looked so peaceful. His hair was cut very short, I remembered that. I could not watch any more.

When I saw the rest of the film, I still felt devastated, almost numb. They showed photos I had never seen before of Jamie Acourt leaving his house with a bulging black bin liner – the photos taken by the police photographer who had no back-up and no mobile phone, so that Jamie was not stopped or followed. Imran Khan was interviewed, reminding us that if you don't get evidence within twenty-four hours in a murder case, you lose what he called 'the golden period'. After that the forensic evidence and every other kind is much harder to pin down.

David Clapperton, the former Assistant Chief Constable of Kent, who was involved in the old Police Complaints Association investigation of the case, remarked that the basic problem in the first police attempt to find the killers 'was one of leadership – it had no direction and it had no idea of what it was trying to achieve'. I thought when I heard him say this that it was an understatement, but later I realised he spoke truer than he knew. There were things, he also said, 'that normally would have been done quickly and that were missed', particularly the gathering of forensic and identification evidence.

That evening I heard for the first time the voices of the gang as they were interviewed by the police back in May 1993. This was from Jamie Acourt's interview:

'Can I ask you where you live?'

'No comment.'

'Would it be right to say that you live at home, with three brothers?'

'No comment.'

And so on. The same quiet, bored voice saying over and over, 'No comment.' They showed his brother knife after knife that they had found in his house, a sword in a scabbard, a butcher's knife, and to each request to identify them as his he responded, 'No comment.'

A different side of Neil Acourt to the controlled voice refusing to admit that he knew where he lived was shown in the video surveillance, some segments of which were included in the film. Once again I saw Acourt in his striped shirt lashing out over arm with his huge knife, practising his stabbing, slashing wildly from left to right in front of his friends' faces. What this meant out on the street was revealed by Lee Pearson, who told how Neil stabbed him while Gary Dobson hit him on the back of the head with a tool. A few months later Neil stopped him again, threatening him with a knife two feet long. He put the point against his chest bone and stood there, menacingly, letting him know he could get him whenever he wished. Perhaps he was afraid that Lee would talk.

And Rico White, a young black man, spoke about how his best friend Darren Giles, who is white, was stabbed in the heart by Jamie Acourt in that Greenwich nightclub. Darren was trying to defend Rico, who had been threatened by Acourt, and was clinging to Acourt's back to get him off his friend. Acourt stabbed behind him wildly and was lucky he did not kill Darren, who was not armed. Though perhaps even then the younger Acourt's luck would have held, because this was the case that a jury decided was one of self-defence and Acourt walked free. Just as David Norris walked free from his trial for stabbing Stacey Benefield.

They also played tape recordings of Gary Dobson denying to the police that he ever knew David Norris, a claim later shown to be a lie. And they had a recording of his Talk Radio interview from 1999, when he was trying to rehabilitate himself. 'I swear to you on my mother's life that I am not guilty of this crime,' he said to one caller to the programme. I do not know who struck the actual blow that killed my son, but I think Gary Dobson does. It was infuriating to hear his pleading voice when he has been deaf to our pleas for so long.

In the film, Superintendent Bill Mellish put Clifford Norris's claims of being an ordinary peace-loving criminal into perspective. 'When we picked him up,' he said, 'there were guns everywhere, 'his minder had guns, there were guns in the car, guns in the golf bag, a sawn-off shotgun and an Uzi sub-machine gun on the bed.' Mellish's comment reminded me of what we had been up against, and that Norris had many friends in the police force. One of them was Detective Sergeant John Davidson.

The film so far had been upsetting, but had not produced any new evidence. Mark Daly reconstructed the movements of the suspects that night, an elaborate recreation of where they might have been from the statements of Witness B (who saw them running along Rochester Way from his bus, and whose evidence was not used at the trial), Witness EE, who claimed to have seen the two Acourts on Well Hall Road near the murder scene three-quarters of an hour after Stephen was killed, and Witness K, the boy who went to the Acourts' house and saw them acting suspiciously at 11.45 that night. (K never co-operated with the investigation, probably out of fear, but a friend of his was quoted as saying that K saw them putting clothes in the washing machine at that late hour.) Daly reckoned that after the stabbing, the five ran to a friend's house on Dickson Road, washed off the blood and got rid of the knives, and then dashed the long way home along Rochester Way, where B saw them. Daly surmised that the two Acourts were drawn by curiosity back to the scene of the murder, and that they must have been confident enough to do that, so Witness EE's sighting of them might well be accurate. This seemed a bit strained to me, but Daly's main point was surely right – this was a lot of sightings (including Duwayne's) for boys who claimed they were home all night. But this would not be enough to reopen the case, I could tell that.

The final fifteen minutes of the film were electrifying for me. There on screen was an ex-policeman called Neil Putnam saying openly, for the first time, that the case had been tainted by corruption. Even to hint at this in relation to individual policemen had been very difficult before, and usually impossible, for the legal reasons I've hinted at. But Putnam said on film that Detective Sergeant John Davidson, who was in charge of interviewing some of the most vulnerable witnesses – young men and women who were in fear of their lives from the gang and their older relatives – was also in the pay of Clifford Norris. 'I would say that John Davidson was receiving cash from Clifford Norris, by the expression he was using that he was getting a little earner out of it, a *good* little earner.'

Davidson had also interviewed some of the suspects. Here was an experienced police officer at the heart of the case being accused of taking bribes to protect Norris's family and friends.

I had always had a deep suspicion of John Davidson, as anyone reading the earlier part of this book can tell. One thing that had soured the case in its early days was the treatment of these young witnesses, many of whom were scared off. Macpherson had probed and probed at him, and had given him a stinging rebuke: 'He was the wrong person to carry out the tasks allocated to him.' But Macpherson could not find any evidence that tied the killers or Norris to Davidson. Davidson had not given an inch. This was, after all, the man who denied there was any racist aspect to the murder in his evidence to the Inquiry. I had found him cold, thuggish and intimidating on the stand. And I knew that if the first investigation had been deliberately corrupted, it needed a safe pair of hands on the street and in the interviewing rooms.

What Putnam's evidence now revealed was that Davidson was part of a web of corrupt policemen in the South East Regional Crime Squad. Putnam himself had been another, until he had blown the whistle on his colleagues. He had been sent to jail, while Davidson had got clean away, though Deputy Assistant Commissioner John Yates was interviewed saying that he had 'no doubt' that Davidson was corrupt. He also described Putnam as 'a witness of truth'.

That phrase came back to haunt him when he was told that Putnam had claimed that he told police investigators during the Macpherson Inquiry about Davidson's relations with Norris. This claim, that Davidson was, in the words reported by Putnam, 'looking after Norris', was never investigated. Nor was Putnam called as a witness during the Inquiry. He claims that his evidence was buried.

Deputy Assistant Commissioner Yates, looking rather flustered, simply denied that he ever knew, and that Putnam never made the allegation. 'To suggest that we would hide references to [his allegation] is simply ridiculous.' He said that eight years is a long time and that many people have put questions to Putnam over the years and maybe he had become confused. Putnam's answer to this was that his word was good enough to convict corrupt officers, and that he had not been wrong about anything else. 'I was a witness of truth – and now all of a sudden I'm mistaken?' He went on to claim that his information was suppressed to protect the Metropolitan Police.

After thirteen years, I do not believe, however, that the hard shell that surrounds the real story of that first investigation has started to crack. I do not believe that the story is about one corrupt detective. When former Assistant Chief Constable David Clapperton said that 'the basic problem was one of leadership' he was not wide of the mark. I disagree with him when he says 'it had no real idea of what it was trying to achieve'. I just don't think that can be true. It is far more likely to me that there was a clear idea giving a kind of sick life to that investigation. It was an anti-investigation, designed to cover up the truth, not find it. Not all officers involved in it can have been corrupt. The question is, who was, and how high did corruption reach? That is what the Metropolitan Police must answer.

I am glad that a new investigation was launched the day after the film was broadcast. There are at least eight new lines of inquiry thrown up as a result of the film and information coming in to the police. The examination of the original investigation will be handled by the IPCC (Independent Police Complaints Commission), and it will be a test of that body's integrity. I have had my criticisms of the IPCC, but I hope that they will not hesitate to expose the truth at last. For years I was accused of bitterness and of making unsubstantiated allegations against the police. Yet any objective person reading the history of my son's case could tell that all was not right with the police who looked into it. Now another policeman has confirmed that we were right.

I know that there will be more smokescreens thrown up as we get closer, and it is sometimes like trying to grasp smoke. The way the police conduct themselves needs to be looked at and reformed more radically than it has been until now. Putnam's briefings to investigators of police corruption were not recorded, for example. We do not know what notes were taken during his interviews. And there must be many with something to hide, and the ability to hide it. However, after Putnam's revelations, it is now just a little less easy for them to do so.

Meanwhile, former Detective Sergeant John Davidson runs a bar on the island of Minorca. It is called El Contrabandista, which I'm told means 'The Smuggler'. I'm sure he and some of his regulars reminisce about the old days in south-east London – the good old days when certain crimes could go unpunished, and corrupt detectives could put a little aside for their retirement. Those days cost me my family, and my beloved son his life. May they never return.

Stephen's Legacy

For several years after Stephen was murdered we wanted to do something that would be a lasting memorial to him. We had long discussions about creating a trust connected with Stephen's desire to become an architect.

Caron Thatcher, Imran's colleague, was writing something about how trusts are set up and she started the process. Then Ros Howells introduced me to Linda Hayes, who had been a senior figure in the Metropolitan Police Authority. She was used to setting up trusts, so I went to see her and she helped draw up the articles and spoke to the Charity Commission. When Neville visited the UK we had another meeting, to which he was invited.

The Trust was set up relatively quickly. We met towards the end of 1997, and then in 1998 we decided on trustees. Neville and Ros Howells and myself seemed obvious choices. I thought Elvin Oduro would be appropriate as a friend of Stephen's, who would bring a lot to the Trust as a young person. I wanted to have Stuart as a trustee, but it was not the right moment. He was still going through a difficult time; I wanted him, however, to have the option to take it up when he was ready. We always knew we wanted to have Arthur Timothy, the black architect with whom Stephen did work experience. Rev. David Cruise was also an easy choice. It was suggested that Jon Snow, the TV journalist and news presenter, would be a good patron; we wrote to ask him and he said would be honoured to be involved.

Linda got all the documents together and spoke to the Charity Commission, and after that it all fell into place relatively quickly.

The Campaign provided about £20,000 in start-up funding, and by the end of July all the papers had been sent to the Charity Commission. We went to their office to meet them and they could not do enough to help. Within six weeks we were given charitable status. One of the principle objectives of the Trust is to give disadvantaged young people the opportunity to study for a profession they might not previously have considered and to develop practitioners in the field of architecture and other related design professions.

The Trust has a vision about education – that education, along with the power and opportunities that it delivers, leads the way out of deprivation. The Trust is a living legacy of Stephen's hopes and aspirations and a fitting tribute to his memory.

We launched the Stephen Lawrence Charitable Trust at the Jamaican High Commission in 1998, when Derek Heaven was High Commissioner. It was quite a low-key event, so after the report came out in 1999 we did a second, more high-profile launch at the South African High Commission. Jack Straw came, and that is when he announced a £300,000 donation. We have managed to do some significant work, thanks to some generous gifts. When Sir Herman Ouseley was stepping down as chair of the Commission for Racial Equality, he donated to the Trust the money that had been collected to buy him a leaving gift. On the tenth anniversary of Stephen's murder, the editor of the *Daily Mail*, Paul Dacre, sent £1000.

Conscious of the fact that architects of black and ethnic minority origin are a rarity in Britain – fewer than 4 per cent – we are seeking to change this by investing in the creative talent of young people through giving them scholarships and bursaries to pursue higher education in this field.

In its first five years the Trust assisted some thirty students working closely with several architectural bodies, including the Architectural Association and the Royal Institute of British

Architecture. Overseas, the Trust has backed students from the University of Technology in Jamaica. In February 2002 our bursary programme was extended to the University of Cape Town in South Africa.

The difference we have been able to make to these young people's lives is remarkable and gratifying, and one or two of them in particular have touched me deeply. You may talk to people on the phone and see their work on paper, but sometimes it is only when you meet them in person that you realise what this chance can mean to them.

A recent bursary winner was a young woman whose story touched me deeply when I met her. She had arrived very late for her interview, which meant that of the forty-five minutes allotted to her only five minutes remained. (Normally interviews take place together with the bursary officer but on that day I was responsible for seeing the candidates.) I told her that there was not enough time at that stage to interview her, since the next candidate was already there. She said she would wait. I agreed, a little reluctantly, since this would make me late, after I had already spent the whole day interviewing. She waited, and during the interview I asked her about herself. I had seen some of her work, and she went on to tell me she was working in a youth club with children aged between fourteen and nineteen.

'How old are you?' I asked her.

She said she was eighteen.

'You're eighteen and you're doing all this?'

The first impression anyone might get from hearing the way she spoke was that she was just another street-wise young person, using the same casual street talk, but I really listened as she began to open up and told me a bit about her background. For whatever reason, she and her brother were not cared for by their mother, so had lived with her grandmother. Her grandmother couldn't cope, and she had lived with an aunt for a time, and now at this young age she was living in a hostel on her own.

Despite her family troubles she had got herself through A-levels and was now preparing to go to university. It was impressive that by herself she had achieved so much more than many youngsters who have positive input from both parents and the support of a stable family structure. I realised that here was an amazing young woman who, despite the odds, had a great deal going for her, and was just looking to be given a chance. Someone like her is what the Trust is about: giving a young person the opportunity to fulfil their dreams.

It is quite a responsibility choosing the students, given our restricted funds and therefore having to turn down applicants, but it is also very rewarding. A young man to whom we gave a one-off award recently stopped by the office to bring us some cakes and a card as a token of his gratitude.

Some of the students whom we have been supporting over a period of time participate at our annual fundraising dinner and reception, which over the years has drawn sponsorship and generous support from many organisations and individuals including the *Daily Mirror*, *The Write Thing*, *The Voice*, HSBC, St James Group, Kwame Kwei-Armah, Moira Stuart, Janet Kay, Carol Thompson, Maya Angelou and her publishers Virago. In November 2004 four government ministers, as well as the Prime Minister's wife, found time to attend.

Our next big project is to set up a Stephen Lawrence Centre, which will open, I hope, in Lewisham in 2007 and will run mentoring and community empowerment programmes, including creative arts.

The Trust has been exhibiting students' work over the years and we include some of Stephen's. His friend Elvin looked through Stephen's work, picked out what he thought would be good and enlarged them. I have paintings of Stephen's at home. He always used bright colours. From a very young age he liked drawing and would be so excited when Neville came home to show him the pictures that he had done. I am sure Neville would have talked to him about architecture, which was what Neville himself had wanted to do when he was growing up, but with the limitations on West Indian finance and opportunity, it was not possible. Neville is quite good at drawing himself; he would sit and draw houses with Stephen, and I think that is where Stephen first picked up the idea of wanting to be an architect. It was always there in his head. He never lost sight of that ambition.

Among the continuing activities of the Trust is the annual Stephen Lawrence Memorial Lecture, inaugurated by Prince Charles in 2000. In the subsequent years it has been delivered by Maya Angelou, Trevor Phillips and MP David Lammy. Imran Khan and Michael Mansfield have also spoken at this event, and spoken well.

As in any organisation, there have of course been occasional difficulties along the way. Stephen's name is a magnet for all sorts of people, and at times I am disappointed that some individuals who at first appeared genuinely committed to working with us had another personal agenda. The truth of it is that no matter how high may be the profile of anyone who associates themselves with the work of the Trust, no single person is bigger than the cause. I acknowledge that there is a certain power and recognition that comes with the name of the Stephen Lawrence Trust that others may in the future try to hijack, but I am determined to protect the integrity of what the Trust stands for: it is a precious legacy to my first-born son, who was not allowed to live to achieve his dreams and fulfil his potential.